International Organizations, 1918–1945
A Guide to Research and Research Materials

Guides to European Diplomatic History
Research and Research Materials

Series Editor
Christoph M. Kimmich

British Foreign Policy, 1918–1945
By Sidney Aster
ISBN: 0-8420-2176-0

French Foreign Policy, 1918–1945
By Robert J. Young
ISBN: 0-8420-2178-7

German Foreign Policy, 1918–1945
By Christoph M. Kimmich
ISBN: 0-8420-2167-1

International Organizations, 1918–1945
By George W. Baer
ISBN: 0-8420-2179-5

Italian Foreign Policy, 1918–1945
By Alan Cassels
ISBN: 0-8420-2177-9

Available from Scholarly Resources Inc.
Wilmington, Delaware

International Organizations
1918–1945

A Guide to Research and Research Materials

Compiled and Edited
by
George W. Baer

Scholarly Resources Inc.
Wilmington, Delaware

Scholarly Resources Inc.
104 Greenhill Avenue
Wilmington, Delaware 19805

Library of Congress Cataloging in Publication Data

Baer, George W.
    International organizations, 1918–1945.

    Includes bibliographies and index.
    1. International agencies—Bibliography.
2. International relations—Bibliography.   3. International agencies—Archival resources.   I. Title.
Z6464.A1B33   [JX1995]   016.3412   80-53893
ISBN 0-8420-2179-5   AACR2

43,153

To my mother
Violet Thornhill Baer
in appreciation

INTRODUCTION TO THE SERIES

This handbook on International Organizations is one in a series of research guides on European diplomatic history between 1918 and 1945. It is intended for scholars doing research for seminar papers, dissertations, and books, who want information to help them plan their work and to guide them on their visits to archives and libraries. It will enable them to find their way quickly and efficiently through the voluminous research and research materials that have become available in recent years and will point them toward solutions to the problems they will encounter in the course of their work.

The handbook is organized to serve the researcher's needs. The introductory chapter describes the various international organizations and multilateral conferences and associations of the period--how they were organized and how they functioned, how they affected the conduct of foreign affairs and diplomacy, and how they were influenced by national interests, bureaucratic politics, official and public opinion. This information will help the reader determine where to concentrate his research, how to allot research time, and, not least, how best to approach the materials in the archives. The next three chapters bring together the most current information on public and private archives, on newspaper collections, libraries, and research institutes. They indicate what work can be undertaken on the basis of resources in repositories on this side of the Atlantic, and what has to be left for a visit to Europe, and further, given the frequent duplication of source material, what repository will be most useful and rewarding. The remainder of the volume is bibliography. Sections on general and bibliographical reference works are followed by a survey of the literature in the field, ranging from documentary series to memoirs to significant secondary sources. Arranged topically within a broadly chronological framework, largely annotated, this bibliography permits ready reference to specific books and articles, historic personalities, and diplomatic events. Together with the archival information, the bibliography will suggest areas for further research or reassessment.

There are five volumes in the series. Besides International Organizations, they cover France, Germany, Great Britain, and Italy. Each has its own distinctive features, for of course the archival holdings and the research based on these holdings vary considerably. They are, however, meant to be complementary. They focus on materials relevant to different subject areas, and, within the limits set by the history of international relations, avoid needless duplication. They are organized along similar lines, and researchers who need to consult several volumes should have no trouble.

Each volume is edited by an authority in the field. Each reflects experience gained on the spot in archives and libraries as well as knowledge shared by colleagues, archivists, and librarians. The volumes therefore are as current and as reliable as possible.

The editors hope that these handbooks will prove to be valuable companions to all who are interested in international affairs and diplomacy.

Christoph M. Kimmich
Series Editor

CONTENTS

Funds provided by the Faculty Research Committee of the University of California, Santa Cruz, helped support my research. I am grateful to Candace Lynn Brown who patiently and carefully typed the manuscript.

I. INTRODUCTION

It is possible, and necessary, to take a new look at the international organizations and the international system of the period 1918-1945. Data are available. Few new sources will appear. Archives are (mostly) open; documents are (many of the most important) published. The memoirs have been (mostly) written. Contemporary accounts abound. The successes and failures of the institutional foci of this book are richly and accurately recorded. And we now have distance enough to see the period as an historic whole, the opportunity to ask historical questions.

Early commentators on the post-war settlements imagined their work in historical dimension. From the beginning a stream of books and articles compared the League of Nations to assumed precedents: the agreement between the Pharaohs and the Hittites; the associations of Greek city-states or Hansa towns; the internationalist thinking of Dante, Sully, Grotius; the synthetic expressions of Kant, Vattel, Rousseau, Bentham; the developments of international jurisprudence; and, of course, the classic political comparison with the Congress of Vienna and the Congress system of the early 19th century. Leagues of Nations: Ancient, Mediaeval and Modern--this title of 1919 (by Elizabeth York) is emblematic of the expectation of finding institutional comparison, and legitimacy, in history.

Such historical excursions were, however, of little significance in the development of modern international organizations, which responded to other ideals of security systems or to the functional needs of complex interdependence in the modern world. But they did express the awareness that during the 18th and 19th centuries there had grown up, as F. A. Hinsley summed it, a "new conception of Europe as an international system; the formulation of modern international law; the experience of an equilibrium of actual power between the leading states; . . . a movement by those states towards the belief that the maintenance of that equilibrium was the true purpose of the balance of power . . . and, after 1815 a determination by the

1

victor governments to establish a European international system incorporating these innovations, and to pursue policies that would safeguard it against further overthrow" (Nationalism and the International System. London: 1973, 83).

For fifty years after Napoleon, European governments based policy--for the first time--on the idea that they had a common interest, perhaps even a duty, to limit (in Hinsley's words) "the pursuit of their individual interests to the point that was consistent with the maintenance of the stability of the European international system as a whole" (ibid., 84). The notion of conference diplomacy, of regulation according to a shared assumption of a balance of power, a norm of equilibrium, of restraint, worked because the expectations of the major powers stayed consonant with the territorial and political realities of the Vienna settlement.

By 1919 this system was in ruins, lost in the world war. It had long been in disintegration, as the vast changes of the final third of the 19th century transformed the character of international affairs, a new world that made obsolescent the predicates of the old. Dynamic and self-defining nationalism, industrial production and finance capitalism, exploded the economic structures of state and created, with the development of new technology in transport and warfare, a global expansion of trade and domination. The states of Europe, and now of the world, shared unequally in these changes, and this inequality made false the assumption of comparability and common interest on which the preindustrial system of restraint had rested. Machtpolitik, independence of action, these became the ambitions of states, replacing a sense of common responsibility for the maintenance of peace, replacing an international system whose goal was stability.

In 1919 the victor powers faced the task of responding to the international disarray. The League was a radical departure from earlier arrangements, meant to be general in scope, universal in membership, permanently established. But in terms of its central political goals the League too failed. It could not secure stability or maintain the peace.

Looking backward, the period 1918-1945 seems a transitional epoch in international affairs. Stability was at last achieved in Europe, not through an international organization or through expressions of popular will but, after thirty years and another world war, only with the exhaustion of European belligerent nationalism and the introduction of two superpowers on Europe's flanks, holding, and they two alone, weapons against which no alliance could stand. It was this balance, with Europe divided on either side, that stabilized the continent after 1945. It was in this circumstance, and through the recognition (imposed or by assent) of interests defined according the dominant ideology of the particular sphere of influence, that a new international system was forged in Europe. Such an end, such an abdication of conventional sovereign prerogatives, was not, and could not have been, foreseen by the statesmen at Paris in 1917, or by national leaders twenty-five years later.

* * *

The modern study of international affairs and the era of diplomatic history defined as a distinct subject began coterminously with the foundation of the League. Emerging academic fields, as the League itself also, reflected an enlarged horizon and contemporary needs. The first chair in international politics, the Woodrow Wilson Chair at the University College of Wales, Aberystwyth, was established in 1919 explicitly to promote the success of the League. Its second incumbent, Charles Webster, expressed the urgency of the postwar mood in his inaugural lecture in 1923.

> Nothing less than the existence of civilization is at stake. Unless we can find a way to a more sanely ordered system of International Politics, nothing good or beautiful that men erect in the world can be considered safe from destruction.[1]

Partisans of associationism during the 1920s and 1930s, tended to share three characteristics.

> First, an emphasis on the prescriptive, normative purpose of solving the problems of the world peace and laying the foundations for a

1. Cited by John, I., Wright, M., and Garnett, J., "International Politics at Aberystwyth, 1919-1979," in International Politics, 1919-1969: The Aberystwyth Papers, edited by Brian Porter (London, 1972), p. 89.

new improved international order; second, a basic optimism as regards the feasibility of a peaceful world order; and third, the concentration of teaching and research on international institutions and law, particularly the structure and working of the League of Nations (ibid.).

Of course the terms varied from country to country, from prescription to prescription. British concern with the League was always tied to an evaluation of the effect on the empire, French to the question of its European security. In Britain the British (later the Royal) Institute of International Affairs (founded 1919) was housed (from 1923) in Chatham House, given by a Canadian to advance imperial ties. In Germany the Institut für Auswärtige Politik in Hamburg originated with members of the German delegation to Versailles--its original title (to 1923) was Archiv der Friedensverträge. There was a Deutsche Liga für Völkerbund (established 1918) but most associationist (non-revisionist) discussion in Germany before Hitler centered less on the question of League membership than on the alternatives of some kind of pan-European federation or some kind of arrangement (perhaps a customs union) of Central Europe, the concept, powerfully evocative, of Mitteleuropa.

The motivation behind most associationist thinking was that men were deeply disturbed by how the war began, fearful of another, distressed at continued jingoism and revisionism, puzzled by destabilizing forces seemingly beyond political control, and appalled by the ignorance and incoherence of analyses about international affairs. In the 1920s and early 1930s associationists were propagandists, carrying new ideas to a public who recognized that international affairs were not any longer a matter of cabinet maneuvers but a matter of life and death. If international affairs through open diplomacy were susceptible to their understanding, were they also susceptible to their influence? Robert Cecil's dictum was that publicity was the life-blood of the League, and the broadened base of political discourse is an important feature of this age, as associationists studied, devised, and lectured (some said miseducated) peoples and governments.

With the disillusionment and discouragement of the 1930s, with the depression, the failures of collective security, the disarmament conferences,

INTRODUCTION

the arbitration agreements, the frailty of efforts
to 'outlaw' war, with the rise of fascist governments, the terms of discussion naturally changed.
Supportive optimism disappeared. The old tenets
of associationist thinking, expectations of harmonization, cooperation, restraint, natural balance,
rationality, institutionalization, seemed hopelessly
misguided. Against what was now called utopian,
idealist, legalist thinking was leveled a 'realist'
critique, stressing what governments had never
forgotten: that international law and treaty
adherence are subject to political interpretation,
that national interest and its public opinion may
not be pacific or aim for stability, that the
Covenant might be broken with impunity, that no
project existed which all major governments were
prepared to support, that no continental, and
certainly no global, harmonization had taken place,
and that traditional practices of power politics
remained the essentials of affairs.

* * *

The job of historians, wrote Jean-Baptiste
Duroselle, is to "ceaselessly enlarge the framework
of explanation." The aim of diplomatic history, he
said, must be an "aspiration vers l'histoire
'totale'," "la synthèse entre l'événement et les
structures."[1] It is with this sentiment one must
approach the study of international organizations
in this period, and with which this book is offered
as a vade mecum.

A. INTERNATIONAL AFFAIRS

1.   Aron, Raymond. Peace and War: A Theory of
       International Relations. Trans. by R. Howard
       and A. B. Fox. Garden City, NY, 1966.

2.   Baumgart, Winfried. Vom europäischen Konzert
       zum Völkerbund. Darmstadt, 1974.

3.   Baumont, Maurice. La faillite de la paix,
       1919-1939. 2 vols. Paris, 1968.

1. "De l' 'histoire diplomatique' à l' 'histoire
des relations internationales,'" in Mélanges Pierre
Renouvin: Etudes d'histoire des relations internationales (Paris, 1966), pp. 14-15.

5

4. Boasson, C. Approaches to the Study of Inter-
    national Relations. 2nd ed. Assen, 1972.

5. Bowman, Isaiah. The New World: Problems in
    Political Geography. 2nd ed. New York, 1928.
    One of the few scholars explicitly addressing
    the place of geography in political decisions.
    A level-headed discussion, by an advisor at
    the Peace Conference.

6. Carmi, Ozer. Le Grand-Bretagne et la petite
    entente. Geneva, 1972. Disappointment with
    Britain's turn-about over the question of
    League sanctions led to the rapprochement of
    Yugoslavia and Rumania with Germany and Italy,
    and their economic dependence, and the isola-
    tion of Czechoslovakia.

7. Cook, Chris, and Paxton, John. European
    Political Facts, 1918-1972. London, 1975.

8. Council on Foreign Relations. Foreign Affairs
    Bibliography. New York, 1933, 1945, 1955,
    1964, 1979. Volumes survey the years: 1919-
    1932, 1932-1942, 1942-1952-1962-1972. There
    is also a Fifty-Year Bibliography, 1920-1970,
    published in 1972.

9. D'Amoja, Fulvio. Decline e prima crisi dell'
    Europa di Versailles: Studio sulla diplomazia
    Italiana et Europa (1931-1933). Milan, 1967.

10. Davis, Calvin. The United States and the
    Second Hague Peace Conference: American
    Diplomacy and International Organization,
    1899-1915. Durham, NC, 1976. The background
    to American non-involvement with the League.

11. De Porte, A. W. Europe Between the Super-
    powers: The Enduring Balance. New Haven,
    1979.

12. Duchhardt, Heinz. Gleichgewicht der Kräfte,
    Covenance, europäisches Konzert: Friedens-
    kongresse und Friendensschlüsse vom Zeitalter
    Ludwigs XIV. bis zum Wiener Kongress. Darm-
    stadt, 1976. The second volume of a survey
    of research into peace congresses in the
    modern period. The next volume will cover
    the 19th century to the Paris conference.
    Some interesting perspectives.

13.   Duchêne, François. "The Study of Interna-
      tional Affairs." _International Affairs_
      49(1973):61-4. By the then head of the
      International Institute of Strategic Studies.

14.   Duroselle, Jean-Baptiste. _La décadence 1932-
      1939_. Paris, 1979.

15.   Duroselle, Jean-Baptiste. _Histoire diploma-
      tique de 1919 à nos jours_. 5th ed. Paris,
      1971.

16.   Duroselle, Jean-Baptiste. "De l' 'histoire
      diplomatique' à l' 'histoire des relations
      internationales.'" In _Mélanges Pierre
      Renouvin: Etudes d'histoire des relations
      internationales_, edited by J.-B. Duroselle.
      Paris, 1966.

17.   Farrell, J. C., and Smith, A. P., eds. _Image
      and Reality in World Politics_. New York,
      1967. Essays include K. Boulding's "The
      Learning and Reality-Testing Process in the
      International System," and O. R. Holsti's
      "Cognitive Dynamics and Images of the Enemy."

18.   Frankel, Joseph. _Contemporary International
      Theory and the Behavior of States_. London,
      1973. Relations between theory and practice
      are necessary but uneasy and distant. Most
      theories are obsessed with method and pay
      too little attention to relevance of practice.

19.   Fry, Michael. _Illusions of Security: North
      Atlantic Diplomacy, 1918-1922_. Toronto,
      1972.

20.   Giraud, Emile. _La nullité de la politique
      internationale des grandes démocraties, 1919-
      1939_. Paris, 1948. An indictment of French
      and British passivity by a former League
      official.

21.   Gregory, Winifred, ed. _International Con-
      gresses and Conferences, 1840-1937: A Union
      List of Their Publications available in
      Libraries in the United States and Canada_.
      New York, 1972.

22. Groom, A. J. R., and Mitchell, C. R. International Relations Theory: A Bibliography. London, 1978.

23. Hauser, Oswald, ed. Weltpolitik 1933-1939. Göttingen, 1973.

24. Hinsley, F. H. Nationalism and the International System. London, 1973. A brilliant study of nationalism, balance of power, and problems of international organizations.

25. Howard, Michael. The Continental Commitment: The Dilemma of British Defence Policy in the Era of Two World Wars. London, 1972.

26. Jervis, Robert. Perception and Misperception in International Politics. Princeton, 1976.

27. Joll, James. "The Decline of Europe, 1920-1970." International Affairs, Special Issue (1970):1-18.

28. Kaufmann, Johann. Conference Diplomacy: An Introductory Analysis. Leyden, 1968. Dutch diplomat discusses all aspects (pitfalls, opportunities, techniques) of international conferences, which have become a normal part of diplomatic life.

29. Knorr, Klaus, and Rosenau, James N., eds. Contending Approaches to International Politics. Princeton, 1969. Does academic study of the subject have useful value or it is merely esoteric entertainment?

30. La Barr, Dorothy, and Singer, J. David. The Study of International Politics: A Guide to the Sources for Student, Teacher, and Researcher. Santa Barbara, 1976.

31. Lyons, F. S. L. Internationalism in Europe, 1815-1914. Leyden, 1963. A fundamental one-volume reference work.

32. Mance, H. O. "The Influence of Communications on the Regulation of International Affairs." Journal of the British Institute of International Affairs. 1(1922):78-79. "Transportation is civilization."

33. Marks, Sally. The Illusion of Peace: International Relations in Europe, 1918-1933. London, 1976.

34. Mitrany, David. The Functional Theory of Politics. London, 1975. Essays on the functional approach by its major spokesman.

35. Morgan, Roger, ed. The Study of International Affairs: Essays in Honour of Kenneth Younger. London, 1972. Essays include Andrew Schonfield on "The Nature of International Studies"; J. E. S. Fawcett, "Human Rights in International Relations"; D. C. Watt, "Contemporary History and the Survey of International Affairs."

36. Nicolson, Harold. The Evolution of Diplomatic Method. London, 1954. The Chichele Lectures, 1953. Ch. IV, "The Transition Between the Old Diplomacy and the New," asserts the value of careful formulation of position.

37. Northedge, F. S. The International Political System. London, 1976.

38. Orvik, Nils. The Decline of Neutrality, 1914-1941. 2nd ed. London, 1971.

39. Peele, Gillian, and Cook, Chris, eds. The Politics of Reappraisal, 1918-1939. London, 1975. Has a good study of Whitehall mandarins by Max Beloff.

40. Pfaltzgraff, Robert L., Jr. "International Relations Theory: Retrospect and Prospect." International Affairs 50(1974):28-48.

41. Pfaltzgraff, Robert L., Jr. The Study of International Relations: A Guide to Information Sources. Detroit, 1977.

42. Porter, Brian, ed. The Aberystwyth Papers: International Politics, 1919-1969. London, 1972.

43. Preston, A., ed. General Staffs and Diplomacy before the Second World War. London, 1978.

9

44. Renouvin, Pierre, and Duroselle, Jean-
    Baptiste. Introduction to the History of
    International Relations. Trans. by M. Ilford.
    New York, 1967.

45. Riker, William. The Theory of Political
    Coalitions. New Haven, 1962.

46. Rodgers, Hugh L. Search for Security: A
    Study of Baltic Diplomacy, 1920-1934. Hamden,
    CT, 1975. What the League offered to the new
    state of Latvia.

47. Romains, Jules. Sept mystères du destin de
    l'Europe. New York, 1940.

48. Rosenau, James N., ed. Comparing Foreign
    Policies: Theories, Findings, and Methods.
    New York, 1975.

49. Rosenau, James N., ed. The Scientific Study
    of Foreign Policy. New York, 1971.

50. Saint-Aulaire, August. La mythologie de la
    paix. Paris, 1930.

51. Scharffenorth, Gerta, and Huber, Wolfgang,
    eds. Neue Bibliographie zur Friedensfor-
    schung. Stuttgart, 1973. Part (volume 12)
    of the series Studien zur Friedensforschung,
    edited by George Picht, et al.

52. Schonfield, Andrew. "The Economic Factors in
    International Relations." International
    Affairs, Special Issue (1970):116-126.

53. Selby, Walford. Diplomatic Twilight, 1930-
    1940. London, 1953.

54. Sworakowski, Witold, S., ed. World Communism,
    a Handbook, 1918-1965. Stanford, 1973.

55. Tabouis, Geneviève. Vingt ans de "suspense"
    diplomatique. Paris, 1958.

56. Toscano, Mario. Lezione di storia dei trat-
    tati e politica internazionale. Turin, 1958.

57. Wolfers, Arnold. Britain and France Between
    Two Wars. New York, 1940.

58. Wright, M., David, J., and Clarke, M. Essay
    Collection in International Relations: A
    Classified Bibliography. New York, 1977.

59. Younger, Kenneth. "The Study and Understand-
    ing of International Affairs." International
    Affairs, Special Issue (1970):150-164.

    B. INTERNATIONAL ORGANIZATIONS

60. Akindele, R. A. The Organization and Promo-
    tion of World Peace: A Study of Universal-
    Regional Relationships. Toronto, 1976.
    Chapters on regionalism under League, which
    concludes local arrangements did not upset
    the constitutional balance established in
    favor of universal principles.

61. Altung von Geusau, F. A. M. European Organi-
    zations and Foreign Relations of States:
    A Comparative Analysis of Decision-Making.
    Leyden, 1964. Concentrating on post-1945
    integration, a suggestive approach to con-
    stitutional and practical problems of cooper-
    ation of states, of executive authority, of
    national administrations. The value of 'con-
    sultation.'

62. Atherton, Alexine L. International Organi-
    zations: A Guide to Information Sources.
    Detroit, 1976.

63. Beales, A. C. F. The History of Peace: A
    Short Account of the Organised Movements for
    International Peace. London, 1931.

64. Chadwick, John. International Organizations.
    London, 1969.

65. Cheever, D., and Haviland, H. F., Jr. Organiz-
    ing for Peace. Boston, 1954.

66. Claude, Inis L., Jr. "The Collectivist Theme
    in International Relations." International
    Journal 24(1969):639-656.

67. Claude, Inis L., Jr. Swords into Plowshares:
    The Problems and Progress of International
    Organization. New York, 1956.

68. Cox, Robert W., Jacobson, Harold K., et al.
     The Anatomy of Influence: Decision Making
     in International Organization. New Haven,
     1973. Cox on the ILO; Jacobson on the Inter-
     national Telecommunications Union; James
     Bell on UNESCO; Jacobson on WHO.

69. Donelan, Michael, ed. The Reason of States:
     A Study in International Political Theory.
     London, 1978. The status of states, and the
     significance of the state system to 'mankind,'
     and to inter-states cooperation.

70. Fawcett, James. International Economic Con-
     flicts: Prevention and Resolution. London,
     1977.

71. Ghebali, Victor-Yves. "The League of Nations
     and Functionalism." In Functionalism: Theory
     and Practice in International Relations,
     edited by A. J. R. Groom and Paul Taylor.
     London, 1973.

72. Goodrich, Leland M., and Kay, David, eds.
     International Organizations: Politics and
     Process. Madison, 1973.

73. Haas, Ernst. B. Beyond the Nation State:
     Functional and International Organization.
     Stanford, 1964. The ILO is used to test the
     theory.

74. Haas, Ernst B. Collective Security and the
     Future International System. Denver, 1968.

75. Haas, Michael, comp. International Organi-
     zation: An Interdisciplinary Bibliography.
     Stanford, 1971

76. Haas, Michael, ed. International System: A
     Behavioral Approach. New York, 1974. Con-
     temporary in focus, yet questions posed about
     leadership, national aims, alliance purpose,
     nature of support, information, conceptuali-
     zation, as features of decision making,
     alternative modalities, implementation, give
     useful terms for historical analysis.

78. Hoffmann, Stanley. "International Organiza-
     tion and the International System." Inter-
     national Organization 24(1970):389-413.

79. Jacobson, Harold K. Networks of Interdependence: International Organizations and the Global Political System. New York, 1979. An outstanding synthetic introduction, with overview of IGOs and INGOs of 1920s and 1930s compared to plethora of organizations since 1945.

80. Jenks, C. Wilfred. The World Beyond the Charter: In Historical Perspective. A Tentative Synthesis of Four Stages of World Organisation. London, 1969. World before the Covenant; World of the Covenant; World of the Charter, World Beyond the Charter. Relative advantages and disadvantages of League and UN systems.

81. Johnson, Harold S., and Singh, Baljit. International Organization: A Classified Bibliography. East Lansing, 1969.

82. Levontin, A. V. The Myth of International Security: A Juridical and Critical Analysis. Jerusalem, 1957.

83. Luard, Evan, ed. The Evolution of International Organizations. London, 1966. F. P. Walters contributes a fine essay on the League.

84. Maza, Herbert. Neuf meneurs internationaux: De l' initiative individuelle dans l'institution des organisations internationales pendant le XIXe et le XXe siècle. Paris, 1965.

85. Orue y Arregui, J. R. de. "Le régionalisme dans l'organisation internationale." Recueil des cours 53(1935):1-95.

86. Pick, Otto, and Critchley, Julian. Collective Security. London, 1975.

87. Rosenau, James N., ed. Linkage Politics: Essays on the Convergence of National and International Systems. New York, 1969.

88. Singer, J. David, and Wallace, Michael. "Intergovernmental Organization and the Preservation of Peace, 1816-1974: Some Bivariate Relationships." International Organization 24(1970):520-547.

89.   Skjelsbaek, Kjell. "The Growth of Interna-
      tional Non-governmental Organization in the
      Twentieth Century." International Organiza-
      tion 25(1971):420-442.

90.   Speeckaert, G. P. Select Bibliography on
      International Organization, 1885-1964.
      Brussels, 1965.

91.   Taylor, Paul, and Groom, A. J. R., eds. Inter-
      national Organisation: A Conceptual Approach.
      London, 1978.

92.   Wallace, Michael D., and Singer, J. David.
      "Intergovernmental Organization in the Global
      System, 1815-1964: A Quantitative Descrip-
      tion. International Organization 24(1970):
      239-287.

93.   Yalem, Ronald J. Regionalism and World Order,
      Washington, D. C., 1965. Regional security
      arrangements arose from crises in collective
      security--survey of developments 1920-1963.

          C. INTERNATIONAL LAW AND DIPLOMACY

94.   Berber, Friedrich, ed. Völkerrecht: Dokumen
      tensammlung. Vol. 1: Friedensrecht, Vol. II:
      Konfliktsrecht. Munich, 1967. Compresses
      into 2,565 pages a representative selection of
      documents of general interest from the some
      800 volumes of treaties published in the last
      sixty years by the League and UN. Included
      are documents dealing with international
      organizations; alliances; neutralization;
      internationalizations of rivers, sea, space;
      disarmament; armistices; peace, and so forth.

95.   Bowett, D. W. The Law of International Insti-
      tutions. London, 1963. Fine text, with
      concise history of development of private
      international bodies, and the League and
      other global institutions.

96.   Brierly, J. L. The Law of Nations: An Intro-
      duction to the International Law of Peace.
      Edited by Sir H. Waldock. 6th edition.
      Oxford, 1963.

97.   Butterfield, Herbert, and Wight, Martin, eds.
      Diplomatic Investigations: Essays in the
      Theory of International Politics. London,

1966. Good discussions of balance of power
ideas, with essays by G. F. Hudson on the
impossibility of detailed planning in collective security arrangements and by Butterfield
on continuity in diplomatic practices.

98. Chiu, Hungadh. The Capacity of International
Organizations to Conclude Treaties, and the
Special Legal Aspects of the Treaties so
Concluded. The Hague, 1966.

99. Craig, Gordon A., and Gilbert, Felix, eds.
The Diplomats, 1919-1939. Princeton, 1953.
Twenty-one essays highlighting the personal
contributions of major diplomats.

100. Dimitch, V. N. La courtoisie internationale
et le droit des gens. Paris, 1930.

101. Dunn, F. S. The Practice and Procedure of
International Conferences. Baltimore, 1929.
At this point, the stress was on its novelty,
a new phenomenon.

102. Ganshof van der Meersch, W. J. Organisations
européennes. vol. I. Brussels, 1966.

103. Gould, Wesley L., and Barkun, Michael. Social
Science Literature: A Bibliography for International Law. Princeton, 1972.

104. Grenville, J. A. S. The Major International
Treaties, 1914-1973: A History and Guide
with Texts. London, 1974.

105. Hankey, Maurice. Diplomacy by Conference:
Studies in Public Affairs, 1920-1946. London,
1946.

106. Hardy, Michael. Modern Diplomatic Law.
Manchester, 1968.

107. James, Alan, ed. The Bases of International
Order: Essays in Honour of C. A. W. Manning.
London, 1973.

108. Jessup, Philip C. A Modern Law of Nations.
4th revised edition. Hamden, CT, 1968.
A modern law of nations should be built on
premise that it must be directly applicable
to an individual, and that international

society must recognize common interests in observance of its law.

109. Ostrower, Alexander. Language, Law, and Diplomacy: A Study of Linguistic Diversity in Official International Law. 2 vols. Philadelphia, 1965. Interesting discussions of: Esperanto as a language accepted by the League; the struggle between English and French in 1919 during the drafting of the Covenant; the adoption of English as the official language of the Court and the second official language of the League; "Danger of the Multiple Authenticity in International Engagements."

110. Pastuhov, Vladimir D. A Guide to the Practice of International Conferences. New York, 1944.

111. Schiffer, Walter. The Legal Community of Mankind. New York, 1954.

112. Schiffer, Walter. Repertoire of Questions of General International Law before the League of Nations, 1920-1940. Geneva, 1942.

113. Schröder, Dieter. Die Volksdiplomatie. The Hague, 1972.

114. Schulzinger, Robert D. The Making of the Diplomatic Mind: The Training, Outlook, and Style of United States Foreign Service Officers, 1908-1931. Middletown, CT, 1975.

115. Shenton, Herbert. Cosmopolitan Conversation: The Language Problems of International Conferences. New York, 1933.

116. Strupp, Karl. Bibliographie de droit des gens et des relations internationales. Leyden, 1938.

117. Thompson, Kenneth W. "The New Diplomacy and the Quest for Peace." International Organization 19(1965):394-409.

II. ARCHIVES OF INTERNATIONAL ORGANIZATIONS

A. LEAGUE OF NATIONS

1. Publications

As befitted an institution committed to open diplomacy, the League far more than any state did its work in public view. One can only hint at the richness of the publication collection. The Covenant in article 18 declared:

> Every treaty or international engagement entered into hereafter by any Member of the League shall be forthwith registered with the Secretariat and shall as soon as possible be published by it. No such treaty or international engagement shall be binding until so registered.

From this stemmed the Treaty Series, of which 205 volumes were published between 1920 and 1946, containing agreements of all kinds, treaties of peace, treaties of commerce, international covenants, adjesions, extensions, notice, and so forth. In the UN Library in Geneva many of these lie, signed, sealed, and ribboned, in elegant ranks in a vault, 'Collection of Conventions, Ratifications, and other Diplomatic Instruments deposited with the League Secretariat.' Each month the Official Journal was published, giving in French and English the record of debates of the open sessions of the Council and presenting all documents received or sent by the Secretariat, including evidence and opinion related to Council debate. The debate of the Assembly and the minutes of its six committees are contained in the Records of the Sessions of the Assembly, published after 1923 as Special Supplements to the Official Journal. These Official Journals are formidable volumes, running, for instance, to 2,600 pages for 1931. Beyond this, on every issue they touched, the organs, agencies, commissions, sections, missions, services, committees, conferences, bureaux, and offices of the League system published their statutes, statistics and evidence, inquiries, studies, reports, surveys, estimates, problems, press clippings, deliberations, recommendations, and conclusions. Over 100,000 items were published in the League's 27 years. A lot in their time, it has been suggested that the UN produces an equivalent mass in about two years. Fortunately, much of this material was widely distributed, and is available in libraries throughout the world. Fortunately, too, guides exist to this wealth of publication.

2. Archives

These are held in the League of Nations Archives and Historical Collection Section of the United Nations Library in the Palace of Nations, Geneva. It helps one's understanding of corridor diplomacy to wander about this vast building, home of the League after 1936. The site is magnificent—the Palace does it no justice. A few hundred yards up the hill is the headquarters of the International Committee of the Red Cross; down by the lake was the International Labor Organization. Except for categories listed below, the archives are open for consultation after forty years. Exemptions may be granted upon application to the Director-General of the UN Office at Geneva, although work benefitting from such exceptions may have to be vetted. Some files are closed for sixty years: documents communicated unofficially to League officials by governments whose archives are not open for the dates in question; documents which might injure reputations, affect the privacy or endanger the safety of individuals; personal files of League officials or agents. It is hard to imagine much of importance is still kept in reserve.

The Archives have only recently become readily usable. Until 1969 there were few, and only partial, guides or indexes, restrictions were narrow and unclear, the administration was unresponsive, it was uncomfortable to work there. Since 1969 definite rules and reasonable cooperation exist, there is a reading room, and, above all, thanks to a major project supervised by the expert archivist Yves Pérotin, there is a Répertoire général enabling rapid review of the whole body of files (of which there are 1,700 linear meters) produced by the units of the Secretariat.

It is to the Répertoire général that most researchers first turn, and so the listings below follow its classifications.

a. The Secretariat Archive Group (1919-1947)

This central collection combines the (administrative) Registry files and the (functional) Section files, two sometimes overlapping, sometimes identical, sometimes different classifications reflecting the complex administrative evolution of the League. The Répertoire général brings these into concordance for research purposes. The main units are:

--Office of the Secretary General (1919-1946)

--Administrative Commissions and Minorities Section

Administrative Commissions; Saar; Saar plebiscite; Danzig; Minorities; Upper Silesia.

--Economic and Financial Section

Economic and Financial Section; Brussels Conference, 1920; Expert missions of economic and financial assistance to Austria, Rumania, Bulgaria, Hungary; Economic Conference, Geneva, 1927; customs, statistical, financial, and economic studies; Monetary and Economic Conference, London, 1933.

--Health and Social Questions Section

Social questions; opium control; Health Organization; international liaison; infants; epidemic control; pharmaceuticals; traffic in women and children; child welfare.

--Information Section

--Legal Section

Labor questions; ILO Conference, Washington, 1919; treaties and codifications of international law; Permanent Court of International Justice.

--International Co-operation and International Bureaux Section

International bureaux; intellectual cooperation; youth.

The Secretariat Archive Group (1919-1947)

--Mandates Section

Mandates; slavery

--Political Section

Political affairs; Upper Silesia and other administrative commissions; Mosul Commission; Lytton Commission. Section files of 1933-1940.

--Communications and Transit Section

Transit issues; International Transit Conference, Barcelona, 1921; river, port, sea, and air navigation; road traffic; electricity; posts and telegraphs.

--Disarmament Section

Disarmament issues; Disarmament Conference; Permanent Military Commission. Some files originating with support furnished by the Section for the following conferences: on the regime of the Straits, Montreux, 1936-1937; on the Mediterranean at Nyon, 1937; on the abolition of the capitulations in Egypt at Montreux, 1937.

--Liaison with Latin America

--Refugee Section

This section existed in the Secretariat between 1920-1924 and in 1930. Refugee matters handled by other Sections are found in the Nansen Mixed Group, wherein are found: Prisoners of War; Russian refugees; famine in Russia; refugees from the Near East; Armenian refugees.

--Several Sections, political and technical

General organization; Assembly; Council; Genoa Conference; Lausanne Conference; from 1933, the Central Section.

--Internal Services and Personnel

--Library

ARCHIVES OF INTERNATIONAL ORGANIZATIONS

The Secretariat Archive Group (1919-1947)

--Publications Service and Reproduction of
  Documents

--Registry

   This contains an elaborate card index file,
   with a 'name index' and a 'subject index,'
   reference being to subjects and not to categories of action before 1928 and, thereafter,
   mainly a file reference.

b. The Nansen Mixed Group

   Refugee problems were treated by different
authorities. The work of Fridtjof Nansen, League
High Commissioner for Prisoners of War and Refugees,
took place under the Secretariat in 1920-1924, then
under the ILO in 1925-1929, then again within the
Secretariat in 1930. In 1931, after Nansen's death,
an autonomous institution, the Nansen International
Refugee Office, was established under League auspices, lasting until 1938. Meanwhile, other authorities acted in differing relations with the League.
This complicated situation ended with the creation
of the International Refugee Organization in 1948.
   In the Nansen Mixed Group are records of activities under League supervision, together with
archives of: missions, offices, or delegations in
Soviet Union, London, Belgrade, Greece, Berlin,
Vienna, and Warsaw; the Evian Conference setting up
the Intergovernmental Committee for Refugees, 1938-
1939; the High Commissioner for Refugees coming from
Germany, 1933-1936; considerations of Russian and
Armenian Refugees in the 1930s; the League delegate
to the London 'Central Committee for Refugees,'
1940-1943. Certain wartime records of the League's
High Commissioner for Refugees are in Archives
Nationales, Paris (series Aj43).

c. Archive Groups of External Origin (also known
    as "Commission Files")

Commissions and Courts of Law

   Financial Reconstruction of Austria (Vienna
      archives), 1922-1927.
   Financial Reconstruction of Hungary (Budapest
      archives), 1923-1939.
   Greek Refugee Settlement, 1925-1930.

Archive Groups of External Origin (also known as
"Commission Files")

Greco-Bulgarian Emigration, 1920-1931.
Exchange of Greek and Turkish populations,
1923-1934.
Saar Basin Governing Commission (Saarbrücken
archives), 1920-1935.
Saar Plebiscite Commission (Saarbrücken
archives), 1934-1935.
Saar Plebiscite Supreme Court (Saarbrücken
archives), 1935-1936.
Upper Silesia Mixed Commission (Katowice
archives), 1922-1937.
Upper Silesia Arbitral Tribunal (Beuthen
archives), 1923-1937.
Electoral Commission for the Sanjak of Alex-
andria, 1937-1938.

(The archives of the High Commission in Danzig,
1920-1939, appear to be destroyed.)

Normal external office

--Berlin Information Office, 1927-1933

--London Office, 1920-1939

When the Secretariat moved to Geneva in 1920
part of the Economic and Financial Section
continued to work in London. The office also
took on other activities, such as recruitment
for the Technical Assistance mission to China.

--Princeton Office

Most of the Economic, Financial, and Transit
Section moved to Princeton in 1940, taking some
of their files.

--Washington Office, 1941-1946

Some items from the Central Opium Board and the
Narcotics Control Bureau.

(International Institute of Intellectual Cooperation archives are with UNESCO in Paris.)

(The fate of the archives of the Information
Office, the Institute for the Codification of
Private Law, and the International Educational

Archive Groups of External Origin (also known as "Commission Files")

Cinematographic Institute in Rome is unknown, as is that of the archives of the Paris and Vichy Offices. Destroyed were the archives of the Tokyo Information Office, the Coordinating Office for Technical Assistance to China located in Hong Kong and then in Hanoi, the Eastern Bureau for Epidemiological Intelligence in Singapore, and the International Center for Research in Leprosy in Rio de Janeiro.)

Collections

The largest is the collection of printed publications and multigraphed 'documents' discussed above, integral to the archives but kept apart in the Reader's Services and Documentation Section of the Library. This constitutes, despite some gaps, the largest existing accumulation of printed or duplicated League documentation. Also under the 'collection' classification are:

--conventions, ratifications, and other diplomatic instruments from which were printed the Treaty Series.

--the 'Daily Synopsis,' duplicated summaries of registered correspondence.

--the 'League of Nations Museum,' documents taken from the archives, by which the Répertoire général makes reference possible to the corresponding file.

--photographs of League personalities and the Palace of Nations. (Films and sound records contemporary to the League are kept in the UN headquarters in New York.)

"Private Papers"

These are records that were in private possession, and are fewer in number and significance than one might imagine.

--Loveday Papers, 1920-1954, 30 boxes

Alexander Loveday joined the Secretariat in 1920 as a member of the Economic and Financial

Archive Groups of External Origin (also known as "Commission Files")

Section, becoming its Director in 1931. From 1940 to 1946 he was also chief of the Princeton Mission (with some authority over the Washington Mission). These papers consist of his yearly official correspondence, 1920-1939, and some subject files on particular issues, e.g., economic and financial problems in eastern Europe.

--Mantoux Papers, 1919-1926, 2 boxes

--Drummond Papers, 1920-1933, 2 files

Eric Drummond (later Earl of Perth) was Secretary-General, 1919-1933. Those of his papers that remained in Geneva were destroyed in 1940, save a few taken with him on his departure and later returned.

--Avenol Papers, 1921-56, 1 box

Joseph Avenol was Deputy Secretary-General, 1923-1933, and Secretary-General, 1933-40. The seventeen files are fragments of varied provenance and content. The greater part of Avenol's papers are deposited in the Archives of Ministère des affaires étrangères, Paris.

--Tyler Papers, 1920-1945, 1 box

Royall C. Tyler was Deputy Commissioner-General of the League in Budapest, 1920-1924, and Representative in Hungary of the Trustees for the Hungarian Loan and Delegate of the Financial Committee in Budapest, 1924-1938.

--Van Asbeck Papers, 1925-1938, 1 box

Frederick N. van Asbeck, of the Netherlands, was a member of Permanent Mandates Commission.

--Records of the International Federation of League of Nations Societies, 1921-1944, 44 boxes.

The secretariat of this organization was located first in Bordeaux, then in Brussels, then in Brussels and Geneva, then in Geneva

Archive Groups of External Origin (also known as "Commission Files")

alone. This record has many gaps, with, for example, files on only seven of the at least twenty-two Assemblies held by the Federation.

--There are additional files and boxes containing papers of:

Adrien Pelt (Director of the Information Section, 1934-1940)

Carlos Garciá-Palacios (member of the Information Section)

René Mayer (member of several sub-committees of the Advisory Committee for Communications and Transit--and French premier in 1953)

Martin Hill (member of the Economic and Financial Section, personal assistant to Under Secretary-General F. P. Walters, 1934-1939, and secretary to the Bruce Committee, which Committee's work this file covers)

Further Holdings

--International Peace Bureau Archives

Founded in 1889 to serve as permanent secretariat to the Universal Peace Congresses, it acted as liaison between various peace organizations, and became secretariat to the International Union of Peace Societies, until dissolved in 1959. Its Secretary-General from 1912 to 1950 was Henri Golay, some of whose correspondence is also in the library.

--Suttner-Fried Papers

Correspondence between the two pacifists Baroness Bertha von Suttner and Alfred Fried. (Fried's diary and additional correspondence is to be found in the Hoover Institution on War, Revolution and Peace).

--Shepardson Papers

Working files of W. H. Shepardson, American secretary of the Commission on the League of Nations at the Peace Conference, Paris, 1919.

Archive Groups of External Origin (also known as
"Commission Files")

--Moderow Papers, 1945-1952

Notable for an unpublished study by a long-
time Polish diplomat: "Die Freie Stadt Danzig.
Ein völkerrechtliches Experiment."

--Martin Papers

William Martin, staff member of the Journal de
Genève and, 1920-1924, in charge of general
studies at the ILO.

--Collection of Caricatures

By Dorso, Kelen, Petovic, and Roth.

--Silbernagel Collection

Publicity material favoring Switzerland's entry
into the League.

* * *

League of Nations Archives and Historical Collection Section--United Nations Library at Geneva,
is located at: United Nations Office at Geneva,
8-14 avenue de la Paix, CH-1211 Geneva, Switzerland
10. Photo-copying machines are available for modest
payment for page; arrangements for microfilming may
be made with a private firm in Geneva. The Library
does not do copying for researchers, and reproduction of large numbers of files is forbidden.

3. Guides to League Archives and Publications

118. Aufricht, Hans. Guide to League of Nations
Publications: A Bibliographical Survey of the
Work of the League, 1920-1947. New York,
1951.

119. Breycha-Vauthier, A. C. de. Sources of Information: A Handbook on the Publications of
the League of Nations. London, 1939.

120. Carroll, Marie J. Key to League of Nations
Documents Placed on Public Sale, 1920-1929,
with supplements for 1930, 1931, 1932-33,
1934-6. Boston, in those years.

121. Ghebali, Victor-Yves and Catherine. A Repertoire of League Serial Documents, 1919-1947. 2 vols. Dobbs Ferry, 1973.

122. Pérotin, Yves. "The League of Nations." In The New Guide to the Diplomatic Archives of Western Europe, edited by D. H. Thomas and L. M. Case. Philadelphia, 1975.

123. Reno, Edward A., Jr. League of Nations Documents, 1919-1946. A Descriptive Guide and Key to the Microfilm Collections. 3 vols. New Haven, 1973-1975.

124. United Nations Educational, Scientific and Cultural Organization. Guide to the Archives of International Organizations. Part I: The United Nations System. Preliminary version. Paris, 1979.

4. A Collection on Microfilm

Research Publication, Inc., of New Haven, has put together, on microfilm, an extensive collection entitled "League of Nations Documents and Serial Publications, 1919-1946," over 25,000 items, some never before published. It includes documents circulated to the Assembly and to the Council, and circular letters from the secretary-general, organized in subject categories and subcategories according to the section listings of the secretariat, in all some 23 separate groupings. In addition the collection includes the documents and minutes of the Permanent Mandates Commission and the reports of the mandatory powers, the minutes of the League of Nations Directors Meetings, 1919-1933, and a set of early documents from the years 1919-1921 dealing with the formation of the organization. A three volume descriptive guide and key to the document collection on microfilm is also available. Also filmed are eleven of the most important of the League's Serial Publications, the Official Journal, the Treaty Series, the Armaments Year Book, the Statistical Year Book, and the International Health Year Book. This extremely valuable collection makes readily accessible much of the archival material noted above hitherto available only in Geneva, and provides a comprehensive and conveniently arranged treasure-trove covering all aspects of the League's work, bringing for the first time much of the League archive to the student's own library.

B. UNITED NATIONS ORGANIZATION

1. Archives

Six archive groups held in the New York headquarters fall in our purview. These are the PAG
(predecessor archive groups) 1 to 6, the records of
defunct organizations. Most have a registration
sheet as a finding aid.

a. The Archives of the International Penal and
    Penitentiary Commission (PAG-1)

A non-government organization, dating from
1872, with a permanent office in Berne after 1927,
its purpose was to "collect documents and information regarding the prevention of crime, and of
prison administration, in order to advise governments on the general measures to be taken to prevent
the violation of the penal law and to provide for
the repression of crime and at the same time of
reform criminals." It held Congresses, published a
Bulletin, and its work was incorporated into the
Department of Social Affairs on the UN Secretariat
in 1950. The archives cover 1893-1951.

b. The Archives of the United Nations Information
    Organization (PAG-2)

These cover 1941-46, during which the UNIO
served as a center for distribution (press, radio,
cinema) of information for the allied governments
and the publicity for the San Francisco Conference.

c. The Archives of the United Nations War Crime
    Commission (PAG-3)

Established in 1943, disbanded in 1948, composed of delegates from allied and dominion governments, the commission was to develop principles of
international and law plan for international tribunals dealing with war crimes. Offices of national
governments submitted charges and evidence on
persons deemed liable to prosecution. The commission recommended if these warranted pressing
charges; the responsibility for detaining and prosecution remaining with the national governments. The
open archives consist of research files, minutes of
meetings, the documents and transcripts of the
International Military Tribunal for the Far East,
and reports of the national military tribunal. The

The Archives of the United Nations War Crime Commission (PAG-3)

formal charge files, periodical lists of war criminals, records of suspects and material with wit-
nesses, lists of war criminals submitted by outside
authorities, and material related to such investigations, are open only for official UN purposes.
The jurisprudential research was published in 1948
as the United Nations War Crimes Commission History
of and Development of the Laws of War (London:
HMSO).

d.   The Archives of the United Nations Relief and
     Rehabilitation Administration (PAG-4)

     This vast collection records the work of war
relief organized by the UN in 1943, continuing until
1948.   It built on work done by the Office of Foreign Relief and Rehabilitation Operations set up by
the US Department of State in 1942, and the International Allied Committee on Post-War Requirements
(the Leith-Ross Committee), established in London
in 1941.   UNRRA, headquartered in Washington with a
major field office in London, was overseen by a
Director General (Herbert H. Lehman, January 1944-
March 1946; Fiorello LaGuardia, April 1946-December
1946; Lowell Rooks, January 1947-September 1948),
had a world-wide staff numbering almost 25,000, with
forty-eight states participating.   Its work is
described in the official history: George Woodbridge
et al., UNRRA: The History of the United Nations
Relief and Rehabilitation Administration (New York,
1950). The value of the archives is suggested by
Robert Claus:

     The UNRRA files contain vast quantities of
     unexploited data on all aspects of UNRRA's
     work, on its policies, techniques, and admin-
     istrative organization and procedures, and on
     economic, social, and political conditions in
     nearly all areas of Europe and China during the
     critical post war years.[1]

1. "The United Nations and Other International
Organizations: 'The United Nations,'" in D. H.
Thomas and L. M. Case, eds., The New Guide to the
Diplomatic Archives of Western Europe (Philadelphia,
1975), p. 379.

The Archives of the United Nations Relief and Rehabilitation Administration (PAG-4)

Associated records outside the UN archives include:

--Office of Foreign Relief and Rehabilitation
Operations, US Department of State, in the
National Archives and the Department of State,
Washington.

--International Refugee Organization, in the
Archives Nationales, Paris.

--UNRRA Bureau of Supply, Medical and Sanitation
Supplies Division, and Bureau of Services,
Health Division, in custody of the World Health
Organization, Geneva.

--UNRRA Library, now incorporated in the UN
Library, New York.

e. The Archives of the United Nations Conference
on International Organization (PAG-5)

This conference met in San Francisco in April
1945, and in June 1945 the delegations of fifty
governments unanimously approved the Charter of the
United Nations Organization, the Statute of the
International Court of Justice, and the 'Interim
Agreements' for the establishment of the Preparatory
Commission of the United Nations. This archive contains the administrative records of the conference
secretariat and the proceedings, and the records of
the various commissions and technical committees, as
well as publicity files, photographs, and sound
recordings. Much of the record was published in
twenty-two volumes between 1946 and 1956 by the UN
as Documents of the United Nations Conference on
International Organization, San Francisco, 1945.

f. The Archives of the United Nations Preparatory
Commission and Temporary London Office (PAG-6)

This group contains records originating from
the two bodies with responsibilities for organizing
the administration of the UNO and its secretariat.
The Preparatory Commission work on the formation of
the organs and committees, the relationships with
specialized agencies, the transfer of the assets of
the League, and the preparation for the first
General Assembly. The organization of the Secre-

ARCHIVES OF INTERNATIONAL ORGANIZATIONS

The Archives of the United Nations Preparatory Commission and Temporary London Office (PAG-6)

tariat was undertaken by the Temporary London Office,
which recruited and staffed the organization, then
liquidated the Preparatory Commission.

* * *

Regulations concerning access to particular UN
archives vary. There is a general restriction of
twenty years, but some records are under special
restriction, and inaccessible without special appro-
val from the Secretary-General's office. It is
advisable to write to the Chief of the Archives
Section.

2. Bibliography

125. Claus, Robert. "The United Nations." In the
New Guide to the Diplomatic Archives of
Western Europe, edited by D. H. Thomas and
L. M. Case. Philadelphia, 1975.

126. United Nations Educational, Scientific and
Cultural Organizations. Guide to the Archives
of International Organizations. Part I: The
United Nations System. Preliminary version.
Paris, 1979.

C. THE PERMANENT COURT OF INTERNATIONAL JUSTICE
AND THE PERMANENT COURT OF ARBITRATION

The Permanent Court of International Justice
was established in 1920 and dissolved in 1946, after
organic association with the League of Nations. Its
archives were entrusted to its successor, the
International Court of Justice, and are kept in the
Peace Palace in The Hague. These Registry archives
are confidential, not open for research purposes.
The Permanent Court issued publications in five
series: Series A/B, Judgements, Orders and Advisory
Opinions; Series C, Pleadings, Oral Statements, and
Documents concerning Cases; Series D, Acts and
Reports; Series E, Annual Reports; Series F, General
Indexes. Important material concerning the esta-
blishment of the court and its administration is
found in the League of Nations archives. Reference
should be made to J. Dunn, Bibliography on the
International Court including the Permanent Court,
1918-1964 (Leiden, 1966).

31

The Permanent Court of Arbitration, founded in 1899, is a panel, or list of persons, nominated by governments signatory to its terms, from which judges may be selected to arbitrate a dispute should the contending parties choose to submit to arbitration. The panel may propose candidates for the Nobel Peace Prize. Its archives are closed to researchers. Its administration (the International Office) is under a Secretary-General and sited at The Hague. It publishes reports, decisions, collections, and analyses of decisions. It dealt with only a handful of cases in the interwar period. In the words of Harold K. Jacobson:

Its significance lies in the fact of its creation rather than in its subsequent accomplishments. It is an important landmark in the development of international governmental organizations because its mandate was not directed toward matters of commercial interest but entered the realm of security affairs and because it included states from Asia and the Americas as well as from Europe. It was the first putting into practice on a substantial scale of any of the elements of the "peace plans."[1]

D. INTERNATIONAL LABOR ORGANIZATION

The annual conference and governing body of the ILO was tripartite, composed of representatives of governments, employers, and workers from the member states. To encourage humane conditions of work, the ILO drafted conventions which the various state legislatures might adopt as national laws governing labor. Its political role encompassed social and economic concerns, and large amounts of data were gathered, organized, and published. Executive heads of the organization's secretariat, the International Labor Office, were, in this period:

Albert Thomas--Director, 1920-1932
Harold Butler--Director, 1932-1938
John Winant--Director, 1938-1941
Edward Phelan--Director-General, 1941-1948

1. Networks of Interdependence (New York, 1979), p. 39.

ARCHIVES OF INTERNATIONAL ORGANIZATIONS

1. Archives

The files, under the Records Management and Communications Section, are classified in series by subject matter. A ten-year rule pertains, save for files marked 'confidential' or considered sensitive--permission for special access may be granted in exceptional cases.
A clear guide and general inventory do not yet exist; only Registry-type indexes are available. The earliest archives consist of papers of the Organizing Committee, set up to prepare for the first session of the Conference, in Washington, 1919. Illustrative of record group holdings are:

--files related to sessions of the Conference and the Governing body, committee reports, correspondence with governments and employers' and workers' delegations.

--papers of Albert Thomas, almost entirely relating to ILO activities, and files from the Director's office under his successors.

--some 10,000 periodical reports of branch offices and national correspondents regarding social conditions in over fifty countries, 1920-1970.

--files concerning technical cooperation in developing countries, concerning hundreds of projects and programs, classified by country and functionally arranged.

--over 200 files on problems arising during and as a result of the second world war, and studies of post-war reconstruction projects.

Of the External Archives Groups, there exist:

--records and printed works of the International Labor Office Basle, 1890-1919, the International Association for Labor Legislation, 1900-1925, and the International Association for Social Progress, 1925-1934, important predecessor or collateral associations.

As the ILO was closely connected to the League, League archives may usefully be consulted in certain cases. The ILO, for instance was in charge of refugee questions, 1925-1929, and these files are in

the Nansen group in the League archives.
The Director-General considers applications for
archival research. Applicants should indicate subject and need, and may be required to sign an agreement of conditions. Access is governed by guide-
lines, not rules. Printed publications and mimeo-
graphed matter are kept not in the archives but with
the Central Library and Documentation Branch. The
ILO published in 1967, a Subject Guide to Publications of the International Labour Office, 1919-1964.
The ILO is located at: 4, route des Morillons,
CH-1211, Geneva, 22.

E. UNITED NATIONS EDUCATIONAL, SCIENTIFIC
AND CULTURAL ORGANIZATION

The Archives Section contains three external
archive groups relevant to our purposes.

1. International Institute of Intellectual
Cooperation

The IICI, created in 1926 by the League in
cooperation with the French government, working
within the League framework but independently of
both the Secretariat and the French government, had
the task of ensuring the continuity of the work of
the League's Committee on Intellectual Cooperation.
Functioning as its executing agency, it prepared
meetings, and maintained the connection with
National Committees for Intellectual Cooperation.
By 1939 forty-four delegates were accredited to the
Institute and National Committees by governments.
UNESCO received the files of the Institute in 1946.
They include administrative and correspondence
files, files of the International Museums Office,
and files of the French Committee for the Inter-
national Educational Cinematographic Institute in
Rome. For work of the League Committee, one should
see the League Archives.

2. Conference of Allied Ministers of Education

In 1942 the British government convened in
London a meeting of allied ministers of education
(representing governments in exile in London) to
discuss problems of education during the war and in
the post-war period. In the course of sixteen meetings (through 1945) the idea of international organization for education was born, to become a specialized agency within the larger system of UN organi-

zations then under consideration. The worth of the
CAME archives is suggested by Luther Evans:

> These materials have importance beyond their
> relevance to the establishment of UNESCO. They
> have much to say about the problems of educa-
> tional reconstruction in occupied European
> countries and about many of the substantive
> matters which have concerned UNESCO: books and
> periodicals, audio-visual aids; scholastic
> equipment; protection and restoration of
> cultural material; denazification education;
> and the problems of teaching science, history,
> etc.[1]

3. Preparatory Commission of UNESCO

From CAME and other work grew article 57 of the
UN Charter adopted on 26 June 1945. Following this,
the British and French governments convened in
November 1945 the Conference for the Establishment
of a United Nations Educational and Cultural Organization. Delegations from the forty-four governments
which had adhered to the Declaration of the United
States of 1 January 1944 attended, added the word
'Scientific' to the proposed organization, and
included in its program the field of mass communications. On 16 November 1945 the conference adopted
the Constitution of the United Nations Educational,
Scientific, and Cultural Organization, as well as
an instrument providing for a Preparatory Commission
and a Secretariat to serve until the official beginnings of the organization, the first General Conference. The Preparatory Commission was based in
London until September 1946 when it transferred to
Paris for the plenary General Conference, 4 November
1946. The records of the Preparatory Commission
show the planning from 16 November 1945 to 6 December 1945, including the work of the Technical Sub-
Committee on the Needs of the War Devastated Areas.
The rules relating to use of the UNESCO
archives are strictly followed. A researcher may
be refused access to material even within the open
period (prior to thirty years), and special arrangements may be necessary. Queries, and a statement of
purpose, should be addressed to: Chief Archivist,
UNESCO, 7 Place de Fontenoy, 75700 Paris.

1. "UNESCO," in D. H. Thomas and L. M. Case, eds.,
The New Guide to the Diplomatic Archives of Western
Europe (Philadelphia, 1975), p. 401.

F. ADDITIONAL ARCHIVES OF INTERNATIONAL
ORGANIZATIONS

1. Food and Agriculture Organization
of the United Nations

In the Central Registry Files of the Archive
are a number of files dealing with the early days
of the FAO. These include: files of the period
from the first Director-General, John Boyd Orr,
1942-1948; files of counsellor Frank Lidgett
MacDougall, cover the period of 1925-1948; papers
on the shaping of policies and early activities;
its position vis-à-vis the UN; and administrative
records. For our purposes the main interest is with
four of the external archive groups.

a. International Institute of Agriculture and
International Forestry Centre, 1905-1946
(Record group 1)

The IIA, an intergovernmental organization of
universal membership, was found in 1905, located in
Rome. Its purpose was to protect the common
interests of farmers by collecting and disseminating
information on agriculture, studying matters
relating to agricultural cooperation, insurance, and
credit; and reviewing technical, economic, social,
and legislative developments pertaining to agriculture. In 1937 the International Forestry Center
was established in Berlin as a branch of the
Institute. By 1939 representatives of sixty-eight
governments were members of the IIA. In 1946 its
functions and assets, were transferred to the FAO--
indeed, at that time (August 1946), the temporary
European office of the FAO was in the IIA headquarters, the villa Umberto.
The IIA archives include files on relations
with the League, the ILO, and the joint IIA/ILO
Agricultural Committee; proposals for international
organizations such as a coffee institute, an animal
production association, and an institute for agricultural engineering; expositions and fairs, 1928-
1942.

b. Combined Food Board, 1942-1946 (Record group 2)

Established in June 1942 as one of four
civilian 'combined boards.' (The others were:
the Combined Raw Material Board, the Combined Production and Resources Board, and the Combined

36

Combined Food Board, 1942-1946 (Record group 2)

Shipping Adjustment Board), set up by the United States and Great Britain to encourage production, facilitate procurement, and conserve the use of supplies from sources remaining open to the United Nations at that point of the war. Joined by Canada in October 1943, the Board recommended the terms of allocation, production, procurement, and distribution of foodstuffs and related commodities. In 1946 it broadened its concern to include problems of post-war supply and trade involving many nations. In July 1946 it was replaced by the International Emergency Food Council.

c. United Nations Conference on Food and Agriculture (Record group 3)

Convened by the US at Hot Springs, Virginia, in May 1943, it has been termed the first of the peace conferences. Attended by representatives of the forty-four states that then comprised the United Nations, and those associated in the war, the purpose of the conference was to exchange information on the plans and prospects of the various countries regarding post-war agricultural production, imports and exports, and questions of nutrition, resources, relative production of commodities, labor, trade, and prices. The conference proposed an interim commission to prepare a permanent international organization on food and agriculture, and to submit a declaration whereby each government would declare a recognition of its obligation to raise the nutritional and living standard of its people.

d. The United Nations Interim Commission for Food and Agriculture (Record group 4)

This group undertook the task, convening in Washington under the chairmanship of Lester Pearson. It prepared the way for the absorption of the IIA and the inclusion of forestry in the program of the new organization, and drafted a constitution for a permanent organization. Its work was completed with the convening of the First Session of the Conference of the Food and Agricultural Organization of the United Nations in October 1945 at Quebec.

e. David Lubin Archives

    Lubin, born near Cracow in 1849, became a
successful merchant and then farmer in California,
where he organized the California Fruit Growers'
Exchange. He founded the IIA, and proposed various
internationalist plans, such as an International
Confederation of Democracies, and an international
parliament to maintain world peace. He died in
1919, his papers together with the IIA collection
becoming the nucleus of the FAO's David Lubin
Memorial Library, wherein are also found exhaustive
collections dealing with the world's agriculture,
all publications of the FAO, and publications of the
UN and its specialized agencies.
    Access to the FAO archives is generally open.
For library research, a written request should be
presented to the Chief Librarian. Address of the
FOA: Viale delle Terme di Caracalla, I-00100 Rome.

        2. International Telecommunication Union

    Founded in Paris in 1865 to regulate the inter-
national use of the Telegraph, and drawing on
regional conventions signed earlier (Austro-German
Telegraph Union, 1850, Western European Telegraphic
Union, 1855), the ITU is the longest-lived international organization, the first potentially universal international governmental organization. It
took its present title in 1932; in 1947 it became a
specialized agency of the UN. Responding to tech-
nological changes in the 20th century, it formulates
agreements and regulations concerning the telegraph,
telephone, and radio. It is of major historical
interest for its pioneering work in international
administration, for its recognition of the functional value of cooperation at the level of supra-
national regulation and coordination.
    The organization was based in Berne from 1896
to 1947 under the surveillance of the Swiss Federal
Council--a model for three other organizations which
followed shortly: The Universal Postal Union of
1874, the International Office for the Protection of
Intellectual Property of 1886, and the Central
Office of International Transportation by Railroad.
There is valuable supplementary material in Series
E of the Federal Archives in Berne, the Swiss
government having had considerable involvement in
the management of these agencies. The ITU moved to
Geneva in 1948. For our purposes, interest centers
on the 'Berne Archives,' the bulk of which is con-

cerned with external relations, and which, as an
archivist who is presently putting the collection
in more usable order wrote, "are far less technical than one would at first think, and . . . con-
stitute an unexplored research area full of
promise."[1] Address: Place des Nations, CH-1211
Geneva 20.

3. Universal Postal Union

This specialized agency of the UN gives as its
aims the 'efficient operation of the various postal
services, thus fostering the development of communications between peoples, and contribution to the
development of international collaboration in the
cultural, social, and economic fields, including
postal technical assistance.' Founded in 1874 it
is an early, and major, functional organization of
continued success. It is therefore with some
surprise one reads its reply to a UN questionnaire
that "only closed files are to be found in the
central archives . . . UPU archives are of no
interest for the origins of other international
organizations."[2] The researcher is advised to
address inquiries to the Information and Documentation Section, UPU, Weltpoststrasse 4, Berne.

4. World Intellectual Property Organization

This is another of the 19th century Berne group
whose line remains unbroken. In 1883 representatives of nine states signed a convention for the
protection of inventors and industrialists and set
up a 'Union' to administer the convention. Three
years later the protection of writers and artists
was added by another convention. The Swiss Federal
Council was entrusted with management and control of
these conventions, and a single administration, the
International Office for the Protection of Intellectual Property, was established in 1893, taking
in areas of competence industrial property (patents,
trademarks, designs, models, etc.) and literary and
artistic property. This office was headquartered

1. Gilberte Pérotin, "The International Telecommuni-
cation Union," in D. H. Thomas and L. M. Case, eds.,
The New Guide to the Diplomatic Archives of Western
Europe (Philadelphia, 1975), p. 396.

2. UNESCO, Guide to the Archives of International
Organizations, Part I (preliminary version) (Paris,
1970), p. 252.

in Berlin, and administratively modeled on the ITU
and UPU. Only one convention was added during our
period, the agreement of The Hague concerning the
International Deposit of Industrial Designs, 1925.
Historical interest lies in the process of administration of the various conventions, of which there
were five by 1945. The WIPO was established in
1967, consolidating the by then dozen or so agreements. Its archives (it is part of the UN system)
are by and large open to consultation. Address:
34 chemin des Colobettes, CH-1211, Geneva 20.

5. World Health Organization

Three external archive groups fall within our
period, involving international organizations concerned with health previous to the foundation of WHO
in 1948. Each group is open; each archive is on
microfilm, the original files having been destroyed.
The OIHP and UNRRA microfilms are fully indexed, and
reference is easily made through the WHO publication:
Catalogue of the Material (Stored in WHO Archives
on Microfilm) from L'Office International d'Hygiène
Publique and the United Nations Relief and Rehabilitation Administration. To understand the work and
relationships of the organizations noted below,
reference should be made to the valuable administrative history published by WHO in 1958: The First
Ten Years of the World Health Organization, chs. 1-3,
and N. Howard Jones, Les bases scientifiques des
conférences sanitaires internationales, 1851-1938
(Geneva, 1975).

a. L'Office International d'Hygiène Publique

Inter-governmental cooperation in questions of
health began in the mid-19th century with conferences to investigate the spread and the possibility
of quarantine of epidemic diseases, cholera in
particular. Lacking knowledge as to the causes and
exact nature of these diseases, conferences passed
sanitary conventions meant to prevent contagion
especially from ports of international commerce.
By the beginning of the 20th century when the causes
of cholera, plague, and yellow fever were, or were
about to be, scientifically understood, the eleventh
International Sanitary Conference (Paris, 1903)
recommended the establishment of a permanent international health office (based on the models of the
International Bureau of Weights and Measures and
other international offices noted above. This gave

L'Office International d'Hygiène Publique

rise to the OIHP (1970), the first international governmental health organization. Responsibilities of the OIHP were the administration and revision of international sanitary conventions, epidemiological intelligence, and public health information. The OIHP was dissolved in 1946, and its epidemiological service transferred to WHO. Its varied archives include correspondence with member states, the record of collaboration with military administrations (Commission sanitaire inter-alliée, 1905-1920), quarantine regulations for shipping and airports, the use of radio for maritime sanitary measures, and questions of transport and sanitation for pilgrims.

b. The Health Organization of the League of Nations

In 1919 the President of the Permanent Committee called upon the OIHP to radically reorient and expand its international health work. This suggestion came to nothing. The limiting condition was the inclusion in the Covenant of a preemptive provision that League members would 'endeavor to take steps in matters of international concern for the prevention and control of disease.' Why the League should take up health concerns when the OIHP already existed, and represented the culmination of some seventy years of international cooperation, was not stated, but the reasons were a desire for coordination of all activities through a central organization, and the breakdown of sanitary conditions in the postwar world (to which was added the influenza pandemic of 1918-1919). These seemed to require reconstruction efforts beyond the scope of the modest resources, limited aims, and restricted jurisdiction of the OIHP.

In 1923 the League set up a Health Committee, transferring health matters within the secretariat (except matters concerning opium and other dangerous drugs) from the Social Section to a newly created Health Section. This, its various commissions on malaria, pilgrimage, cancer, etc., together with the Eastern Bureau, and groups offering technical assistance to, e.g., China, were called the 'Health Organization.'

During this time the OIHP continued a separate, autonomous, and parallel existence, never joining with the League organization because the United States refused its consent. For thirty years the

41

The Health Organization of the League of Nations

two organizations existed side by side, one in Paris
and the other in Geneva. The Registry files of the
Health Section are with the League Secretariat
Archive group. The rest of the extensive section
files are in the WHO archives.

c. United Nations Relief and Rehabilitation
   Administration

UNRRA was founded in 1943 to assist recovery
from the effects of the war. Its Health Division
took over the epidemiological work of the Health
Section of the League and assumed responsibility
for the OIHP's duties regarding sanitary conventions.
It gave health care to displaced persons, provided
medical supplies, and revived the interchange of
information on epidemic diseases, and aided governments of fifteen countries to rebuild their health
services. UNRAA provided the link between intergovernmental health activities before and after the
war. The UNRAA records are in the UN archives in
New York (PAG-4), and 100 microjackets covering
1943-47, with the files of 22 country and area
missions, are in the WHO archives.
WHO archives are located at the headquarters,
Avenue Appia, 1221, Geneva 27. The WHO library
(a separate unit) contains materials inherited from
the various predecessors.

6. The International Committee of the Red Cross

The ICRC archives are not as a rule open to
inspection. Confidentiality is based on the
neutrality of the ICRC. Authorization may be given
for consultation on the condition that ICRC
interests (relations with member states, protection
of victims) are respected. Historical and juridical
studies are favored. Persons who wish to use the
archives should apply to the archivist, giving the
purpose of research. Authorization is strictly on
a personal basis, and researchers must sign an
agreement not to publish their findings without the
assent of the ICRC. Texts must be submitted, and
are subject to having material deleted. Applications should be made to the Head of Research,
Publications and Documentation Department, ICRC,
Geneva.
The ICRC Library is open to the public, containing its publications, appeals to governments,

documents prepared for the international conferences of the Red Cross, etc. Of particular interest is the International Review (originally: International Bulletin of the Red Cross, which appeared monthly after 1919, and is the source of suggestive information, such as, during the 1930s, articles on the protection of civilian populations against chemical warfare and 'passive defence' in the case of air attack.

III. STATE ARCHIVES, PUBLISHED
DOCUMENTS, PRIVATE PAPERS

It is impossible to consider the workings of
international organizations and conferences without
reference to the formulations of policy by the
states which composed them. Other volumes in this
series give detailed references; it is appropriate
here to say some words about those of three states
which played the most influential roles in international organizations during our period.

A. GREAT BRITAIN

1. Archives

Here are the most accessible of European
national archives. Thanks to the Public Records Act
of 1967, a victory for historians, a thirty-year
rule prevails. The archives are well catalogued;
detailed minutes on despatches permit close reconstruction of the thinking behind the decisions; and
ministerial responsibility to the Cabinet, and
thence to Parliament, offers a look at how broader
considerations (political, economic, military)
played their part. The amount of material is huge.
In 1913 the Foreign Office received 68,119 despatches and reports. In 1935 it received 169,248;
in 1938 it received 223,879. There are, for
instance, 101 volumes on international conferences
between 1916 and 1922; 35 on the Washington Disarmament Conferences. But it is all well-ordered, and
while cross-reference is always necessary, and
while all Foreign Office material must be supplemented by use of Cabinet Office records, Treasury
documents, the files of the armed services, Parliamentary debates, and private papers, clear, reliable
studies of British positions may now be made.
Unique among the powers, Britain for a time had a
Minister of League of Nations Affairs, a post with
Cabinet status, held by Anthony Eden from June 1935
to January 1936, by which the government acknowl-
edged popular concerns for international cooperation as a means of preventing war. British delegates at conferences and at Geneva followed, as a

45

rule, Whitehall's direction.

Records for our period are stored at the Public Record Office in Kew, Richmond, Surrey, TW9 4DU. Here are the files of the Cabinet, Treasury, Admiralty, Foreign Office, Colonial Office, and War Office. Application for use is made at Kew. There are reading rooms, facilities for typing, and photocopying (undertaken by the Office upon request). There are many guides, of increasing complexity and refinement, the most initially being the Guide to the Contents of the Public Record Office, which is being revised to describe the contents of classes of holdings, and is available in printout at Kew. One may find in many libraries, or purchase from HMSO, publications listed in handbooks on the British National Archives (1979), The Records of the Colonial and Dominions Office (1964), Classes of Departmental Papers for 1960-1939 (1966), The Records of the Cabinet Office to 1922 (1966), The Records of the Foreign Office 1782-1939 (1969), Records of Interest to Social Scientists 1919-1939 (1971), The Cabinet Office to 1945 (1973), and a guide to PRO documents on The Second World War (1972).

Also for sale, reprinted by the Kraus Reprint Corporation (KTO Press, Milwood, NY), are lists of FO records, General Correspondence, Embassy and Consular Archives, and Indexes to FO General Correspondence, by year, from 1920-1948, a set of 119 volumes, and containing the indexes to the 'Secret' (or 'Green') papers. Of particular help is the fact that the PRO will sell microfilms of F.O. Confidential Prints, the final incoming and outgoing correspondence of the FO.

For A Catalogue of Microfilm (1976) write the Photo-Ordering Section at Kew. On microfilm, then, is available the all-important Cabinet minutes and Cabinet papers, records of CID reports to the Cabinet, files concerning economic and monetary conferences, records of the Interallied Armistice Commission, FO Private Collections, and all the registered files on the League of Nations. This material is in final draft, however, and for study of policy formation one must go to the minutes, the intra-departmental notations, found only in the jackets in the files.

2. Published Documents

The printed collection is Documents on British Foreign Policy, 1919-1939. This covers the period

28 June 1919 to 3 September 1939, that is, from the
signature of the Versailles treaty to the outbreak,
for Britain, of the war. The first series, and its
cohort series IA, covers the 1920s; the second
series takes its point of departure 1930 (or, more
precisely, begins with the preparations the year
preceding for the London Naval Conference); the
third series (the only one now complete) covers
1938-1939, commencing 9 March 1938 with Schuschnigg's
decision to hold a plebiscite in Austria. Each
volume is organized around particular themes. To
suggest the pertinence to our studies, I list simply
a few chapter headings, from volumes sometimes
devoted entirely to these issues: "The Reference
of the Question of Upper Silesia to the Council of
the League of Nations, July 9, 1921-November 2,
1922"; "The Genoa Conference, April 9-May 19, 1922";
"The Reference of the Saar Problem to the League of
Nations, April 24-December 16, 1923"; The "American
Proposal for the Renunciation of War: Discussions
at Geneva on Security, December 30, 1927-April 13,
1928"; "British Signature of the Optional Clause,
July 24-December 31, 1929"; "First Report of the
Sub-Committee of the Committee of Imperial Defence
on Belligerent Rights, February 13, 1929"; "The
London Naval Conference, January 21-April 22, 1930";
"Outbreak of the Italo-Ethiopian War: Condemnation
of Italian Action by the League Assembly, October
3-10, 1935."
     The remarkable engagement of the public with
foreign affairs, and in particular the interest in
the League, and the fact that the League was a
forum for open discussion, meant that many issues
concerning international organization were dealt
with in the public sphere. The record of Parliament, both Commons and Lords, is found in Parliamentary Debates, aka Hansard. One finds something
about the official mind here, including its capacity
to conceal, and the temper of opinion. For a list
of Parliamentary papers relevant to international
relations see: Robert Vogel. A Breviate of British
Diplomatic Blue Books, 1919-1939. Montreal, 1963.

3. Private Papers

     For private papers, no nation has more exten-
sive collections than Britain. One begins with the
Historical Manuscripts Commission, Quality House,
Quality Court, Chancery Lane, London. Collections
include those of:

Stanley Baldwin (Cambridge University Library)
Robert Cecil (British Library)
Austen Chamberlain (University Library,
   Birmingham)
Neville Chamberlain (University Library,
   Birmingham)
David Lloyd George (Beaverbook Library)
Maurice Hankey (Churchill College, Cambridge)
Arthur Henderson (Public Record Office)
Samuel Hoare (Cambridge University Library)
Philip Kerr (National Library of Scotland)
Ramsay MacDonald (Public Record Office)
Gilbert Murray (Bodleian Library, Oxford)
Herbert Samuel (House of Lords)
Robert Vansittart (Churchill College,
   Cambridge)
C. K. Webster (London School of Economics)

B. FRANCE

1. Archives

Archives of the Ministère des affaires étrangères are located at 37 quai d'Orsay, Paris 75700.
Access is not certain, and a thirty-year rule does
not pertain. The opening of records to 10 July 1940
applies to the National Archives, not to the AEME.
Admission is granted only after submission of a
letter to the Conservateur en Chef des Archives,
detailing the aim and nature of research. This
must be accompanied by a letter of identification,
and support, from the researcher's academic director
or from the cultural attaché of the person's
national embassy in Paris. A sentence in Vincent
Confer's introduction to the AEME sums up the first
problem the researcher will encounter: "Archival
losses during the Second World War have created
difficulties for researchers concerned with peace
plans in 1914-1919, or with French participation in
international conferences and the League of Nations
after 1919."[1] The story of the destruction of
records of the 1930s by French authorities in the
face of German invasion is told in the general
introduction to volume 1, second series, of Documents diplomatiques français, 1932-1939. Further
complications, which apply even more to the Italian
records, are noted by Anthony Adamthwaite:

1. "France," in D. H. Thomas and L. M. Case, eds.
The New Guide to the Diplomatic Archives of Western
Europe (Philadelphia, 1975), p. 73.

48

Despite the proliferation of paper from the chancelleries, many key decisions went unrecorded. A Minister or senior official communicated many decisions by voice, instead of official meetings . . . Thirdly, an unknown quantity of papers have been lost or destroyed . . . Missing are many of the memoranda of conversations held for the Foreign Minister of the day, also the minister's informal instructions and private correspondence, internal Foreign Ministry minutes and secret documents not passed through the official register of correspondence . . . The methods of working in the Quai d'Orsay account for some of the gaps in the archives. It was quite common in the inter-war years for a Minister or senior official to retain in his personal files, papers which should have gone to the archives . . . Also, it was not unknown for a Minister to have certain papers removed from the official record. Moreover, there was no equivalent in the Quai d'Orsay of the Foreign Office practice of minuting incoming papers.[1]

Still, substantial material exists, much retrieved from missions or embassies abroad, from other departments, or from collateral material. Open for consultation in the AEME, relevant to our investigations, are the following.

Open Series

>   1918-1929 Europe, Etats-Unis, Levant, Asie-
>   Océanie et Tunisie
>   1918-1940 Afrique
>   1918-1949 Amérique
>   A Paix--1914-1920
>   Maison de la Presse--1914-1928.

Series open but limited for investigation upon previous authorization and subject to some exclusions

>   1930-1939 (on this is based the published
>   Documents diplomatiques français)
>   Société des Nations--1917-1940

1. France and the Coming of the Second World War (London, 1977), pp. 397-98.

Use of these series is made more easy by following typewritten inventories available in the Reading Room. These include inventories for:

Correspondance politique et commerciale de 1897 à 1929

Correspondance politique et commerciale de 1918 à 1940
   Afrique
   Y série Internationale

Séries complémentaires
   B Relations commerciales--1920-1929
   A Paix--1914-1920
   Maison de la Presse--1914-1928

The AEME published in 1917 a Guide du lecteur detailing conditions of admission and listing the series open to inspection. An example from this pamphlet shows how a researcher would approach a study of the Genoa conference of April 1922. Call, based on the inventories, would go for:

Série B Relations commerciales, vols. 85-135

Série Y Internationale, vols. 29-36

Série S.D.N. (limited, by authorization), vols. 1204-1206 (September 1921-May 1922)

Papiers d'agents:
   Millerand, vols. 72-93
   Alphand, files III and IV
   Charles-Roux, file X, international conferences
   Defrance, vol. 1
   Henri de Jouvenel (limited, by authorization)
   Plaisant, box 3

2. Published Documents

For the 1930s one turns to the Ministry of Foreign Affairs's Commission de publication des documents aux origines de la guerre 1939-1945, Documents diplomatiques français, 1932-1939. This is being published by the Imprimerie nationale in two series, the first covering 1932-1935, the second 1936-1939. To fill, partially, the tremendous gaps caused by the destruction of the war, documents

were repatriated from Germany, recalled from posts
abroad, taken from coding office records, and from
other non-diplomatic departments, and, in a few
cases, borrowed from private holdings such as that
of René Masigli. Much remains absent, and files
are incomplete concerning internal discussions in
the Foreign Ministry, the execution of treaties,
many international conferences, separatist movements,
the Austro-German customs union, the Manchurian
crisis, and so on. Still the DDF has vital material
concerning the League, the disarmament conferences,
the Saar plebiscite, the economic conference of
1933, and the Ethiopian affair.

3. Private Papers

Private papers of ministers and secretaries
of state held by the government include those of:

Vincent Auriol (Fondation nationale des
    Sciences politiques)
Paul Baudouin (Ministère des affaires
    étrangères)
Léon Blum (Fondation nationale des Sciences
    politiques)
Georges Bonnet (MAE)
Georges Clemenceau (variously at the Service
    historique de l'Armée de Terre, Bibliothèque
    Nationale, MAE, and Musée Georges
    Clemenceau)
Edouard Daladier (Fondation nationale des
    Sciences politiques and the MAE)
Marcel Déat (Bibliothèque nationale)
Pierre Flandin (Bibliothèque nationale and MAE)
Paul Boncour (MAE)
Raymond Poincaré (Bibliothèque nationale, and
    the Service historique de l'Armée de Terre)
Albert Thomas (Archives Nationales)

Further information on these papers is found in
C. de Tourtier-Bonazzi and F. Pourcelet, Guide des
papiers des ministres et secrétaires d'état de 1871
à 1974, volume 1 (Paris, 1978).

4. Other Sources

Few if any minutes were taken of meetings of
the Council of Ministers, so 'cabinet' records do
not exist for France. However, records of certain
important sessions may be reconstructed from memoirs
of participants, such as, the formulation of League

and sanctions policy during the Italian-Ethiopian
conflict found in the autobiography of League delegate and minister Edouard Herriot, Jadis, volume 2,
D'une guerre à l'autre, 1914-1936 (Paris, 1952).
Official thinking may be found in such other sources
as:

> Archives du Sénat. Palais de Luxemburg.
> Archives de la Chambre des Députés. Palais
> Bourbon. In particular here are the rather
> complete Procès-Verbaux des séances de la
> commission des Affaires Etrangères.
> Sénat, Annales du Sénat, débats parlementaires.
> Chambre des Députés, Journal officiel, débats
> parlementaires.
> Assemblée Nationale, Rapport fait au nom de la
> commission chargée d'enquêter sur les
> événements survenus en France de 1933 à 1945.
> C. Serre, ed. 9 volumes. Paris, 1951-1952.

See also:

127. Hartmann, P. C. Pariser Archive, Bibliothe-
ken, und Dokumentationszentren zur Geschichte
des 19. and 20. Jahrhunderts. Munich, 1976.

128. Welsch, E. K. Libraries and Archives in
France. Pittsburgh, 1973.

C. UNITED STATES

1. Archives

The Records of the Department of State repose
mainly with the National Archives and Records
Services, Washington, D.C. Service there is
prompt, guides abundant, and copying services
available. The records are open according to a
thirty-year rule. A systematic microfilming is
underway, and over 100,000 rolls are presently
available for sale. Two National Archives publications are useful to the researcher: the Guide to
the National Archives of the United States (Washington 1974), and M. O. Gustafson, ed., The National
Archives and Foreign Relations Research (Athens, OH,
1974). Documentation is located along the following
groups of State Department records:

a. General Records of the Department of State
   (Record Group 59)

   These comprise the topically arranged central
decimal file. Particularly relevant are classes 5
(international conferences), 6 (commerce), 7 (political relations between states), and 8 (international affairs of states). The 'purport lists,' or
subject indexes, are available for the period 1910-
1944 as National Archives Microfilm Publication
M973, also available as a pamphlet published in 1976.
The Catalog of National Archives Microfilm
Publications (1974) gives a more detailed breakdown,
and shows as well the decimal files from classes 7
and 8 which have been filmed.

b. Records of International Conferences, Commissions, and Expositions (Record Group 43)

   This includes records of the United States
delegates to the conferences on arms limitation
(1921-1922, 1927, 1930, and 1935), and conferences
on regional, technical, and humanitarian cooperation.

c. Records of Foreign Service Posts (Record
   Group 84)

   These consist of files maintained at individual
U.S. diplomatic and consular posts overseas, of
which in 1939 the U.S. maintained approximately
sixty diplomatic and 300 consular posts. These are
distinct from State Department records, mostly in
bound volumes, for which registeries and some card
indexes are to be found.

d. Records of the American Commission to Negotiate
   Peace (Record Group 256)

   All Commission records except those of the
Inquiry are filmed as National Archives Microfilm
Publication M820. An inventory is available com-
piled by Sandra Rangel (1974).

e. Presidential Papers

   Of presidential papers, Wilson's are in the
Library of Congress, Hoover's in the presidential
library in West Branch, Roosevelt's in Hyde Park,
and Truman's in Independence. These libraries are
administrated by the National Archives, and contain

as well papers deposited by officials of those presidencies.

2. Published Documents

The essential publication series, a model of thoroughness and accuracy, is the Department of State's Foreign Relations of the United States. These many volumes offer quite comprehensive policy-making documents and correspondence. The series is complete for our period, readily available, and can be very informative.

3. Private Papers

--Ray Stannard Baker (Library of Congress)
--Joseph C. Grew (Houghton Library, Harvard University)
--Harry Hopkins (Roosevelt Library, Hyde Park)
--Edward House (Sterling Library, Yale University)
--Cordell Hull (Library of Congress)
--Robert Lansing (Library of Congress)
--David Hunter Miller (Library of Congress)
--Elihu Root (Library of Congress)
--Henry L. Stimson (Sterling Library, Yale University)
--Arthur Sweetser (Library of Congress)
--Hugh R. Wilson (Hoover Library, West Branch)

4. An Additional Resource

Two series recently published by Garland Publishing Company provide new data on American policy. In the series "The Legislative Origins of American Foreign Policy" two volumes give the minutes of the executive sessions of the Senate Foreign Relations Committee, 1913-1933, including the closed discussions of the Kellogg Pact, the Manchurian Crisis, and the World Court. The series "United States Military Intelligence, 1917-1927" contains interesting assessments of many events affecting the League, notably the disarmament conferences.

D. OTHER STATES

As for all states, reference should be made initially to the companion volumes in this series, such as on Germany by Christoph Kimmich, and in Italy by Alan Cassels. Below I note mainly printed materials from European states, general references that contain mention of international organizations.

1. Germany

The central diplomatic collections are the Documents on German Foreign Policy, 1918-1945, based on captured material and the Akten zur deutschen auswärtigen Politik, 1918-1945, which complements it. These are in several series, sensibly ordered, and may be supplemented by:

129. Kent, George O. A Catalogue of Files and Microfilms of the German Foreign Ministry Archives, 1920-1945. Stanford, 1962.

Two other published collections are Ursachen und Folgen: Vom deutschen Zusammenbruch 1918 und 1945 bis zur staatlichen Neuordnung Deutschlands in der Gegenwart, and Akten der Reichskanzlei, both large scale presentations of the policy-making processes. Helpful overview of the archives are:

130. Epstein, Fritz T. "Germany." In The New Guide to the Diplomatic Archives of Western Europe, edited by D. H. Thomas and L. M. Case. Philadelphia, 1975. This has a good bibliography, discusses the holdings of private papers, and notes research instruction in Germany.

131. Haase, D., ed. The Records of German History in Germany and certain other Record Offices. Boppard am Rhein, 1975.

132. Welsch, E. K. Libraries and Archives in Germany. Pittsburgh, 1975.

2. Italy

The Ministero degli affari esteri is publishing I Documenti diplomatici italiani, the fifth through ninth series of which cover 1914-1943. This is arranged chronologically, and is difficult to follow topically. There are informative introductions which in certain instances describe the composition and method of work of the foreign ministry, and relate these to Italy's position towards conferences and the League. After 1922, and particularly in the early 1930s, the tono fascista disrupted regular diplomatic routines, and one must go increasingly to Mussolini's papers (in the Archivio Centrale dello Stato), his speeches, and private accounts to follow the Italian line. Use of material in the Archivio Storico Diplomatico del Ministero degli Affari Esteri is, formally, governed by a fifty-year rule, but one may ask permission to see material after thirty years. Of note here are the Carteggio serie politica, and the Archivio di Gabinetto.

3. Belgium

Documents diplomatiques belges, 1920-1940 is issued in five volumes, but has little on the League. The Archives Générales du Royaume in Brussels contains some interesting papers, such as those of Paul Hymans. For the foreign ministry refer to:

133. Thomas, D. H., "Belgium." In D. H. Thomas and L. M. Case, eds., The New Guide to the Diplomatic Archives of Western Europe. Philadelphia, 1975.

4. The Netherlands

Documentation betreffende de buitenlandse politiek van Nederland, 1919-1945 is a new and very rich collection with relevant documents from archives outside the Netherlands, and extensive summaries in English of each document.

IV. OTHER COLLECTIONS AND RESOURCES

The experience of the war, the notion of 'open diplomacy,' the newly organized League of Nations, the realization that foreign affairs intimately affected civilian life, and that, reciprocally, foreign policy was subject to public debate, opened an era of greatly increased interest in international affairs. The ideology of Wilsonianism, with its predicates of rational discourse and political democratization, the fact that the League was an open forum, gave rise to lively discussion in the democracies, while, in the dictatorships, there was a conscious effort to orchestrate support behind government policy.

A. LIBRARIES

The United Nations Library in the Palace of Nations in Geneva houses the most complete collection in Europe of works on international administrative law, a collection international in scope on economic, financial, and social questions, and a large number of maps and geographical works. Admission is upon application; books may be checked out or set aside for extended use.

The Dag Hammarskjöld Library adjoins the Secretariat building at the United Nations headquarters in New York City. Its general collection, reference collection, and periodical and newspaper collections are broad and current. For our purpose, the center is the Woodrow Wilson Collection, a gift to the United Nations in 1950 of the Woodrow Wilson Foundation, of some 15,000 documents and books relating to the League, world organizations, diplomatic history, peace movements, and international relations during the period of the League's existence. These materials do not circulate, and must be consulted in the Woodrow Wilson Reading Room. They are catalogued, indexed, and with various reference guides.

The Library of the Peace Palace at The Hague opened in 1913, and is an outstanding collection of reference and research materials on international law, peace, and internationalism. A catalogue of about half its entries has been published on microfiche by the Clearwater Publishing Co., New York, in two volumes, Periodicals Reference Guide, and Universal Bibliographical Catalogue. Each state archive has attached to it a library where basic published state collections are usually to be found, together with essential reference aids for use in the archive itself. A good deal of information can be picked up readily and efficiently by perusing these stacks.

The great state libraries, the great university and municipal libraries, are no doubt well known to the researcher. The British Library (aka until recently the Reading Room of the British Museum), the Bibliotheque Nationale, the Library of Congress, need no introduction, and catalogues of their holdings are widely available. Mention might be made additionally of particular rich collections in schools of law, such as the Law Library of Columbia University and the International Legal Studies Library at Harvard.

The Library of the Hoover Institute on War, Revolution and Peace at Stanford has extremely rich western and eastern European holdings for our period, including many periodicals and journals, interesting ephemera, hard-to-find documents and studies, and some collections of interest, such as the Alfred Fried Collection concerning peace movements from 1892-1921, and the W. D. Hines Collection concerning post-war agreements and operations concerning Rhine and Danube shipping. Researchers should consult: Agnes F. Peterson, Western Europe: A Survey of Holdings at the Hoover Institution on War, Revolution and Peace (1970), and The Library Catalogue of the Hoover Institution on War, Revolution and Peace, published by G. K. Hall, particularly the 63 volumes (1,087,000 cards) of the Western Language Collections, published in 1969 with a 5-volume supplement in 1972 and a 6-volume supplement in 1977, and the Western Language Serials and Newspaper Collections, 3 volumes (46,800 cards).

The Bibliothek für Zeitgeschichte-Weltkriegsbücherei in Stuttgart was founded in the late 1920s and has holdings similar to the Hoover Institution. This is the largest German special collection in contemporary history. Its catalogues too have been published by G. K. Hall, an Alphabetischer Katalog in 11 volumes and a Systematischer Katalog in 20 volumes.

The Ullstein Archiv in Berlin has 3 million clippings and over 16,000 volumes of German and

foreign newspapers and periodicals from the 1920s
and 1930s, and is comparable for the continent to
the Chatham House Press Library.

The Oral History Collection of Columbia University contains the 'reminiscences' of the following
members of the League Secretariat: Thanassis
Aghnides, Pablo de Azcárate y Florez, Edouard de
Haller, Branko Lukac, and Van Asch van Wijck.

B. INSTITUTES

Expressive of the sense that foreign affairs
were now public affairs was the foundation of institutions and university positions devoted to contemporary international affairs. The first professor-
ship in international politics was established in
1919 at the University College of Wales and named
for Woodrow Wilson. Its purpose was to be both
academic and practical, to disseminate the fruits
of research to the public at large. Similarly, the
purposes of institutes was both study and publicity,
research and public education, aiming at certain
cases to influence policy as well. To these ends
journal series were established, which contain a
vivid record of inter-war thinking about international relations and organizations.

1. The Royal Institute of International
Affairs (London)

Founded in July 1920 as the British Institute
of International Affairs (it received a royal
charter in 1926), this was the exemplar of liberal
internationalist thinking, private, unofficial,
without policy-making dimensions. Independent of
government, political party, or obvious pressure
group, it held regular meetings, informed speeches,
and lively discussions. Its annual dinner, from
1930, was usually addressed by the Foreign Secre-
tary--who proposed a research agenda. The reports
of its study groups, its constant attention to
League and Commonwealth affairs, its stress on
change, on economic and social as well as political
issues, and its publications, made Chatham House
(as it is often referred to after its establishment
there in 1923) a major forum for opinion and information, as it sought to place British thinking in
the context of world concerns. Its journal, International Affairs (originally, and to 1930, the
Journal of the British [then Royal] Institute of
International Affairs), contains the record of

speeches and discussions, often by foreign visitors, and a comprehensive review of internationalist bibliography.

Its publications began with its sponsorship of A History of the Peace Conference of Paris, a collective undertaking of great value, and, after 1922, the Institute became affiliated with The British Year Book of International Law (founded 1920), a work comparable to the Recueil des cours in its illuminating, expert articles by legal authorities. From 1925 the annual Survey of International Affairs, supplemented after 1928 with the volumes of Documents on International Affairs, provided a thematic overview of (mainly European) political events, in which the League, especially during the Manchurian and Ethiopian crises, figured prominently. G. M. Gathorne-Hardy's study of the post-war world, A Short History of International Affairs (various editions after 1934) reflects the lines of Chatham House thinking, and a number of studies dealing with the Near East and Africa show the mandate mentality at its most generous. The Institute created a remarkable Press Library of well classified clippings, that is open to post-graduate students at Chatham House, St. James's Square, London.

2. The Council on Foreign Relations (New York)

This was the American counterpart, closely associated with the RIIA. Less visible to non-members as a forum of discussion (speeches and discussions were not printed in its journal), it took a more lofty and limited view of its educational function. It published Foreign Affairs Quarterly, the most prestigious outlet for liberal American internationalism in an era when the major domestic opposition to this attitude came from isolationism. From 1928 the Council published two annual volumes, American Foreign Relations (comparable to the Royal Institute's Survey) and Political Handbook of the World: Parliaments, Parties and Press. The Council's membership has been studied as an elite group. Pushing this assertion back into the 1920s and 1930s would be an interesting study. The tenor of Council thinking may be grasped in the autobiography of the long-time editor of Foreign Affairs:

134. Armstrong, Hamilton Fish. Peace and Counter-
     peace: From Wilson to Hitler. New York, 1971.

The Foreign Relations Library was established in 1930, aiming to cover all aspects of international relations since 1918, and reference to its 55,000 volumes may be found in the Catalog of Foreign Relations Library, published in nine volumes in 1969 by G. K. Hall, Boston.

3. Institut für Auswärtige Politik (Hamburg)

The idea for this was born at Versailles with Delbrück, Montgelas, Weber, and Mendelssohn-Bartholdy, that some group should speak for Germany. Its original title was Archiv der Friedensverträge, and under early directorship of Albrecht Mendelssohn Bartholdy it published the Archiv der Friedensverträge and cooperated in the publication of the great document series Die Grosse Politik der Europäischen Kabinette, 1871-1914. In 1923 the name was changed to Institut für Auswärtige Politik, and it began publication of Europäische Gespräche, a fairly even-handed monthly of articles, documents, reviews, and bibliography.

4. Hochschule für Politik (Berlin)

This was closer to the Royal Institute of International Affairs in educational function, giving distinguished foreigners a podium in Germany. Together with the Institut für Auswärtige Politik it published the series Politische Wissenschaft.

5. Henri Dunant Institute (Geneva)

Closely associated with, but distinct from, the International Committee of the Red Cross, its work has been to put the Red Cross in historical perspective and context. In 1968 it published the history of the ICRC, the second volume of which, De Sarajevo à Hiroshima, was written by André Durand. At present it and the ICRC are publishing a bibliography on international humanitarian law.

6. Istituto per gli studi di politica internazionale (Milan)

An example of an institute in the service of government and official policy. Founded in 1933, backed by business interests, publishing the Rassenga di politica internazionale and the Annuario de politica internazionale, its purpose was to organize a consensus for a more active Italian foreign policy. In this sense, being founded in the absence of a developed academic or popular interests in international political science, Ispi was an interesting corporatist venture. Similarly, it should be noted that the review Affari Esteri was edited in the Foreign Ministry.

135. Montenegro, Angelo. "Politica estera e organizzazione del consenso: Note sull'istituto per gli studi di politica internazionale, 1930-1943," Studi Storici 19(1978):735-776.

7. Carnegie Endowment for International
Peace (New York)

Founded in 1910, and established with a European office, it was, during our period, a very important source for serious and comprehensive studies on many important institutional matters. It published International Conciliation, a year book, and pamphlets, as well as its important monographs.

8. Geneva Research Center (Geneva)

Noted for its series Special Studies (which items are listed in the bibliography below by author, as they were self-contained works) the Center drew authors from the League milieu, and its monographs on current issues often have a special immediacy as a result.

9. L'Académie de Droit International
de la Haye (The Hague)

Speeches delivered here were published, as authoritative articles concerning international law, the work of the Permanent Court, and the League, in the Recueil des cours de l'Académie de Droit International de la Haye.

10. Institute of Pacific Relations

For this institute, reference should be made to:

136. Angus, Henry F. The Problem of Peaceful Change in the Pacific Area. London, 1937.

C. ADDITIONAL PERIODICALS

In addition to journals mentioned earlier, associated with an institute concerned with international affairs, the following are useful:

Annuaire de la Société des Nations, edited by Georges Ottlick in Geneva. There are 8 volumes of this informative yearbook, full of facts about the League, details of leading figures, institutional information, and so on. The first volume, covering 1920-1927, was published in 1927, with subsequent volumes published in 1928, 1929, 1930, 1931, 1936, 1937, and 1938.

Zeitschrift für ausländisches öffentliches Recht und Völkerrecht, similar to the above, published in Berlin in the late 1920s and early 1930s.

Annuaire, Institut de droit international (Basle).

The Europe Year-Book: An Annual Survey of European Politics, Art and Literature, a European Who's Who and Directory, and a Statistical Review of Europe began in 1926, improved in sophistication, and was incorporated into The Europa Service (London), inaugurated in 1930, and beginning in 1933 published The Encyclopedia of Europe and the European's Who's Who.

Die Friedenswarte was founded in Berlin in 1899 by Alfred H. Fried, the noted pacifist, internationalist, for 'international understanding and international organization,' and moved to Zurich in the 1930s where it was edited by Hans Wehberg, a professor of international law at the Institut Universitaire des Hautes Etudes Internationales in Geneva. It drew on League observers and notables, and contains much of an informal, as well as an analytic nature, giving fresh perspectives on Geneva in the 1930s.

International Conciliation, in New York, was begun in 1907 by the American Association for International Conciliation and published 1924-1972 by the Carnegie Endowment as a journal of explication.

Problems of Peace was published annually 1926-
1938 by the Institute of International Relations in Geneva, with interesting speeches and
commentaries by important figures on the Geneva
scene.

L'Europe nouvelle, founded in 1918 by Louise
Weiss to 'promote peace and understanding'
gives a record of contemporary thinking.
Edited by Weiss until 1934 its interest is
enhanced by the record Weiss left in the second
volume of her autobiography:

137. Weiss, Louise. Mémoires d'une Européenne.
     Paris, 1970.

This book covers the period 1919-1934, in two parts,
'Genève ou Moscou,' and 'Apostolat pour la Société
des Nations.' She like Wehberg was much in atten-
dance in Geneva and various international conferences, and interviewed League participants.
Newspapers may be used to contrast what was
known to the public and what officialdom was thinking and doing. Papers which covered the League and
international organizations are: Le journal de
Genève, Le journal des nations, La tribune de Genève,
L'écho de Paris, Le temps, The Manchester Guardian,
The Times (London), and The New York Times. The
latter two are well indexed, and there are various
inside accounts, such as following for The Times:

138. Morrison, Stanley. The History of the "Times":
     volume 4, part 2, The 150th Anniversary and
     Beyond, 1912-1948. New York, 1952.

139. Wrench, J. D. Geoffrey Dawson and Our "Times."
     London, 1955.

140. McLachlan, D. In the Chair: Barrington-Ward
     of the "Times," 1927-1948. London, 1971.

D. SCHOLARLY JOURNALS

Scholarly work since 1945 appears in journals
of history, international affairs, and political
science. International Affairs and Foreign Affairs
carry on the traditions of their foundation,
although without the optimism that distinguished
the period of the Great Experiment. The following
may be consulted for articles offering analytical
perspectives or which study the period historically.

Comparative Politics
Europa Archiv
Historian
History
Historical Journal
Historische Zeitschrift
International Journal
International Organization
International Studies Quarterly
Journal of International Affairs
Journal of Contemporary History
Journal of Modern History
Political Science Annual
Political Science Quarterly
Politische Vierteljahresschrift
Revue historique
Revue d'histoire de la Deuxième Guerre Mondiale
Revue d'histoire moderne et contemporaine
Round Table
Vierteljahrshefte für Zeitgeschichte
World Politics

E. CONTEMPORARY SKETCHES

Geneva was a small town. This was an era
fascinated with public figures. Many worthwhile
details are found in journalistic accounts, of which
there are a vast amount. Among them:

141. Azcárate, Pablo de. William Martin: Un grand
     journaliste à Genève. Geneva, 1970.

142. Barman, Thomas. Diplomatic Correspondent.
     London, 1968.

143. Benjamin, R. S., ed. Eye Witness, New York,
     1940.

144. Crozier, W. P. Off the Record: Political
     Interviews, 1933-1934. Edited by A. J. Taylor.
     London, 1974.

145. Dell, Robert. The Geneva Racket, 1920-1939.
     London, 1940.

146. Géraud, André, Pertinax (pseud.). Les
     fossoyeurs. 2 vols. New York, 1943.

147. Hillson, Norman. Geneva Scene. London, 1936.

148. King-Hall, Stephen. Our Times, 1900-1960. London, 1961.

149. Ludwig, Emil. Nine Sketched from Life. New York, 1934.

150. Matthews, Herbert L. A World in Revolution: A Newspaperman's Memoir. New York, 1972.

151. Romains, Jules. Seven Mysteries of Europe. Trans. by G. Brée. New York, 1940.

152. Sava, George. A Tale of Ten Cities. London, 1942.

153. Slocombe, George. A Mirror to Geneva: Its Growth, Grandeur and Decay. New York, 1938.

154. Sulzberger, C. L. A Long Row of Candles: Memoirs and Diaries, 1934-1954. New York, 1969.

155. Tabouis, Genevieve. They Called Me Cassandra. New York, 1942.

156. Tabouis, Genevieve. Vingt ans de "suspense" diplomatique. Paris, 1958.

157. Temperley, Arthur C. The Whispering Gallery of Europe. London, 1938.

158. Ward-Price, George. Extra-Special Correspondent. London, 1957.

159. Waterfield, Gordon. Morning Will Come. London, 1944.

160. Wiskemann, Elizabeth. The Europe I Saw. London, 1968.

Three works of fiction that use the League as their scene:

161. Cohen, Albert. Belle du Seigneur. Paris, 1968.

162. Oldfield, Peter (pseudo.). The Alchemy Murder. London, 1929.

163. Oldfield, Peter (pseudo.). The Death of a Diplomat. London, 1928.

These last two are detective stories, co-written by the director of the League Office in London, Vernon Bartlett, and a member of the Finance Committee, Per Jacobsson.

For representation through the eyes of two notable cartoonists:

164. Kelen, Emery. Peace in Their Time: Men Who Led Us In and Out of War. New York, 1963. Kelen, drawing often with Alois Derso, was caricaturist-in-residence of the League, and his cartoons still decorate private and public places in Geneva today.

165. Low, David. Europe since Versailles. Harmondsworth, 1946. Drawing for the London Evening Standard, Low's pen captured conferences and personalities. This book, one of his several, is good on the mood of the time.

V. PLANNING FOR PEACE, 1919

Faced with the herculean tasks of formulating terms of peace with the defeated states and establishing an entirely new system of collective security, the victorious powers meeting in Paris differed among themselves as to the nature of the settlement and the purpose of a new international order. The history of the conference and the founding of the League of Nations is the study of uneasy compromises between ideologies and traditional interests. The Covenant was made an integral part of the treaties, its principles viewed by some with derision and suspicion, and by others as the main hope for the creation of a lasting peace.

A. PEACE CONFERENCES

166. Albrecht-Carrié, R. Italy at the Paris Peace Conference. New York, 1938.

167. Antonelli, E. L'Afrique et la paix de Versailles. Paris, 1921.

168. Baker, Ray Stannard, ed. Woodrow Wilson, Life and Letters. 8 vols. New York, 1927-39.

169. Baker, Ray Stannard. Woodrow Wilson and World Settlement. 3 vols. New York, 1922.

170. Bariety, Jacques. "La haute commission interalliée des territoires Rhénans." In Problèmes de la Rhénanie, 1919-1930, by M. Vaïsse, et al. Metz, 1975.

171. Baumgart, W., et al. Versailles--St. Germain-- Trianon: Umbruch in Europa vor fünfzig Jahren. Munich, 1971. Nine scholarly essays with central European perspective.

172. Beau de Loménie, Emmanuel. Le débat de ratification du traité de Versailles à la chambre des députés et dans la presse en 1919. Paris, 1945.

69

173. Beer, G. L. African Questions at the Paris Peace Conference. New York, 1923.

174. Berger, Marcel, and Allard, Paul. Les dessous du traité de Versailles. Paris, 1933.

175. Binkley, Robert C. "New Light on the Paris Peace Conference." Political Science Quarterly 46 (1931):335-61, 505-47.

176. Binkley, Robert. "Ten Years of Peace Conference History." Journal of Modern History 1 (1929):607-629.

177. Birdsall, Paul. Versailles Twenty Years After. New York, 1941.

178. Bonsal, Stephen. Suitors and Suppliants: The Little Nations at Versailles. New York, 1942.

179. Bonsal, Stephen. Unfinished Business. Garden City, NY, 1944. Conference diary of an aide to House and Wilson.

180. Bourgeois, Léon. La traité de paix de Versailles. Paris, 1919.

181. Bunselmeyer, Robert E. The Cost of War, 1914-1919: British Economic War Aims and the Origins of Reparation. Hamden, CT, 1975.

182. Carnegie Endowment for International Peace. Official Statements of War Aims and Peace Proposals, December 1916 to November 1918. New York, 1921.

183. Clemenceau, Georges. Grandeurs et misères d'une victoire. Paris, 1930.

184. Clémentel, Etienne. La France et la politique économique interalliée. Paris, 1931.

185. Conférence de la Paix. Recueil des actes de la conférence. 28 vols. Paris, 1922-34. These have been printed in microfilm and published by the Hoover Institution.

186. Conference of Ambassadors. The Minutes of the Conference of Ambassadors, 26 January 1920 - 12 January 1931. These 97 volumes,

the procès-verbaux taken by the American Diplomatic Mission, have been reproduced in microfilm and are sold by Bay Microfilm, Palo Alto, in 97 reels.

187. Curry, George. "Woodrow Wilson, Jan Smuts, and the Versailles Settlement." American Historical Review 66(1961):976-83.

188. Deák, Francis. Hungary at the Paris Peace Conference. New York, 1942.

189. Dockrill, M. L., and Steiner, Zara. "The Foreign Office at the Paris Peace Conference in 1919." International History Review 2(1980):54-86.

190. Duroselle, Jean-Baptiste. De Wilson à Roosevelt: Politique extérieure des Etats-Unis, 1913-1945. Paris, 1960.

191. Elcock, Howard. Portrait of a Decision: The Council of Four and the Treaty of Versailles. London, 1974.

192. Fellner, Fritz, and Maschl, Heidrun. "Saint-Germain, im Sommer 1919:" Die Briefe Franz Keleins aus der Zeit seiner Mitwirkung in der österreichischen Friedensdelegation. Mai-August 1919. Salzburg, 1977.

193. Fisher, H. A. L. James Bryce. 2 vols. New York, 1927.

194. Fitzhardinge, L. F. "Hughes, Borden, and Dominion Representation at the Paris Peace Conference," Canadian Historical Review 49(1968):160-9.

195. Floto, Inga. Colonel House in Paris. Princeton, 1979. An excellent study of American policy and a superb single volume study of the conference.

196. Fowler, Wilton B. British-American Relations, 1917-1918. Princeton, 1969.

197. Gelfand, Lawrence E. The Inquiry: American Preparations for Peace. New Haven, 1963.

198. Genov, G. P. Bulgaria and the Treaty of Neuilly. Sofia, 1935.

199. Gunzenhäuser, Max, ed. Die Pariser Friedens-
     konferenz 1919. Frankfurt a. Main, 1970.
     Comprehensive bibliography of conference and
     its aftermath.

200. Hankey, Maurice. The Supreme Council: At
     the Paris Peace Conference, 1919: A Commen-
     tary. Good on the formation of the Council of
     Four by an important member of the British
     secretariat at the conference.

201. Harrod, Roy. The Life of John Maynard Keynes.
     London, 1953.

202. Haupts, Leo. Deutsche Friedenspolitik, 1918-
     1919: Eine Alternative zur Machtpolitik des
     Ersten Weltkrieges. Düsseldorf, 1976. Full
     use of German records, with excellent bibli-
     ography.

203. Headlam-Morley, James. A Memoir of the Paris
     Peace Conference. London, 1972. Especially
     useful for the decisions on the Saar and
     Danzig.

204. Hendrick, Burton J. The Life and Letters of
     Walter H. Page. 2 vols. New York, 1923.

205. House, E. M., and Seymour, C. What Really
     Happened at Paris. New York, 1921.

206. Kedourie, Elie. "The End of the Ottoman
     Empire." Journal of Contemporary History
     3(1968):19-28.

207. Keynes, John Maynard. The Economic Con-
     sequences of the Peace. London, 1920.

208. Keynes, John Maynard. A Revision of the
     Treaty. London, 1922. A sequel to The
     Economic Consequences of the Peace.

209. King, Wunsz (Chin, Wen-ssu). China at the
     Peace Conference in 1919. New York, 1961.

210. Kitsikis, Dimitri. Le rôle des experts à la
     conférence de la paix de 1919: Gestation
     d'une technocratie en politique internation-
     ale. Ottawa, 1972.

211. Krüger, Peter. Deutschland und die Repara-
     tionen 1918/19: Die Genesis des Repara-

tionsproblems in Deutschland zwischen Waffenstillstand und Versailler Friedensschluss. Stuttgart, 1973.

212. Lansing, Robert. The Peace Negotiations: A Personal Narrative. Boston, 1921. Secretary of State to February 1920, setting forth his opposition to Wilson's policy. The Department of State in 1939 and 1940 published two volumes of The Lansing Papers, 1914-1920, as part of the series Foreign Relations of the United States.

213. La Pradelle, A. de., ed. La paix de Versailles: La documentation internationale. 12 vols. Paris, 1929-39.

214. Lederer, Ivo J. Yugoslavia at the Paris Peace Conference: A Study in Frontier Making. New Haven, 1963.

215. Leon, George B. Greece and the Great Powers, 1914-1917. Thessaloniki, 1974.

216. Leopold, Richard W. Elihu Root and the Conservative Tradition. Boston, 1954.

217. Link, Arthur S., et al., eds. The Papers of Woodrow Wilson. Princeton, 1966 et seq.

218. Link, Arthur S. Woodrow Wilson: Revolution, War and Peace. Arlington Heights, IL, 1979. A short synthesis by the leading Wilson scholar.

219. Lloyd George, David. Memoirs of the Peace Conference. 2 vols. New Haven, 1939.

220. Lloyd George, David. The Truth about the Peace Treaties. London, 1938.

221. Lloyd George, David. War Memoirs. 6 vols. London, 1933-6.

222. Luckau, Alma. The German Delegation at the Paris Peace Conference. New York, 1941.

223. McDougall, Walter A. "Political Economy versus National Sovereignty: French Structures for German Economic Integration after Versailles." Journal of Modern History 51(1979):4-23.

224. Mantoux, Paul. Les délibérations du conseil des quatres (24.3-28.6. 1919): Notes de l'officier-interprète. 2 vols. Paris, 1955. There is an English translation by J. B. Whitton: Paris Peace Conference, 1919: Proceedings of the Council of Four, Geneva, 1964.

225. Marston, F. S. The Peace Conference of 1919: Organisation and Procedure. New York, 1944.

226. Martet, Jean. "M. Clemenceau and the Versailles Peace Treaty." Journal of the Royal Institute of International Affairs 6(1930): 783-800.

227. Mayer, Arno J. Political Origins of the New Diplomacy, 1917-1918. New Haven, 1959.

228. Mayer, Arno J. Politics and Diplomacy of Peacemaking: Containment and Counterrevolution at Versailles, 1918-1919. New York, 1967.

229. Mosca, Rodolfo, ed. Vittorio Emanuele Orlando: Memorie, 1915-1919. Milan, 1960.

230. Nicolson, Harold. Peacemaking 1919. New York, 1939.

231. Noble, George B. Policies and Opinions at Paris, 1919: Wilsonian Diplomacy, the Versailles Peace, and French Public Opinion. New York, 1955.

232. Opie, Redvers, et al. The Search for Peace Settlements. Washington, D.C., 1951.

233. Page, Stanley W. The Formation of the Baltic States: A Study of the Effects of Great Power Politics upon the Emergence of Lithuania, Latvia, and Estonia. Cambridge, MA. 1959.

234. Parrini, Carl P. Heir to Empire: United States Economic Diplomacy, 1916-1923. Pittsburgh, 1969. Foundation of American international economic policy laid by Wilson administration.

235. Pink, Gerhard P. The Conference of Ambassadors, Paris 1920-1931. Geneva, 1942.

236. Renouvin, Pierre. Le traité de Versailles. Paris, 1969.

237. Riddell, Lord. Lord Riddell's Intimate Diary of the Peace Conference and After, 1918-1923. London, 1933.

238. Rössler, Hellmuth, ed. Die Folgen von Versailles, 1919-1924. Göttingen, 1969.

239. Stadler, K. R. "The Disintegration of the Austrian Empire." Journal of Contemporary History 3(1968):177-90.

240. Salter, J. A. Allied Shipping Control: An Experiment in International Administration. Oxford, 1921.

241. Satow, Ernest. "Peacemaking, Old and New." Cambridge Historical Journal 1(1923):23-60.

242. Schwabe, Klaus. Deutsche Revolution und Wilson-Frieden. Düsseldorf, 1971.

243. Seymour, Charles. Letters from the Paris Peace Conference. Edited by H. B. Whiteman, Jr. New Haven, 1966. Member of the Inquiry, then head of the Austro-Hungarian division of the American commission to negotiate the peace. Shows above all problems of attempting a comprehensive settlement in a single conference, and the problems of varying moods in the absence of clear policy.

244. Spector, S. D. Rumania at the Paris Peace Conference: A Study of the Diplomacy of Ioan I. C. Bratianu. New York, 1962.

245. Stein, Boris E. Die russische Frage auf der Pariser Friedenskonferenz, 1919-1920. Leipzig, 1953.

246. Stirling, Alfred. Lord Bruce: The London Years. Melbourne, 1974.

247. Tardieu, André. The Truth About the Treaty. London, 1921.

248. Temperley, H. W. V., ed. A History of the Peace Conference of Paris. 6 vols. London, 1920-24.

249. Thompson, John M. Russia, Bolshevism, and the Versailles Peace. Princeton, 1966.

250. Tillman, Seth. Anglo-American Relations at the Paris Peace Conference of 1919. Princeton, 1961.

251. Tittoni, Tommaso, and Scialoja, V. L'Italia alla conferenza della pace. Rome, 1921.

252. Toynbee, A. J. The World after the Peace Conference. London, 1925. This is an epilogue to the six volume Chatham House study A History of the Peace Conference of Paris, and a prologue to the first volume of the Survey of International Affairs, 1920-1923.

253. Trachtenberg, Marc. "Reparation at the Paris Peace Conference." Journal of Modern History 51(1979):24-55. Reparations were the central problem of Europe after Versailles. Here the French are portrayed as moderates, the British as hardliners.

254. Widenor, William. Henry Cabot Lodge and the Search for an "American" Foreign Policy. Berkeley, 1979.

B. FOUNDING THE LEAGUE

255. Birn, Donald S. "The League of Nations Union and Collective Security." Journal of Contemporary History 9(1974):131-59.

256. Bourgeois, Leon. Le pacte de 1919 et la Société des Nations. Paris, 1919. The chief French delegate in the drafting committee.

257. Buzenkai, D. I. "Bolsheviks, The League of Nations, and the Paris Peace Conference, 1919." Soviet Studies 19(1967):257-63.

258. Curry, George W. "Woodrow Wilson, Jan Smuts, and the Versailles Settlement." American Historical Review 66(1961):968-86.

259. Dubin, Martin David. "Toward a Concept of Collective Security: The Bryce Group's 'Proposals for the Avoidance of War,' 1914-1917." International Organization 24(1970):288-318.

260. Egerton, George W. "Britain and the 'Great Betrayal': Anglo-American Relations and the Struggle for the United States Ratification

of the Treaty of Versailles, 1919-1920." The
Historical Journal 21(1978):885-911.

261. Egerton, George W. Great Britain and the
Creation of the League of Nations: Strategy,
Politics, and International Organization,
1914-1919. Chapel Hill, 1978. Although
British leaders made the principal contribution to drafting the Covenant, the bureaucratic and political elite, especially around
Lloyd George, opposed, doubting the viability
of collective security and wanting a world
conference system, bringing America into a
new balance of power focused on the Rhine.

262. Fortuna, Ursula. Der Völkerbundsgedanke in
Deutschland während des Ersten Weltkrieges.
Zurich, 1974.

263. Fosdick, Raymond B. Letters on the League of
Nations: From the Files of Raymond B. Fosdick.
Foreword by Arthur S. Link. Princeton, 1966.
Reflects idealism and hopeful expectations of
American liberals in 1919-20, when Fosdick
was Under Secretary General of the League.
Beginning of series "Supplementary Volumes
to The Papers of Woodrow Wilson".

264. Fowler, Wilton B. British-American Relations,
1917-1918: The Role of Sir William Wiseman.
Princeton, 1969.

265. Fraenkel, Ernest. "Idee und Realität des
Völkerbundes im deutschen politischen Denken."
Vierteljahrshefte für Zeitgeschichte 16(1968):
1-14.

266. Gunzenhäuser, Max. Die Pariser Friedenskonferenz 1919 und die Friedensverträge 1919-
1920. Frankfurt am Main, 1970.

267. Honigsheim, Paul. "An der Wiege der Völker-
bundidee." Die Friedenswarte (1938):209-35.

268. Latané, J. H., ed. Development of the League
of Nations Idea: Documents and Correspondence
of Theodore Marburg. 2 vols. New York, 1932.

269. Miller, David Hunter. The Drafting of the
Covenant. 2 vols. New York, 1928. An essen-
tial source, with many documents. With Cecil
Hurst, Miller, who was legal advisor to the

American delegation, was responsible for the wording of the Covenant. The first volume discusses the work of the League of Nations Commission. The second volume collects drafts and documents.

270. Miller, David Hunter. My Diary at the Conference of Paris: With Documents. New York, 1924.

271. Munch, P., ed. Les origines et l'oeuvre de la Société des Nations. 2 vols. Copenhagen, 1923-4. 33 articles on all phases of the early period by notables and experts.

272. Raffo, Peter. "The Anglo-American Preliminary Negotiations for a League of Nations." Journal of Contemporary History 9(1974):153-76.

273. Robbins, Keith. The Abolition of War: The 'Peace Movement' in Britain, 1914-1919. Cardiff, 1976.

274. Rublee, George. "Inter-Allied Machinery in War-Time." In The League of Nations Starts: An Outline by its Organisers, edited by R. B. Fosdick, et al. London, 1920.

275. Shotwell, James T., ed. The Origins of the International Labor Organization. 2 vols. New York, 1934.

276. Smuts, Jan Christian. The League of Nations: A Practical Suggestion. London, 1918.

277. Stone, Ralph. The Irreconcilables: The Fight against the League of Nations. Lexington, KY, 1970.

278. Wilson, Florence. The Origins of the League Covenant. London, 1928. Only woman full member of the U.S. Peace Commission, shows development of the Phillimore Reports of June 1918 onwards.

279. Wimer, Kurt. "Woodrow Wilson's Plans to Enter the League of Nations Through an Executive Agreement." Western Political Quarterly 9(1958):800-12.

280. Wimer, Kurt. "Woodrow Wilson Tries Concilia-
     tion: An Effort that Failed." The Historian
     25(1963):419-38.

281. Winkler, Henry R. The League of Nations Move-
     ment in Great Britain, 1914-1919. New Bruns-
     wick, NJ, 1952. Shows nature of public
     opinion.

282. Woolf, Leonard S. International Government.
     London, 1916. An early inspirational source.

VI. THE LEAGUE OF NATIONS

With the League one begins by noting its uniqueness, or, at any rate, understanding it as an institution. In Gerhard Neimeyer's succinct description, the League may be considered as:

> an organization of nations, an organization
> of potentially universal character, centering
> in a general and representative organ as well
> as in a small and "executive" organ, based on
> a Covenant containing elaborate procedure for
> the peaceful settlement of international
> disputes, a universal guarantee of terri-
> torial integrity, a promise of a grand coali-
> tion against any state that illegally resorted
> to war, and [holding out] the prospect of
> eventual universal disarmament.[1]

The founders of the League determined to repattern international relations away from the old concentration on national autonomy based on power, away from arms competition, away from changeable alliances. The maintenance of peace through organized, collective action offered, it appeared, a new form of political control. The League's claim to be an institution devoted to peaceful settlement and collective security gave it an assertion of centrality, while its constitution caused it to be seen as a form of world community. Yet of course for the various member states it was only one of their instruments of action, and it is inadequate to focus narrowly on the Covenant or on simply institutional analysis. The problems facing the League were formidable. There was the funda-mental incoherence of international relations, and the persistence of the autonomous right to wage war. The United States never joined, Russia was for a long time held away, and eventually expelled. France blew hot and cold, seeking increasingly to find defensive alliance outside the League. British priorities were often elsewhere, viewed in

1. "The Balance-Sheet of the League Experiment," International Organization 6(1952):540.

terms of imperial commitments, Japan and Germany joined, and then withdrew. Predominant power could never be located at Geneva. There was never a collectivist 'balance.' The great issues of the 1920s, reparations and disarmament for instance, were usually dealt with outside the framework of the Covenant, even when sentiment towards the League was at its most optimistic. In the 1930s when postwar settlements were breaking down, the testing of the League over Manchuria and Ethiopia showed that nothing could be accomplished without close cooperation and determination on the part of the major powers, and, here again, Geneva often took second place. Never universal despite its assumptions, the League as a political agency could not fulfill universal roles. Never sovereign, nor meant to be, it never replaced the sovereign autonomy of its members. Yet it played an important role, of a particular kind. As Niemeyer wrote, we need to "appraise the League not merely in terms of the ideal goal but above all as an institution situated in the mainstream of world politics, and intended to affect the conditions of war and peace" (_ibid._, 557). Indeed, it seems that international organizations have functioned most successfully 'not as participants in, or masters over, but as adjuncts to the multistate system."[1]

A. GENERAL STUDIES

283. Avenol, Joseph. "The Future of the League of Nations." _International Affairs_ 13(1934): 143-158. The minimalist position of the pessimistic Secretary-General.

284. Beer, Max. _The League on Trial_. Trans. by W. H. Johnston. London, 1933. Prominent German journalist, for some years member of the Information Section, very critical of Drummond, and bitterly dissatisfied with League results.

285. Bendiner, Elmer. _A Time for Angels: the Tragicomic History of the League of Nations_. London, 1975.

1. Inis L. Claude, Jr., "The Growth of International Institutions," in B. Porter, ed., _International Politics, 1919-1969_ (London, 1972), p. 293.

286. Bregman, Alexandre. La politique de la
     Pologne dans la Société des Nations. Paris,
     1932.

287. Caioli, Aldo. L'Italia de fronte a Ginevra.
     Rome, 1965.

288. Cecil, Robert. The Moral Basis of the League
     of Nations. London, 1923.

289. Charvet, Jean-Félix. L'influence britannique
     dans la S.D.N. (Des origines de la S.D.N.
     jusqu'à nos jours). Paris, 1938.

290. Dexter, Byron. The Years of Opportunity: The
     League of Nations, 1920-1926. New York,
     1967. Notes that "if the peace becomes the
     overriding objective . . . the influence of
     the organization will be used to advance the
     objectives of the most warlike power." Die
     cast in 1924-1925. Condemns Locarno which
     limited commitment to collective security.

291. Edwards, Augustin. "Latin America and the
     League of Nations." Journal of the Royal
     Institute of International Affairs 8(1929):
     134-140. Discusses absence of Mexico, and
     concludes influence of United States in
     western hemisphere much greater than that of
     the League.

292. Fleming, D. F. The United States and the
     League of Nations, 1918-1920. New York,
     1932. Strongly pro-Wilson and hard on Lodge.

293. Fosdick, Raymond B., et al. The League of
     Nations Starts: An Outline by its Organisers.
     London, 1920. Essays by notables of the
     early days.

294. Fosdick, Raymond B. Letters on the League of
     Nations from the Files of Raymond B. Fosdick.
     Princeton, 1966.

295. Giraud, Emile. "La Société des Nations:
     L'expérience de vingt ans." Revue générale
     de droit international public (1940):45-65.
     A sobering overview.

296. Goodrich, Leland M. "From League of Nations to United Nations." International Organization 1(1947):3-21.

297. Gorgé, Camille. La neutralité helvétique: Son évolution politique et juridique des origines à la seconde guerre mondiale. Zurich, 1947.

298. Guggenheim, Paul. Völkerbund, Dumbarton Oaks und die schweizerische Neutralität. Zurich, 1945.

299. Gunzenhäuser, M. "Der Genfer Völkerbund, 1920-1946." Bibliothek für Zeitgeschichte, Jahresbibliographie 41(1969):425-536.

300. Henig, Ruth B., ed. The League of Nations. Edinburgh, 1973. A good selection of speeches and writings.

301. Hewes, J. E., Jr. "Henry Cabot Lodge and the League of Nations." Proceedings of the American Philosophical Society 114(1970); 245-55.

302. Hildebrand, Klaus. Das deutsche Reich und die Sowjetunion im Internationalen System, 1918-1932: Legitimität oder Revolution? Wiesbaden, 1977.

303. Hsia, Chi-Feng. China and the League and My Experiences in the Secretariat. Shanghai, 1928.

304. Institute of International Relations. Pacifism is Not Enough. London, 1935. Three noteworthy essays are: W. Rappard, "Small States in the League of Nations"; Alvarez del Vayo, "The Chaco War" (he was chairman of the Commission of Inquiry); and R. MacIver, "National Planning and International Organization." A volume in the 'Problems of Peace' series.

305. Jackson, Judity, and King-Hall, Stephen, eds. The League of Nations Yearbook. London, 1932, 1933, 1934.

306. Jones, Samuel S. The Scandinavian States and the League of Nations. Princeton, 1939.

307. Joyce, James A. Broken Star: The Story of
     The League of Nations (1919-1939). Swansea,
     1978.

308. Juntke, F., and Sveistrup, H. Das deutsche
     Schrifttum über den Völkerbund, 1917-1925.
     Berlin, 1927. List compiled from books in
     the Prussian State Library.

309. Kidd, George. The Role of the Council in
     Execution of Frontiers Assigned to the League
     of Nations by the Treaty of Versailles.
     Geneva, 1935.

310. Kuehl, Warren F. Seeking World Order: The
     United States and International Organization
     to 1920. Nashville, 1969.

311. Larus, Joel, ed. From Collective Security to
     Preventive Diplomacy: Readings in Inter-
     national Organization and the Maintenance of
     Peace. New York, 1965.

312. League of Nations. Liste mensuelle d'ouvrages
     catalogués à la Bibliothèque de la Société
     des Nations, 1928-1946.

313. League of Nations. Ouvrages sur l'activité
     de la Société des Nations catalogués à la
     Bibliothèque du Secrétariat. Geneva, 1928,
     supplement, 1931.

314. League of Nations. Ten Years of World Co-
     operation. Geneva, 1930. A well-ordered
     summary of activities, leaving the reader
     with the conclusion that the first decade was
     constructive and promising.

315. Mantoux, Paul. "On the Procedure of the
     Council of the League of Nations for the
     Settlement of Disputes." Journal of the
     Royal Institute of International Affairs
     6(1926), 16-31. Based upon his experiences as
     director of the Political Section.

316. Matshushita, Masatoshi. Japan in the League
     of Nations. New York, 1929.

317. Mervin, D. "Henry Cabot Lodge and the League
     of Nations." Journal of American Studies,
     4(1970):201-4.

318. Munch, P. La politique de Danemark dans la Société des Nations. Geneva, 1931.

319. Nicholas, H. G. "From League to United Nations." International Affairs, Special Issue (1970):8-100.

320. Niemeyer, Gerhart. "The Balance-Sheet of the League Experiment." International Organization 6(1952):527-58. Seminal article. Good critique of Walters's book, and opens broader discussion.

321. Noel-Baker, P. J. The League of Nations at Work. London, 1926.

322. Ostrower, Gary B. Collective Insecurity: The United States and the League of Nations During the Early Thirties. Lewisburg, 1979.

323. Ostrower, Gary B. "Secretary of State Stimson and the League." The Historian 41(1979):467-82.

324. Ottlik, Georges. Annuaire de la Société des Nations. Eight volumes published at Geneva for the years 1920-27, 1928, 1929, 1930, 1931, 1932-36, 1937, 1939.

325. Pfeil, Alfred. Der Völkerbund: Literaturbericht und kritische Darstellung seiner Geschichte. Darmstadt, 1976.

326. Raffo, P. The League of Nations. London, 1974.

327. Rappard, William E. L'entrée de la Suisse dans la Société des Nations. Geneva, 1923. Motta writes the preface. Shock of League supporters when U.S. failed to join. Election campaign to decide issue, famous plebiscite of May 1920, would, Motta thinks, have resulted in refusal except for active interest of Federal Government in support of adherence. An interesting study, parallel to the American experience.

328. Rappard, William E. The Geneva Experiment. London, 1931. Sees 'Europeanization' as greatest threat to League.

329. Redmond, Kent G. "Henry L. Stimson and the
      Question of League Membership" The Historian
      25(1963):211-12.

330. Rolin, Henri A. La politique de la Belgique
      dans la Société des Nations. Geneva, 1931.

331. Scott, George. The Rise and Fall of the
      League of Nations. London, 1973. A super-
      ficial account, even though some Cabinet
      papers are used.

332. Schwarz, Wolfgang. "Germany and the League
      of Nations." International Affairs 10(1931):
      197-207. Editor of Vorwärtz. "The attitude
      of Germany to the League of Nations and to
      peace can only be completely satisfactory
      when this national question is solved too."
      A statement truer than he knew then.

333. Sharma, Shiva-Kumar. Der Völkerbund und die
      Grossmächte: Ein Beitrag zur Geschichte der
      Völkerbundpolitik Grossbritanniens, Frank-
      reichs, und Deutschlands, 1929-1933. Frankfurt
      a. Main, 1978. A good study of the critical
      years with exhaustive bibliography.

334. Smuts, J. C. "The Present International
      Outlook." International Affairs 14(1935):3-
      19. Assumes 'people' want peace, with jejune
      parallels between individual and national
      'pyschologies.'

335. Stone, R. The Irreconcilables: The Fight
      Against the League of Nations. Lexington,
      KY, 1970.

336. Veatch, Richard. Canada and the League of
      Nations. Toronto, 1975. Excellent study,
      showing with regard to the Ethiopian affair
      how the Canadian minister took advantage of
      the domestic political campaign to put forward
      the proposal for further (oil) economic
      sanctions, and how the Hoare-Laval debacle
      saved the Canadian government from having to
      make a commitment.

337. Verma, D. N. India and the League of Nations.
      Patna, 1968.

338. Walters, F. P. A History of the League of
     Nations. London, 1952. The classic, detailed,
     pro-League study. Still by far the best
     introduction to the League.

339. Walters, F. P. "The League of Nations," in
     The Evolution of International Organisations,
     edited by E. Luard. London, 1966.

340. Wehberg, Hans. "Zur Methode der Vorbereitung
     des Völkerbundes während des Weltkrieges."
     Die Friedenswarte 5/6 (1939):177-201.

341. Wigniole, Albert. La Société des Nations et
     la revision des traités. Paris, 1932. An
     exhaustive, pessimistic legal study, a narrow
     interpretation of article 19.

342. Windass, Stan. "The League and Territorial
     Disputes," in The International Regulation of
     Frontier Disputes, edited by E. Luard.
     London, 1970.

343. White, Ralph. "Regionalism vs. Universalism
     in the League of Nations." Annales d'études
     internationales (1970):88-114.

344. Wright, Quincy, and Kidd, G. "Reform of the
     League of Nations." Geneva Special Studies,
     V, 7-8. Geneva, 1934.

345. Zimmern, Alfred. The League of Nations and
     the Rule of Law, 1918-1935. London, 1936. A
     second, revised edition published in 1939.

B. INSTITUTION

346. Aufricht, Hans. A Guide to League of Nations
     Documents. New York, 1951.

347. Barros, James. Betrayal from Within: Joseph
     Avenol, Secretary General of the League of
     Nations, 1933-1940. New Haven, 1969.

348. Barros, James. Office Without Power: Secre-
     tary General Sir Eric Drummond, 1919-1933.
     New York, 1979. The most complete history of
     Drummond as Secretary General, in the forma-
     tive years of the post.

349. Basdevant, Suzanne. Les fonctionnaires internationaux. Paris, 1931. International officials in the League, the Court, and the ILO.

350. Boudreau, F. G. "International Civil Service," in Pioneers in World Order, edited by H. E. Davis. New York, 1944.

351. Deibel, Terry L. Le secrétariat de la Société des Nations et l'internationalisme américain, 1919-1924. Geneva, 1972. An outstanding study, one of the Carnegie Foundation's 50th anniversary monographs.

352. Elès, Georges. Le principe de l'unanimité dans la Société des Nations et les exceptions à ce principe. Paris, 1935.

353. Fosdick, Raymond B. The League of Nations and the United Nations after Fifty Years: The Six Secretaries-General. Newton, CT, 1972.

354. Fourès, Roger. Des développements apportés par la SDN à la notion de représentation étatique. Paris, 1939.

355. Frei, Paul H. De la situation juridique des représentants des membres de la Société des Nations et ses agents. Paris, 1929.

356. Greaves, H. R. G. The League Committees and World Order: A Study of the Permanent Expert Committees of the League of Nations as an Instrument of World Government. London, 1931. This assembles the widely diverse activities of the League committees and discusses their roles, with some speculation as to their future function in a more powerful League.

357. Hill, Martin. Immunities and Privileges of International Officials: The Experience of the League of Nations. New York, 1947. An informed study by an expert in League activities and reform plans.

358. Jacklin, Seymour. "The Finances of the League." International Affairs 13(1934):689-704. Treasurer of the League since 1926, defending the League and showing how moderate the expenses of the organization are.

359. Jordon, Robert S. International Administration: Its Evolution and Contemporary Applications. New York, 1972.

360. Koh, Byung Chul. The United Nations Administrative Tribunal. Baton Rouge, 1966. Discusses need of employee security in any international or organization. Shows work of League Tribunal, which delivered 37 judgments between 1928-1946, and its relation to UN Tribunal which began work in 1950.

361. Kohlhase, N., Altung von Geusau, F. A. M., Siotis, J., Gerbet, P., and Louis, J.-V. Les missions permanentes auprès des organisations internationales. Brussels, 1973.

362. Langrod, Georges. The International Civil Service: Its Origins, its Nature, its Evolution. Trans. by F. G. Berthoud. Leyden, 1963. The administrative as well as political aspects, evolution under the League and ILO, and the drafting of articles 94-101 of the Charter concerning the Secretary General.

363. Loveday, Alexander. Reflections in International Administration. Oxford, 1956. Sums up his conclusions from his work in League.

364. Prevost, Marcel. Les commissions de l'assemblée de la Société des Nations. Paris, 1937.

365. Purves, Chester. The Internal Administration of an International Secretariat: Some notes based on the Experience of the League of Nations. London, 1945.

366. Ranshofen-Wertheimer, Egon. The International Secretariat. Washington, 1945. The most comprehensive treatment of the subject based on League experience.

367. Riches, Cromwell A. The Unanimity Rule and the League of Nations. Baltimore, 1934.

368. Rovine, Arthur W. The First Fifty Years: The Secretary-General in World Politics, 1920-1970. Leyden, 1970. Drummond's impartiality and discretion served as model. A redeeming feature of Avenol's tenure was the work of the Bruce Committee and its concept of central administration for economic and social programs.

369. Schwebel, Stephen M. The Secretary-General of the United Nations. Cambridge, 1952.

370. Singer, J. David. "The Finances of the League of Nations." International Organization 13(1959):255-73.

371. Siotis, Jean. Essai sur le secrétariat international. Geneva, 1963. Reflections by a close student of the League and UN and head of Carnegie Foundation's European office in Geneva.

372. Siraud, Pierre. Le tribunal administratif de la Société des Nations. Paris, 1942.

373. Wilson, Clifton E. Diplomatic Privileges and Immunities. Tucson, 1967.

374. Wilson, Joseph. "Problems of an International Secretariat." International Affairs 20(1944): 542-554.

VII. PRESERVING THE PEACE

A. Peace Settlements: The 1920s

Some thirty political disputes were brought
before the League during its first decade, submitted
to the Council or the Assembly under articles of the
Covenant pertaining to various procedures for
settlement such as arbitration, enquiry, conciliation, or judgment. The goal of the League was
peaceful settlement, the avoidance of a war from
which would have to follow the application of sanctions under article 16, the ultima ratio of the
system of collective security. These cases show
the League and the Permanent Court acting with
considerable resourcefulness. Most of the disputes
were legacies of the war, unsettled issues conse-
quent upon territorial or political changes. In no
case was the interest of a great power seriously
involved, or, at any rate, none was committed to
unilateral action against the wishes of the League.

1. The Aland Islands, 1920-1921

Territorially part of newly independent Finland,
they were claimed by Sweden by right of self-determination, a majority of the islanders wishing to
change national identity. At issue was a number of
problems typical of immediate post-war disputes:
territorial jurisdiction over fragments of old
empires, traditional notions of sovereignty versus
claims of submerged nationalists, and minority
rights. Britain brought the problem to the Council
as a threat to peace. The Council recommended
recognition of Finnish sovereignty with a League
guarantee to safeguard the Swedish character of the
population, and an international agreement to neu-
tralize and demilitarize the archipelago, as the
Swedes wanted.
The capacities of the League, the conciliatory
initiative of the Secretary-General, and the cooperation of the States concerned, gave a compromise
settlement. The British representative on the
Council concluded: "the dispute could never have
been settled by the ordinary means of diplomacy."

375. Barros, James. The Aland Islands Question:
     Its Settlement by the League of Nations. New
     Haven, 1968. The best study, fully documented.
     The quotation above is from p. 333.

376. Raschhofer, H., ed. Selbstbestimmungsrecht
     und Völkerbund: Das Juristengutachten im
     Aalandstreit vom 5. September 1920. Cologne,
     1969.

2. Vilna

     Part of the unsettled situation on Russia's
western frontier, Vilna changed hands five times in
1920. The dispute was between Lithuania, claiming
Vilna as a capital city, and Poland, which brought
the matter to the Council in 1920 to prevent an outbreak of war. The Council proposed a demarcation
line, sent a military commission, and recommended a
plebiscite organized by the League. Initially
accepted by both sides, the Council gave up these
proposals in 1920 following Poland's preemptive
occupation, Lithuanian intransigence, the Soviet
threats. Unprepared for such opposition, unsup-
ported by any greater power, the League undertook
a long search for a compromise settlement, until the
Conference of Ambassadors (outside League authority)
awarded the city to Poland. In this case the League
deflected a threat of imminent hostilities, but
failed (lacking enforcement powers) to solve the
dispute.

377. Grauzinis, C. La question de Vilna. Paris,
     1927.

378. Meriggi, L. Il conflitto lituano-polacco e
     la questione di vilna. Milan, 1930.

379. Moresthe, Georges. Vilna et la problème de
     l'est europèen. Paris, 1922.

380. Senn, A. E. The Great Powers, Lithuania and
     the Vilna question, 1920-1928. Leyden, 1966.

3. Upper Silesia

     Who was to control the second richest industrial
area of the continent? Poland claimed Upper Silesia
by ethnic right, and in fear of economic domination
if it was returned to German hands. Germany claimed
it by ethnic right, and as essential to economic

recovery. At Versailles it was the only German border question left unsettled. The Supreme Council could not decide. Clemenceau favored Polish claims, to keep Germany weak. Lloyd George, and Keynes, favored the German claim, to renew the strength of middle Europe's economic leader. Friction on the spot was exacerbated by the pro-Polish attitude of French forces there. A plebiscite in March 1921 gave no clear answer. Territorial division according to population wish seemed as difficult and as controversial as deciding who was to get what of the industrial and mining network. Deadlocked, the Supreme Council, in August 1921, gave the problem to the League.

Working with great technical skill, benefitting from not having the main contestants as parties to the case, and supported by the promise of the Supreme Council to abide by its decision, a Council committee in six weeks presented a plan that laid a boundary while maintaining intact the existing inter-dependent mining, manufacturing, trading, and trans-portation connections. To Germans it appeared to deliver the main wealth to Poland, a 'partition' which many never accepted and for which many never forgave the League. Yet the Geneva Convention on Upper Silesia (May 1922) was signed by both sides, and a Mixed Commission kept it in force for fifteen years. Walters (A History of the League of Nations, 156) called the convention "a document unique in international history as providing for the mainten-ance of economic unity across a political frontier," and as a precursor of, say, the Schuman Plan, it is worth study by those interested in economic inte-gration.

The most serious continuing problem was that of minorities, and complaints to the League by German minorities kept alive (or were created by) German grievances for many years. The Permanent Court was asked for several judgments in property disputes and with regard to minority schools.

381. Campbell, F. Gregory. "The Struggle for Upper Silesia, 1919-1922." Journal of Modern History 42(1970):360-385. A fine monograph-- the issue as considered in the Supreme Council.

382. Clarke, R. W. "The Influence of Fuel on International Politics." Journal of the British Institute of International Affairs 2(1923):107-118. By the British expert on the plebiscite commission. France's interest was

in keeping coal out of German hands, so that, aside from Russia, France and its Polish ally would control 85% of continental coal.

383. Kaeckenbeeck, Georges. The International Experiment of Upper Silesia: A Study in the Working of the Upper Silesian Settlement, 1922-1937. London, 1942. The best work on the subject, by a member of the Secretariat in charge of legal questions at the German-Polish Conference and then President of the Mixed Tribunal. Includes tests of reports and the convention.

384. Paton, H. J. "Upper Silesia." Journal of British Institute of International Affairs 6(1922):14-28. Very informative.

385. Rosenthal, Harry K. "National Self-Determination: The Example of Upper Silesia." Journal of Contemporary History 7(1972):231-42. The historical ambiguities of national self-determination. A large number could not be classified by nationality. Rather than satisfying a real demand, many forced to acquire a nationality.

386. Stone, Julius. Regional Guarantees of Minority Rights: A Study of Minorities Procedure in Upper Silesia. New York, 1933.

387. Wambaugh, Sarah. Plebiscites Since the War, with a Collection of Official Documents. 2 vols. Washington, Carnegie, 1933. Volume I is the best secondary account of the plebiscite of May 1921.

388. Wandycz, Piotr S. France and Her Eastern Allies, 1919-1925. Minneapolis. 1962. Explores French interests in detail, with rich use of Polish studies.

4. Albania

The Treaty of London which brought Italy into the war promised annexations from Albania to Serbia in the north and Greece in the south, and promised dominant political and economic control over the remainder of the state of Italy. Positions changed during the war and at the peace settlement. In 1921 Albania's frontiers were still unsettled.

Responsibility for determining post-war boundaries
was given to Supreme Council and the Conference of
Ambassadors, but no final action was taken. Albania
lay exposed. Yugoslav troops occupied territory in
the north; Greece claimed parts of the south (northern Epirus). The League's role was indirect,
although Walters' conclusion is fair: "There can
be little doubt that Albania owed her survival as
an independent State to the action of the League."
(A History of the League of Nations, 161). The
First Assembly admitted Albania, a generous and
legitimizing concession, and the Second Assembly
broadcast warnings against delay. Investigation of
the archives of the Ambassadors' Conference and
Britain will show whether it was exposure to such
publicity or promptings from the other sources that
prompted the conference to settle the boundary, and
the Yugoslavs to withdraw in the face of the British
threat to call the Council to consider enforcing
compliance with the new decision. The League aided
Albania in famine relief and reconstruction, but
increasingly the state became a satellite of Italy,
having been made virtually a mandate by the Conference of Ambassadors which, without regard to the
League, gave Italy its long promised protectory
power.

389.   Baerlein, H. A Difficult Frontier: Yugoslav-
       ians and Albanians. London, 1922.

390.   Lederer, Ivo J. Yugoslavia at the Paris
       Peace Conference: A Study in Frontiermaking.
       New Haven, 1963.

391.   Mousset, Albert. L'Albanie devant l'Europe,
       1912-1929. Paris, 1930.

392.   Stickney, E. P. Southern Albania or Northern
       Epirus in European International Affairs,
       1922-1923. Stanford, 1926.

393.   Yugoslavia. Dokumenti o Pitanju Granice sa
       Albanijon. Belgrade, 1924.

5. Corfu

To delimit the frontier between Albania and
Greece the Conference of Ambassadors sent forth a
boundary commission of which the Italian leader and
three Italian members were murdered on Greek
soil. Demanding but not receiving satisfac-

tion from the Greek government, Italy bombarded and occupied Corfu. The Greeks appealed to the Council, the most important political issue yet brought before the League, and, as an important power was directly involved there were in Geneva thoughts of Sarajevo. Italy denied the competence of the League, as the murdered men were agents of the Conference of Ambassadors, and threatened to resign membership if the Greek appeal were taken up. But with all except French opinion strongly against him, Mussolini did accept the jurisdiction of the Conference to settle the dispute. There thus arose in League circles a sense of competition if not contest between two international authorities, for the League, with the Covenant part of the Versailles treaty, had its own claim to action in the settlement of disputes. The Corfu incident showed the limitations of the League unless the powers themselves decided to put it to use.

394. Anchieri, Ettore. "L'affare di Corfù alla luce dei documenti diplomatici italiani." Il Politico (1955):374-395.

395. Barros, James. The Corfu Incident of 1923: Mussolini and the League of Nations. Princeton, 1965. The fundamental study, an excellent diplomatic history, with thorough bibliography.

396. Cassels, Alan. Mussolini's Early Diplomacy. Princeton, 1970.

397. Rumi, Giogria. Alle Origini della Politica Estera Fascista (1918-1923). Bari, 1968.

6. Mosul

This boundary dispute between Iraq and Turkey related to conflicting interpretations of the Treaty of Lausanne. It was referred to the Council by Britain, acting as mandatory for Iraq. It is of interest on several counts. One is because a decision of the Permanent Court declared the Council's decision in this case to be binding (not recommendatory) even though Turkey voted against it (because Turkey was an interested party). Second, it was acquiescence in the Council decision by the new nationalist government of Kemel which ended the dispute. Third, the real issue here was economic, control of Mosul oil. This is illustrated in the following. In 1927 Leon Crutainsky wrote a thesis entitled: La question de Mossoul devant le conseil de la Société des Nations (Paris, 1927). The same year he (as Leon Crutains) published the thesis under a new title: La Mésopotamie et la lutte pour les pétroles de Mossoul (Paris, 1927).

7. Greek-Bulgarian Frontier Incident, 1925

Prevention of war in this clash was hailed as a great political success. It was important that the great powers worked through the "marvelous instrument" of the Covenant, as a Council delegate called it, coming at the time of the Locarno agreement, it seemed propitious. The League's self-assessment of 1930 suggested that had the article XI been likewise applied in 1914 that crisis might have ended differently (Ten Years of World Co-operation, 33). The comparison is not apt. In a careful study based on archival sources, James Barros concluded that success was based on unique circumstances (weakness of Greece, marginality of Bulgaria, spirit of Locarno, unity of interest among the great powers with Briand as president of the Council seconded by Austen Chamberlain) in which the disputants had no choice but to accept the Council's proscription of further incidents. The British Foreign Office rejected this precedent of League action as inapplicable at the time of the Manchurian crisis.

398. Ahooja-Patel, Krishna. The Greco-Bulgarian Dispute Before the League of Nations, 1925-1927: An Experiment in Peaceful Settlement. Geneva, 1974.

399. Barros, James. The League of Nations and the Great Powers: The Greek-Bulgarian Incident, 1925. Oxford, 1970.

8. The Saar Territory

When the mines of the Saar Basin were handed to France as compensation for the destruction of French coal manufacturing the administration of the territory was given, by the Treaty of Versailles, to the League. Local authority was vested in a Governing Commission appointed by the Council; at the end of fifteen years a plebiscite was to be held to determine national allegiance. The Commission reported to the Council; the population had the right of petition to the Council through the Commission.

Controversy concerning the Commission's fairness, nationalist press opinion, periodic statements from Paris and Berlin, the Council's occasional intercession, and, after a famous Council debate between Stresseman and Briand, the withdrawal of the French garrison in 1927, all kept the League and its administration visible, contentious, and, gradually, the subject of acceptance if not admiration. In 1935 the famous and meticulously conducted plebiscite was held in an intensely nationalistic atmosphere, with an International Force in the service of the League to keep order (3,300 Colombian soldiers under a British commander, wearing armlets with the letters 'S.D.N.') The results gave sovereignty back to Germany and this ended the most important instance of international government in the League's history.

League documents contain the periodical reports of the Governing Commission, the Council debates, some petitions, and the monthly reports of the Plebiscite Commission. Questions concerning the creation of the international police force are in the Council minutes for December 1934. An unpublished report of the force by its commender is in the League archives.

400. Florinsky, Michael T. The Saar Struggle. New York, 1934.

401. Great Britain, Foreign Office, Historical Section. Plebiscite and Referendum. London, 1920.

402. Hill, C. J. "Great Britain and the Saar Plebiscite of 13 January 1935." Journal of Contemporary History 9(1974):121-142.

403. Hirsch, Helmut. Die Saar von Genf: Die Saarfrage während des Völkerbundregimes von 1920-1935. Bonn, 1954. Short, with interesting comments on the pro-French movement from the memoir of Robert Herly.

404. Hirsch, Helmut. Die Saar in Versailles: Die Saarfrage auf der Friedenskonferenz von 1919. Bonn, 1951.

405. Lambert, Margaret. The Saar. London, 1934. A solid, impartial study by a knowledgeable participant.

406. Russell, F. M. The International Government of the Saar. Berkeley, 1926.

407. Russell, Frank M. The Saar: Battleground and Pawn. Stanford, 1951.

408. Wambaugh, Sarah. "Control of Special Areas." In Pioneers in World Order, edited by Harriet E. Davis. New York, 1944

409. Wambaugh, Sarah. A Monograph on Plebiscites with a Collection of Official Documents and a Chronological List of Cases of Change of Sovereignty in Which the Right to Self-Determination Has Been Recognized. New York, 1920.

410. Wambaugh, Sarah. The Saar Plebiscite with a Collection of Official Documents. Cambridge, Mass., 1940. Author helped plan and direct plebiscite.

411. Wehberg, Hans. Saargebiet: Die Staats-und Völkerrechtliche Stellung des Saargebietes. Berlin, 1974.

9. Danzig

The Free City of Danzig was decreed at Versailles to ensure Poland's access to the sea while preserving the mainly German city's separate existence. The League got guardianship of the constitution of the Free City, a High Commission appointed by the League was resident in Danzig to deal with disputes between the Free City and the Polish state, and the territory of the Free City was placed under League protection. The High Commissioner possessed no attributes of government, serving only as a mediator, dependent on cooperation from Danzigers and the neighboring states. This cooperation waxed and waned and it need hardly be said that the nationalist conflicts between Poland and Germany, the nature, legitimacy, and control of the corridor, the ports, the citizens, and the political apparatus of the Free City were among the most complicated and intractable problems of the 1930s. In all this the League had a central but limited role (for example, it had no direct control over the internal politics of the Free City), and its capacity to influence events, or to protect its charge, disappeared when its own authority collapsed at Geneva, and when there was a heating up of the Nazi policy of attrition,

and Poland rejected League mediation. Yet it was
through League involvement that the Free City lasted
twenty years without a clash of arms--in fact this
internationalized solution permitted it to exist at
all, and, in the 1920s, this was the better alter-
native than either leaving Danzig with Germany by
right of self-determination or giving it to Poland
for an access to the sea.

High Commissioners of the League of Nations
were:

Reginald Tower (U.K.), January 1920-November
1920

E. L. Strutt (U.K.), November 1920-December
1920

Bernardo Attolico (Italy), December 1920-
January 1921.

Richard Haking (U.K.), January 1921-February
1923

M. S. MacDonnell (U.K.), February 1923-February
1926

J. A. van Hamel (Netherlands), February 1926-
June 1929

Manfredi Gravina (Italy), June 1929-September
1932

Helmer Rosting (Denmark), October 1932-October
1932

Sean Lester (Ireland), October 1933-January
1937

Carl Burckhardt (Switzerland), February 1937-
September 1939.

Documents published by the government of the Free
City, cases submitted to the Council, advisory
opinions by the Permanent Court (and six of the
twenty-seven advisory opinions rendered by the Court
dealt with Danzig), reports of League committees,
are easily accessible in the publications of the
relevant authorities. The archives of the Office
of the High Commission in Danzig, 1922-1937, appear
destroyed. Files of the Administrative Commissions
and Minorities Section are in the League's Secretariat Archive Group.

412. Burckhardt, Carl J. Meine Danziger Mission,
1937-1939. Munich, 1960.

413. Denne, Ludwig. Das Danzig-Problem in der
deutschen Aussenpolitik, 1934-39. Bonn, 1959.
How the Nazis dealt with Danzig in the late
1930s.

414. Forster, Albert. Das national-sozialistische
     Gewissen in Danzig: Aus Sechs Jahren Kampf
     für Hitler. Berlin, 1936. Leader of the
     Nazis in the Free City. This is what the
     High Commissioner had to put up with.

415. Hamel, Joost Adriaan van. Danzig and the
     Polish Problem. New York, 1933.

416. Harder, H. A. Danzig, Polen und der Völker-
     bund. Berlin, 1928. The German case, arguing
     for revision of the peace treaties and rein-
     corporation of the corridor in Germany.

417. Kimmich, Christoph M. The Free City: Danzig
     and German Foreign Policy, 1919-1934. New
     Haven, 1968. The best study of the most
     significant years of League authority.

418. Leonhardt, Hans. Nazi Conquest in Danzig.
     Chicago, 1942. He was there, and opposed the
     Nazis.

419. Levine, H. S. Hitler's Free City: A History
     of the Nazi Party in Danzig, 1925-1939.
     Chicago, 1973.

420. Levine, H. S. "The Mediator: Carl J. Burck-
     hardt's Efforts to Avert a Second World War."
     Journal of Modern History 45(1973):439-55.

421. Mason, John Brown. The Danzig Dilemma: A
     Study in Peacemaking by Compromise. Stanford,
     1946. Favorable to the League, excellent
     study of personalities and records of the
     time.

422. Moderow, W. Die Freie Stadt Danzig: Ein
     Völkerrechtliches Experiment. 1970. An
     unpublished MS in the Historical Collections
     Section, UN Library, Geneva, by a long-time
     Polish diplomat in Danzig.

423. Morrow, I. F. D. The Peace Settlement in the
     German Polish Borderlands. London, 1936.
     Good geo-political overview.

424. Newman, Simon. March 1939: The British
     Guarantee to Poland. A Study in the Continu-
     ity of British Foreign Policy. Oxford, 1976.
     Seen as not the end of appeasement but natur-

ally corollary of a policy of commitment short of war.

425. Prill, Felician. "Sean Lester: High Commission in Danzig, 1933-1937." Studies (Dublin) 49(1960):259-65.

426. Ramonat, Wolfgang. Der Völkerbund und die Freie Stadt Danzig, 1920-1934. Osnabrück, 1979.

427. Sahm, Heinrich. Erinnerungen aus meinen Danziger Jahren, 1919-1930. Marburg, 1955. President of the Danzig Senate, 1920-1931, the crucial years of League stabilization.

428. Smogorzewski, Casimir. Poland's Access to the Sea. London, 1934.

429. Weck, Nicolas de. La condition juridique du conseil du port et des voies d'eau de Dantzig. Paris, 1933. Inside report of the workings of the Council of the Port of Danzig and the importance of the President, who was appointed by the League in case of deadlock.

B. TERMS OF SECURITY

The Covenant did not, and could not, prohibit war, a sovereign right of states which remained unchallenged. League members were bound only to submit disputes to arbitration, or to an inquiry and report of the Council. Members were obliged to defer hostilities for a period of time only, during which processes for peaceful settlement were undertaken. After that, it was no violation of the Covenant to go to war.

To ensure compliance, article 16 stated that if a state went to war in disregard of these agreements "it shall ipso facto be deemed to have committed an act of war against all other Members of the League," and thus open the possibility of action against it, the so-called sanctions.

These formulations were meant to establish an entirely new foundation for international relations. Yet a stable order required the cooperation of all major states, and that meant a general sense of confidence in the system, patently not present in 1920. The terms of collective security were binding only on members, and then only to a point. Article 16 did not bind members to automatic appli-

cations of sanctions. For reasons of its own, any
state might or might not decide to cooperate.
Important states were never members of the League,
or came and left. The anchor states, Britain and
France, held different views of the organization's
role. German hostility lent weight to revisionist
demands. Who could tell how Russia, Japan, or the
United States might act? Perhaps these difficulties were insurmountable. So unstable was the
international scene, so much a compromise were the
terms of the Covenant, so incomplete the League's
membership, and with so many uncertain of its
value, one might dismiss the Covenant as a failure,
fundamentally flawed, and in pursuit of a utopian
goal. Yet so far had its articles advanced the
prospect of international cooperation, so keen were
members to avoid another war, that one can admire
the determination and imagination of League leaders
in the 1920s who sought to work within rather than
reject the new (if incomplete) system, as the best
hope for world peace.

1. The Permanent Court and
the Optional Clause, 1920

The First Assembly considered the establishment of the Permanent Court of International
Justice its major achievement. The Council had
appointed a Committee of Jurists to draft its
statute. The Committee wanted to give the Court
compulsory jurisdiction, but on British objections
this was retracted by the Council in October 1920.
The Assembly of December 1920 adopted a draft of
reduced competence, and urged member states to
adhere. To put some force behind the Court the
Assembly added an 'optional clause' by which signa-
tors agreed to accept as binding a Court decision
if all parties to a dispute had also agreed. The
Court will be discussed in a later section. Here
attention is called to the important discussions in
the 1920s and 1930s of sovereignty, international
law, and alternatives to unilateral action that
were associated with the drafting and possible
adoption of the statute and the optional clause.
Ratification was not the subject of international
diplomacy.
The Advisory Committee of Jurists which
drafted the statute included Rafael Altamira,
Francis Hagerup, Albert de Lapradelle, Lord
Phillimore, and Elihu Root. The sub-committee of
the Assembly which brought it to the League was

chaired by Leon Bourgeois and included Hagerup,
Cecil Hurst, and Nicolas Politis, some of whom have
written of their experiences, or about whom (Root,
for example) there are good biographies. The work
of these teams is recorded in three compendia:

Advisory Committee of Jurists. Documents
Presented to the Committee Relating to
Existing Plans for the Establishment of a
Permanent Court of International Justice.
The Hague, n.d. (1920).

Advisory Committee of Jurists. Procès-
Verbaux of the Proceedings of the Committee,
June 16th-July 24th, 1920, with Annexes. The
Hague, 1920.

League of Nations. Documents Concerning the
Action Taken by the Council of the League
under Article 14 of the Covenant and the
Adoption by the Assembly of the Statute of
the Permanent Court. Geneva, n.d.

The advisor to Root was James Scott Brown,
who wrote a thorough account:

430. Brown, James Scott. The Project of a Perma-
nent Court of International Justice and
Resolutions of the Advisory Committee of
Jurists. Washington, 1920.

2. Treaty of Mutual Guarantee, 1922;
Draft Treaty of Mutual Assistance, 1923;
Geneva Protocol, 1924

The Council had responsibility for submitting
a plan for disarmament to member states. This was
a constant preoccupation of the League in the
1920s. No issue seemed more important. Yet non-
member states refused cooperation, and members
demanded security and peaceful settlement linked to
the charge of disarmament. If a climate of peace
existed, if security seemed assured, then disarmament had a chance. The Assembly of 1924 expressed
the linkage in its formula: Arbitration, Security,
Disarmament.
Security first. The Third Assembly, of 1922,
proposed a defensive Treaty of Mutual Guarantee
open to all states on the condition they cooperate
in the search for general disarmament. This was
followed by preparation of a Treaty of Mutual

Assistance, prepared by Robert Cecil and Réquin
over the objection of military experts who thought
no state would reduce its armed forces on the basis
of a general treaty. The draft was presented to
the Fourth Assembly in 1923 and circulated to all
member states. It never came to force, torpedoed
by British opposition. The Fifth Assembly of 1924
thereupon put aside a search for guarantee and
renewed the approach to security through arbitration. Led by Herriot and MacDonald the Assembly
sought to close the 'gap' in article 15, by which a
member state could go to war without violation of
the Covenant. Committees under Benes and Politis
presented to the Assembly the Protocol for the
Pacific Settlement of International Disputes. This
'Geneva Protocol' was meant to tie together compulsory arbitration (all signatories were to adhere to
the Optional Clause or submit disputes to the
Council and abide by the decision of its arbitra-
tors), security (sanctions against violators), and
disarmament (the Council would call a conference of
all states). A signator to the protocol would
contract to definite obligations of mutual assistance, and to a process of peaceful settlement, and
the way would be paved for general security leading
to disarmament.
       Again, failure. France and its clients
signed; Britain and the Commonwealth did not.
Concern over future actions of the United States,
unwillingness to get involved in European troubles,
and a dislike of compulsory arbitration led to the
rejection. A weakness of the League throughout its
history was the failure of cooperation by the
British and French governments.

431. Burks, David D. "The United States and the
      Geneva Protocol of 1924: 'A New Holy Alli-
      ance'?" American Historical Review 64(1959):
      891-905.

432. Cecil, Viscount (Robert). "The Draft Treaty
      of Mutual Assistance." Journal of the
      British Institute of International Affairs
      3(1924):45-82. In discussion here Balfour
      states: "Well, frankly, I cannot accept with
      equanimity the idea that even possibly half
      our Empire should be fighting and the other
      half looking on." This sums British opposi-
      tion.

433. Miller, David Hunter. The Geneva Protocol.
New York, 1925.

434. Noel-Baker, P. J. The Geneva Protocol for
the Pacific Settlement of International Disputes. London, 1925. A clear exposition of
its relation to League.

435. Rappard, William E. International Relations
as viewed from Geneva. New Haven, 1925.

436. Stuyt, A. M. Survey of International Arbitra-
tions, 1794-1970. Leyden, 1972.

437. Wehberg, Hans. Das Genfer Protokoll: Betr.
die friedliche Erledigung internationaler
Streitigkeiten. Berlin, 1927.

438. Williams, John Fischer. "The Geneva Protocol
of 1924 for the Pacific Settlement of International Disputes." International Affairs
3(1924):288-304.

439. Williams, John Fischer. The Geneva Protocol
of 1924. London, 1925.

440. Williams, John Fischer. "Treaty Revision and
the Future of the League." International
Affairs 10(1931):326-51. Argues organization
of peace should precede organization of justice, and the Protocol and Geneva Act cut
across the proper development of the League.

3. Locarno, 1925

The search for security went on, next outside
the League, with the negotiation of the Locarno
agreements between Germany, Belgium, France, and
Britain. Locarno bore the imprint of the earlier
efforts, and must be seen in the context noted
above. Germany, and Belgium, France, Poland, and
Czechoslovakia also signed arbitration conventions
to take force upon Germany's admission to the
League. The suggestion of Locarno was that disarmament was the next step in international stabilization.

441. Bariety, Jacques. "Der Versuch einer europäischen Befriedung: Von Locarno bis Thoiry."
In Locarno und die Weltpolitik, 1924-1932,
edited by Hellmuth Rössler and Erwin Hölzle,
Göttingen, 1969.

442. Benes, Eduard. Les accords de Locarno. Prague, 1925.

443. Benes, Eduard. "After Locarno: The Security Problem Today." Foreign Affairs 4(1926):195-210.

444. Enssle, M. J. "Stresemann's Diplomacy Fifty Years after Locarno: Some Recent Perspectives." Historical Journal 20(1977):937-48.

445. Gasiorowski, Zygmunt T. "Benes and Locarno: Some Unpublished Documents." Review of Politics 20(1958):209-24.

446. Grigg, Edward. "The Merits and Defects of the Locarno Treaty as a Guarantee of World Peace." International Affairs 14(1935):176-97. Sees it part of pactomania. Austen Chamberlain in discussion argues for fewer pacts and more strength to the League.

447. Grun, George A. "Locarno: Idea and Reality." International Affairs 31(1955):477-85.

448. Jacobson, Jon. Locarno Diplomacy: Germany and the West, 1925-1929. Princeton, 1972. The best modern study, with comprehensive bibliography.

449. Johnson, Douglas. "Austen Chamberlain and the Locarno Agreements." University of Birmingham Historical Journal 8(1961):62-81.

450. Laroche, Jules. Au quai d'Orsay avec Briand et Poincaré, 1913-1926. Paris, 1957.

451. Maurras, Charles. Le mauvais traité: de la victoire à Locarno: chronique d'une décadence. Paris, 1928.

452. Megerle, Klaus. Deutsche Aussenpolitik 1925. Bern, 1974. By signing Locarno and joining the League German policy lost flexibility that Stresemann hoped to have regarding the Soviet Union.

453. Nathusius, Martin. Das Vertragswerk von Locarno und der Völkerbund. Würzburg, 1926.

454. Rössler, Hellmuth, and Hölzle, Erwin, eds.
Locarno und die Weltpolitik, 1924-1932.
Göttingen, 1969.

455. Ruge, Wolfgang. Stresemann: ein Lebensbild.
Berlin, 1965.

456. Schuker, Stephen A. The End of French Predominance in Europe: The Financial Crisis of
1924 and the Adoption of the Dawes Plan.
Chapel Hill, 1976. Fully detailed account of
the end of reparations in international context.

457. Stambrook, F. G. "'Das Kind'--Lord D'Abernon
and the Origins of the Locarno Pact."
Central European History 1(1968):233-63.

458. Steed, Wickham. "Locarno and British Interests." Journal of the British Institute of
International Affairs 4(1925):286-303.

459. Thimme, Annelise. "Gustav Stresemann:
Legende und Wirklichkeit." Historische
Zeitschrift 181(1956):287-338.

460. Turner, Henry A., Jr. "Eine Rede Stresemanns
über seine Locarnopolitik." Vierteljahrshefte für Zeitgeschichte 19(1967):412-36.

461. Walsdorff, Martin. Westorientung und Ostpoli-
tik: Stresemanns Russland-politik in der
Locarno-Ära. Bremen, 1971.

4. Germany's Admission to the League, 1926

This passage, long sought, was unexpectedly
bitter, and the arguments about rights to Council
seats led to delays, sour debate, intrigue, and the
withdrawal of Brazil and Spain. At the Sixth
Assembly small powers, who felt shunted aside, who
thought that due process had not been followed,
showed their bitterness. The controversy led to
some internal reform (expansion of Council seats)
but the acrimony discredited the League in some
quarters.

462. Carlton, David. "Great Britain and the
League Council Crisis of 1926." Historical
Journal 11(1968):354-64.

463. Freytagh-Loringhoven, Axel von. Von Locarno nach Genf und Thoiry. Berlin, 1926.

464. Kimmich, Christoph. Germany and the League of Nations. Chicago, 1976. A thorough, exacting treatment with a full bibliography.

465. Scelle, Georges. Une crise de la Société des Nations: La réforme du conseil et l'entrée de l'Allemagne à Geneve (mars-septembre 1926). Paris, 1927. A lengthy account of the work of the Motta Committee.

466. Spenz, Jurgen. Die diplomatische Vorgeschichte des Beitritts Deutschlands zum Völkerbund, 1924-1926: Ein Beitrag zur Aussenpolitik der Weimarer Republick. Göttingen, 1966. Entry of Germany, prestigious for the Germans, reinforced British view of League as platform for meetings, versus the French view of it as in the service of France's European security system.

5. The Kellogg-Briand Pact, and the General Act, 1928

The Pact for the Renunciation of War was also negotiated outside the League. Its significance for Geneva was that it involved the United States in the process of international stabilization. Its terms supported ideas only recently reaffirmed by the Assembly in 1927 that war should be renounced and disputes settled by peaceful means. The pact was full of loopholes, however, subject to varying interpretations and lacking the institutional and political bases of security the League was so patiently working towards. It was an event, not part of an international security system. It is well studied in association with the General Act for the Pacific Settlement of International Disputes adopted by the Ninth Assembly in 1928 by which the League sought to implement the Kellogg-Briand Pact by sets of model conventions and treaties proposed to all governments encouraging them to undertake agreements of conciliation, judicial settlement, and arbitration. After limited response, this came to nothing.

467. Borel, Eugène. "L'acte Général de Genève." Recueil des cours (1929):501-95.

468. Ellis, Lewis Ethan. Frank B. Kellogg and American Foreign Relations, 1925-1929. New Brunswick, NJ, 1961. The American perspective--no works of continental European origin used.

469. Ferrell, Robert H. Peace in Their Time: The Origins of the Kellogg-Briand Pact. New Haven, 1952. A good one-volume study.

470. Geigenmüller, Ernst. Briand: Tragik des grossen Europäers. Bonn, 1959.

471. Geneva Research Center. "The Covenant and the Pact." Geneva Studies 1(1930):1-23.

472. Hirsch, Felix. Gustav Stresemann: Patriot und Europäer. Göttingen, 1964.

473. Hudson, Manley O. By Pacific Means: The Implementation of Article Two of the Pact of Paris. New Haven, 1935. Good appraisal of the Pact.

474. Kerr, Philip. "The Outlawry of War." Journal of the Royal Institute of International Affairs 6(1928):361-77. Notes that "the foundation of the British Empire is the absolute outlawry of war within it."

475. Krüger, Peter. "Friedenssicherung und deutsche Revisionspolitik: Die deutsche Aussenpolitik und die Verhandlungen über den Kellogg-Pakt." Vierteljahrshefte für Zeitgeschichte 22(1974):225-57.

476. Maza, Herbert. "James Thomson Shotwell: Le pacte de Paris--1928." In Neuf meneurs internationaux, edited by H. Maza. Paris, 1965.

477. Maza, Herbert. "Salmon Oliver Levinson: Le pacte de Paris--1928." In Neuf meneurs internationaux, edited by H. Maza. Paris, 1965.

478. Miller, David Hunter. The Peace Pact of Paris: A Study of the Briand-Kellogg Treaty. New York, 1928.

479. Myers, Denys P. "The Modern System of Pacific Settlement of International Disputes." _Political Science Quarterly_ 46(1931): 548-88.

480. Rutgers, V. H. "La mise en harmonie du pacte de la Société des Nations avec le pacte de Paris." _Recueil des Cours_ 38(1931):5-123.

481. Schücking, Walther. _Die Revision der Völkerbundssatzung im Hinblick auf den Kelloggpakt._ Berlin, 1931. A German judge on the Permanent Court argues revision of the Covenant to bring it into harmony with the Pact.

482. Shotwell, James T. _War as an Instrument of National Policy and Its Renunciation in the Pact of Paris._ New York, 1929.

483. Stimson, Henry L. "The Pact of Paris: Three Years of Development." _Foreign Affairs_ 11(1932):i-ix.

484. Stoner, John E. _S. O. Levinson and the Pact of Paris._ Chicago, 1942.

485. Suarez, Georges. _Briand: sa vie--son oeuvre avec son journal et de nombreux documents inédits._ 6 vols. Paris, 1938-52.

486. Wehberg, Hans. _Die Ächtung des Krieges._ Berlin, 1930.

487. Williams, John Fischer. "The Geneva Protocol of 1924 for the Pacific Settlement of International Disputes." _International Affairs_ 3(1924):288-304. Fischer Williams was British Legal Representative on the Reparations Commission, 1920-1930.

488. Williams, John Fischer. "Recent Interpretations of the Briand-Kellogg Pact." _International Affairs_ 14(1935):346-68.

489. Williams, John Fischer. "Treaties for the Pacific Settlement of Disputes--Mutual Assistance and Non-Aggression." _International Affairs_ 7(1928):407-21.

6. European Union and the Austro-German Customs Union, 1930-31

A proposition of long standing, the idea of European union had various attributes, showed many faces, served many needs. For some the League was, in Herriot's words, "the first rough draft of the United States of Europe," a form of political federation. For others, such as Richard N. Coudenhove-Kalegri whose ideas of Paneurope received considerable attention in the 1920s and who founded the Pan-Europe Union in 1926, the League was a "lasting menace to the independence of Europe," for it permitted meddling in European issues by non-European states. His idea of "Europe for Europeans" was meant to focus identity in a specific non-national locale, which, while preventing war and economic ruin between competing units, would defend Europe against communism. This followed Friedrich Naumann's ideas of Mitteleuropa, some form of only central European association between France and Russia, with strong overtones of economic union. Ideas as to the constituent nature of this union were vague and contradictory, and not formerly considered by any international organization until 1930.

In May 1930 Briand circulated to the governments of Europe a plan for a European Federal Union. It was opposed by the British, yet, as closer cooperation in security and economics was deemed desirable, the matter was referred to the Eleventh Assembly, which set up a Commission of Enquiry for European Union to pursue the question in the framework of the League. The Soviet Union and Turkey, still not members of the League, and previously excluded from Briand's invitation, were invited to join the Commission. In all, some 28 continental states participated. The result was a year of sittings, and a good deal of information about economic cooperation, but fundamental political issues remained unresolved. When the Chancellor of Austria heard of Briand's plan he declared it unlikely. "What he hoped for some day was an economic union of Central Europe." (Documents on British Foreign Policy, second ser., vol. I, n. 187).

When in March 1931 an Austro-German Customs Union was concluded, the argument was that this was a step toward the goals enunciated by Briand and under consideration by the League. To the French, Czechs, Yugoslavs, and Italians, however, it ap-

peared rather as a step toward the forbidden
Anschluss, and a violation of Austria's agreements
with the League of 1922 by which it received financial assistance on the promise not to enter into
special economic arrangements. The violent reaction was reflected in Council debate; the proposal
was submitted to the Permanent Court; and financial
pressure brought to bear on Vienna. Central Europe
was in disarray--the failure of the Credit-Anstalt
came that May--and in the face of fierce opposition
the proposal was dropped, just as the Court ruled
(by a majority of one vote) against it. The incident left all parties frustrated and perplexed, and
showed, in the context of spreading economic disas-
ters and rising nationalism, the persistent impossibility of finding terms of political and economic
security. The 1930s, therefore, opened with the
forthcoming disarmament conference as the last main
hope for institutional pacification.

490. Agnelli, Giovanni, and Cabiati, Attilo.
     Fédération européenne ou ligue des nations?
     Paris, 1919.

491. Amery, L. S. "The British Empire and the
     Pan-European Idea." Journal of the Royal
     Institute of International Affairs 9(1930):
     1-22. Discusses the various problems and
     opportunities connected with the idea of a
     Europe for Europeans.

492. Bastid, Paul. "L'Idée d'Europe et l'organi-
     sation de l'Europe." L'Europe du xix et du
     xx siècles: Interprétations historiques.
     Vol. V. Paris, 1964.

493. Baumgart, Winfried. Vom europäischen Konzert
     zum Völkerbund: Friedensschlüsse und Friedens-
     sicherung von Wien bis Versailles. Darmstadt,
     1974.

494. Benes, Eduard. Das österreichisch-deutsche
     Abkommen. Prague, 1931.

495. Bonneville, G. Prophètes et témoins de
     l'Europe: Essai sur l'idée d'Europe dans la
     littérature française de 1914 à nos jours.
     Leyden, 1961.

496. Brugmans, Hendrik. "The Evolution of the European Idea." 20th Century Studies 1(1969): 6-17.

497. Brugmans, Hendrik. L'Idée européenne 1918-1965. Bruges, 1965.

498. Cordier, Andrew. European Union and the League of Nations. Geneva, 1931.

499. Coudenhove-Kalergi, Richard N. Eine Idee erobert Europa: Meine Lebenserinnerungen. Cologne, 1958.

500. Coudenhove-Kalergi, Richard N. Kampf um Europa: Aus meinem Leben. Zurich, 1949.

501. Coudenhove-Kalergi, Richard N. Kampf um Paneuropa. 3 vols. Vienna, 1925-28.

502. Coudenhove-Kalergi, Richard N. Pan-Europa. Vienna, 1923. Earliest statement--his journal Paneuropa followed in 1924, and the Pan-Europa Union was founded in 1925.

503. Coudenhove-Kalergi, Richard N. Paneuropa: 1922 bis 1966. Vienna, 1966.

504. Coudenhove-Kalergi, Richard. "The Pan-European Outlook." International Affairs 10(1931):638-651. This, as the others, sets forth the three main reasons: prevention of war, prevention of economic ruin, defense against Bolshevism. Takes as its model unification movements, Commonwealth, and the Pan American experience.

505. Coudenhove-Kalergi, Richard N. Vom ewigen Krieg zum grossen Frieden. Göttingen, 1956.

506. Elisha, Achille. Aristide Briand: Discours et écrits de politique étrangère. La paix, l'union européenne, la Société des Nations. Paris, 1965.

507. Fleissig, Andreas. Paneuropa: Die soziale und wirtschaftliche Zukunft Europas. Munich, 1930. An attack on Coudenhove-Kalergi as unrealistic and too purely political. Wants great international cartels, to plan and stabilize the economic structure of Europe.

508. Foerster, R. H. Europa: Geschichte einer politischen Idee, mit einer Bibliographie von 182 Einigungsplänen aus den Jahren 1306 bis 1945. Munich, 1967.

509. Frommelt, Reinhard. Paneuropa oder Mitteleuropa: Einigungsbestrebungen im Kalkül deutscher Wirtschaft und Politik 1925-1933. Stuttgart, 1977. An excellent monograph, based on all relevant archival and secondary sources. Includes a useful appendix of organizations.

510. Gürge, Wilhelm. Paneuropa oder Mitteleuropa. Berlin, 1929. Another rejection of Paneuropa, arguing for German influence in middle Europe, for unity, and for an extension of Germany's home market.

511. Hauser, Oswald. "Der Plan einer deutsch-österreichischen Zollunion von 1931 und die europäische Föderation." Historische Zeitschrift 179(1955):45-92.

512. Ionescu, Ghita. "Portrait of the Federalist as a Young Man." International Affairs 45(1969):481-88. Denis de Rougemont's ideas of European federalism in the late 1930s and early 1940s.

513. Jahrreiss, H. Europa als Rechtseinheit. Leipzig, 1929. Outline and commentary on various schemes for legal unification.

514. Jouvenel, Bertrand de. Vers les états-unis d'Europe. Paris, 1930. Criticizes the nationalist nature of the peace treaties, and argues for unity to solve problems of minorities, security, and disarmament.

515. Leonard, Raymond. Vers une organisation politique et juridique de l'Europe: Du project d'union fédérale européenne de 1930 aux pactes de sécurité. Paris, 1935.

516. Lipgens, Walter, comp. and ed. Europa-Föderationspläne der Widerstandsbewegungen, 1940-1945: Eine Dokumentation. Munich, 1968. 176 memoranda, manifestos, declarations on future of Europe.

517. Lipgens, Walter. "Europäische Einigungsidee 1923-1930 und Briands Europaplan im Urteil der deutschen Akten." Historische Zeitschrift 203(1966):46-89, 316-363.

518. Lipgens, Walter. "Towards a History of European Integration." Journal of Common Market Studies 17(1978):83-96. The European University Institute at Florence is promoting a multivolume work on the History of European Integration, of which project Lipgens has a leading part.

519. Marchal, Jean. Union douanière et organisation européenne. Paris, 1929.

520. Margueritte, Victor. La patrie humaine. Paris, 1931. Peace through Pan European association.

521. Mayrisch, Emile. Précurseur de la construction de l'Europe. Lausanne, 1967.

522. Meyer, Henry Cord. Mitteleuropa in German Thought and Action, 1815-1945. The Hague, 1955.

523. Preradovisch, Nikolaus von. Die Wilhelmstrasse und der Anschluss Österreichs 1918 bis 1933. Bern, 1971.

524. Rappard, William E. Uniting Europe: The Trend of International Cooperation since the War. New Haven, 1930.

525. Richthofen, Wilhelm von. Brito-Germania: Ein Weg zu Pan-Europa? Warum wieder Weltkrieg? Berlin, 1930.

526. Ruge, Wolfgang, and Schumann, Wolfgang. "Die Reaktion des deutschen Imperialismus auf Briands Paneuropaplan, 1930." Zeitschrift für Geschichtswissenschaft 20(1972):40-70.

527. Scheer, Friedrich-Karl. Die Deutsche Friedensgesellschaft, 1892-1933. Bochum, 1974.

528. Siebert, Ferdinand. Aristide Briand, 1862-1932: Ein Staatsman zwischen Frankreich und Europa. Erlenbach, 1973.

529. Union Douanière Européenne. _Les premiers
     européens._ Paris, 1931. Picking up Briand's
     call for unity, this volume is full of photo-
     graphs, biographies, and pro-union sentiments.

530. Vergnand, Pierre. _L'idée de la nationalité
     et de la libre disposition des peuples dans
     ses rapports avec l'idée de l'état: Etude des
     doctrines politiques contemporaines, 1870-
     1950._ Geneva, 1955.

531. Wehberg, Hans. "Ideen und Projekte betref-
     fend die Vereinigten Staaten von Europa in
     den letzten 100 Jahren." _Friedenswarte_
     41(1941):49-122.

532. White, Ralph. "Regionalism vs. Universalism
     in the League of Nations." _Annales d'Etudes
     internationales_ (1970):88-114.

VIII. DISARMAMENT

What happened to disarmament? The issue was
a central matter on the League's agenda for a
decade. The Covenant (article 8) read that "the
maintenance of peace requires the reduction of
national armaments to the lowest point consistent
with national safety and the enforcement by common
action of international obligations." It gave the
Council the job, "taking account of the geographical situation and circumstances of each State," of
formulating "plans for such reduction for the
consideration and action of the several Governments." As the League's self-assessment in 1930
stated: "The touchstone of the more general work of
organising peace is success in disarmament." (Ten
Years of World Co-operation, p. 49).
    Were arms the cause, or the symptom, of
international insecurity? Some held that
general political agreements must be obtained
before disarmament was possible. Thus the search
for terms for collective action against aggression,
for agreements on arbitration, were closely related
to, and pursued simultaneously with, plans for arms
reduction. For others, arms themselves were held
the cause of war, and disarmament itself was the
decisive first step to security. For each school
disarmament had to be a part of a new world order.
Intense public interest followed, and encouraged,
disarmament proposals.
    Problems were manifold. Definitions of
equity, of proportions, of the nature of arms
themselves had to be made. To long standing concerns about control of weapons of sea and land, to
concerns about the private manufacture of and
traffic in arms, were added, as the years went on,
fears of new instruments of war, weapons of the
air, weapons of chemical and biological nature,
and, increasingly, fear of growing militarism and
belligerent nationalism as threats to peace. The
context of disarmament was worldwide. The United
States and Japan, for instance, were not members of
the League, but their power and intentions were of
greatest importance to Britain's concerns in the
east, and hence to its concerns in Europe. One

question was: would disarmament be best served through a general plan sponsored by the League, or by multilateral agreements outside the organization? And, if disarmament failed, could other security arrangements hold. It did fail. Despite partial agreements, no plan of international control was ever accepted. States refused to give up their sovereign right to judge their own level of arms.

A close study of disarmament issues reveal, as perhaps no other general issue of these times, the political realities and perceptions of national interests, the narrowness of the range of options, and the limitations of the League.

***

The Washington Conference (1921-22) was called by the American government. The League played no part. The conference established ratios for battleships between the five major naval powers. It did not discuss land or air armaments, or troop strengths, and it did not agree on limitations for other types of naval war craft. The ratios confirmed Japan's strong position in the Pacific. The conferees pledged to cooperate in the Pacific, and, by a nine-power treaty, confirmed China's independence. The Washington Conference was a model of the limited, numerical form of arms limitation. Its success inspired the League to act.

In 1921 the Council set up a Temporary Mixed Commission of experts to study "the political, economic, social, historical and geographical aspects" of disarmament. This broad charge was narrowed by the commission, which collected vast amounts of information on existing stocks of arms. In 1922 a plan drawn by Lord Esher presented a formula for the establishment of ratios for land and air forces around which negotiations among European powers might proceed. The Esher plan, like the Washington formulas a type of 'direct method' reduction, was rejected by League agencies as overly technical, and by governments worried about German aggression as premature so long as basic security fears of a political nature remained. For the next few years therefore the League searched for security through treaties, mutual assistance pacts, and arbitration agreements. The connection was summarized by the formula of the 1924 Assembly: Arbitration, Security, Disarmament.

The Locarno agreements appeared to provide some measure of assurance. The final protocol called for states to "give their sincere co-operation to the work relating to disarmament already undertaken by the League of Nations and to seek the realization thereof in a general agreement." In a spirit of optimism the Council set up the Preparatory Commission for the Disarmament Conference, a general conference some hoped would be in session by 1927. Germany and the United States cooperated from the beginning, as did the USSR after 1927 and Turkey from 1928. The Commission's hope for an early conference was not realized, as its debates could not resolve complicated, essential problems of definition (e.g., what was meant by 'armaments, what was the difference between 'defensive' and 'offensive' weaponry), equity (the terms by which ratios were to be set), and methods (e.g., how to go from regional to general arrangements). By 1927, instead of a conference, the commission was deadlocked. A Three Power Naval Conference was held in 1927 in Geneva but formally outside the League, called again by America, seeking agreement on naval armaments in categories not covered at the Washington Conference, but this came to nothing. Somewhat more successful was the London Naval Conference of 1930 which established ratios for cruisers, destroyers, and submarines among Britain, the U.S., and Japan, but which hardly constituted a general agreement, and stayed within the narrow scope of naval arms.

By 1930 economic crises, rising nationalism, the death or departure of some champions, and the rising calls for security or honor based on military strength, led many to think existing agreements were on the verge of collapse, and that the last opportunity for disarmament was at hand. In an anxious mood the Preparatory Commission met for the last time in November and submitted a much compromised draft Disarmament Convention based on the hope that despite great power disunity a general conference might make something of contending views. In February 1932 representatives of over fifty states assembled in Geneva for the long awaited "Conference for the Reduction and Limitation of Armaments."

The conference, under the presidency of Arthur Henderson, lasted two years, and came to nothing. When Roosevelt in May 1933 warned that "confused purposes still clash dangerously" this

was a correct assessment. No proposal found
general acceptance. The failure of the conference
was confirmed with the withdrawal of Germany, and
its notice of intention to leave the League.
  There was no further talk of disarmament.
Proposals floated for an international police force
went nowhere. Fears of war heightened as predicted
horrors of aerial bombardment were added to memories of trenches and submarines. Nowhere in Europe
seemed safe any longer.

* * *

  The files of the Disarmament Section are in
the League's Secretariat Archive Group, in Geneva.
The published diplomatic documents of the major
states each devote much space and attention to
disarmament issues and conferences. There is a
great deal of material here to be investigated.

A. General Works

533. Angell, Norman. The Great Illusion. London,
      1910.

534. Burns, R. D., Urquidi, D., and Chapin, S.
      Disarmament in Perspective: An analysis of
      selected arms control and disarmament agree-
      ments between the World Wars, 1919-1939. Los
      Angeles, 1968.

535. Carlton, David. "Disarmament with Guaran-
      tees: Lord Cecil, 1922-1927." Disarmament
      and Arms Control 3(1965):143-64. Notes
      hopelessness of Cecil's conception of disar-
      mament as linked to security guarantees.

536. Churchill, Winston S. Arms and the Covenant.
      London, 1936.

537. Davies, David. "Disarmament." Transactions
      (Grotius Society) 5(1919):109-17.

538. Gardes, André. Le désarmement devant la
      Société des Nations. Paris, 1929. Examines
      work of Preparatory Commission.

539. Glinberg, Aron. Le problème du désarmement
      devant la Société des Nations et en dehors
      d'elle. Paris, 1930.

540. International Affairs. "Some References on
     Disarmament and Security." International
     Affairs 10(1931):666-83.

541. League of Nations. Armaments Year-Book. 16
     vols. Geneva, 1924-1939/40.

542. League of Nations. Annotated Bibliography on
     Disarmament and Military Questions. Geneva,
     1931.

543. League of Nations. The Reduction of Arma-
     ments and Organisation of Peace. Rev. ed.
     Geneva, 1928.

544. League of Nations. Statistical Yearbook of
     the Trade in Arms and Ammunition. 14 vols.
     Geneva, 1924-1938.

545. Madariaga, Salvador de. Disarmament.
     London, 1929. An influential argument
     against treating disarmament as only a tech-
     nical matter, and for a general security
     settlement.

546. Morgan, L. P. "Disarmament." In Pioneers in
     World Order, edited by H. E. Davis. New
     York, 1944.

547. Naylor, John F. Labour's International
     Policy: The Labour Party in the 1930s.
     Boston, 1969.

548. Noel-Baker, Philip J. Disarmament. London,
     1926. A standard general review.

549. Salewski, Michael. Entwaffnung und Militär-
     kontrolle in Deutschland, 1919-1927.
     Enforcement of disarmament agreement had
     internal consequences for Germany, and the
     Weimar government subordinated disarmament
     issues to more traditional foreign policy
     interests. Detailed exposition of the Allied
     Control.

550. Shotwell, James T., and Salvin, Marina.
     Lessons on Security and Disarmament from the
     History of the League of Nations. New York,
     1949.

551. Sloutzki, Naoum. La Société des Nations et le contrôle du commerce international des armes de guerre (1919-1939). Geneva, 1969. Author was member of the Disarmament Section, 1922-1940, and editor-in-chief of Annuaire militaire and Annuaire statistique du commerce international des armes de guerre. This is the best introduction to the subject.

552. Sloutzki, Naoum. The World Armaments Race, 1919-1939. Geneva, 1941.

553. Smith, H. A. "The Problem of Disarmament in the Light of History." International Affairs 10(1931):600-21. Review of 19th century concepts and approaches. Disarmament must be seen in broadest construction of national power and national will.

554. Wehberg, Hans. The Limitation of Armaments: A Collection of the Projects for the Solution of the Problem (Preceded by an Historical Introduction). Washington, 1921.

555. Winkler, Henry R. "Arthur Henderson." In The Diplomats, 1919-1939. Edited by G. Craig and F. Gilbert. Princeton, 1953. His work with the League and the Disarmament Conference evaluated.

R. The Washington Conference and the London Naval Conference

556. Archimbaud, Léon. La Conférence de Washington. Paris, 192?.

557. Berg, Meredith William. "Admiral William H. Standley and the Second London Naval Treaty, 1934-1936." Historian 23(February 1971):215-236.

558. Bickel, Wolf-Heinrich. Die Anglo-Amerikanischen Beziehungen 1927-1930 im Licht der Flottenfrage: das Problem das Machtansgleichs zwischen Grossbritannien und den Vereinigten Staaten in der Zwischenkriegzeit und seine Lösung. Zurich, 1970.

559. Bouy, Raymond. Le désarmement naval: La Conférence de Londres. Paris, 1931.

560. Bridgemen, W. C. "Naval Disarmament."
     Journal of the Royal Institute of Inter-
     national Affairs 6(1927):335-45. Insight
     into the Genoa conference from British
     representative.

561. Buckley, Thomas. The United States and the
     Washington Conference, 1921-1922. Knoxville,
     1970.

562. Buell, Raymond Leslie. The Washington
     Conference. New York, 1922.

563. Carlton, David. MacDonald versus Henderson.
     London, 1970. Assessments of the policy of
     the second Labor government towards repara-
     tions, the Haque Conference, and, especially,
     the London Conference.

564. Diqman, Roger. Power in the Pacific: The
     Origins of Naval Arms Limitation, 1914-1922.
     Chicago, 1976.

565. Géraud, André. "The London Naval Conference:
     A French View." Foreign Affairs 8(1930):519-
     32.

566. Gordon, Michael R. Conflict and Consensus in
     Labour's Foreign Policy, 1914-1965. Stan-
     ford, 1969.

567. Halpern, Paul G. Keyes Papers. 2 vols.
     London, 1979, 1980. Admiral Keyes's papers
     deal in part with the Washington Naval
     Conference and various disarmament issues.

568. Harada, Kumao. Fragile Victory: Prince
     Saionji and the 1930 London Treaty Issue from
     the Memoirs of Baron Harada Kumao. Intro-
     duced and translated by T. F. Mayer-Oakes.
     Detroit, 1968. Harada's report of the polit-
     ical intelligence he gathered for Saionji,
     last of the genro, whose policies of inter-
     national cooperation on disarmament influ-
     enced the Naval Conference, and who fought
     against renewed Japanese militarism.

569. Hoag, Charles L. Preface to Preparedness:
     The Washington Disarmament Conferences and
     Public Opinion. Washington, 1941.

570. Ichihashi, Yamato. The Washington Conference
     and After: A Historical Survey. Stanford,
     1928. Author was interpreter for senior
     Japanese delegate.

571. Kennedy, Malcom D. The Fstrangement of Great
     Britain and Japan, 1917-1935. Berkeley,
     1969.

572. MacDonald, J. Ramsay. "The London Naval
     Conference, 1930." Journal of the Royal
     Institute of International Affairs 9(1930):
     429-51.

573. Morgan, Laura Puffer. The Background of the
     London Naval Conference. Washington, D.C.,
     1931.

574. O'Connor, Raymond G. Perilous Equilibrium:
     The United States and the London Naval
     Conference of 1930. Lawrence, 1962.

575. Scheer, Reinhardt. Amerika und die Abrüstung
     der Seemachte. Berlin, 1922.

576. Tucker, William R. The Attitude of the
     British Labour Party Towards European and
     Collective Security Problems, 1920-1939.
     Geneva, 1950.

577. Vinson, John C. William E. Borah and the
     Outlawry of War. Athens, 1957.

578. Willoughby, W. W. China at the Conference.
     Baltimore, 1922.

579. Wu, Saofong. La Chine et la Conférence de
     Washington. Paris, 1927.

     C. The League and the World Disarmament
         Conference, 1932-34

580. Arnold-Forster, William. "British Policy at
     the Disarmament Conference." Political
     Quarterly 3(1932):365-80.

581. Arnold-Forster, William. The Disarmament
     Conference. London, 1931.

582. Arnold-Forster, William. "Policy for the
     Disarmament Conference." Political Quarterly
     2(July 1931):378-93.

583. Berdahl, Clarence A. "Disarmament and Equality." Geneva Studies 3(1932):1-16.

584. Böhmert, Victor. Die Rechtsgrundlagen für Deutschlands Recht auf Abrüstung seiner Vertragsgegner. Berlin, 1931. The German view, against the French.

585. Brouckère, Louis de. "Les travaux de la Société des Nations en matière de désarmement." Recueil des Cours (1928):365-450.

586. Carnegie, David. "The Private Manufacture of Arms, Ammunition and Implements of War." International Affairs 10(1931):504-23. Discusses the recommendations, eight years previous, of the Temporary Mixed Commission for the Reduction of Armaments, which recommended control of private manufacture, and the League's "Draft Convention for the Supervision and Publicity of the Private Manufacture of Arms" of 1929.

587. Cecil, Viscount. "Facing the World Disarmament Conference." Foreign Affairs 10(1931): 13-22.

588. Cot, Pierre. "Disarmament and French Public Opinion." Political Quarterly 2(1931):367-77.

589. Cushendun, Lord. "Disarmament." International Affairs 7(March 1928):77-90. A pessimistic report by British delegate.

590. Davis, Malcolm W. "The Draft Disarmament Convention: A Synthesis of Conference Decisions." Geneva Studies 4(1933):1-16.

591. Davis, Norman H. "The Disarmament Conference." International Conciliation 285(1932): 470-76.

592. Disarmament Information Center, Geneva. Disarmament: A Review of the Acts of the League of Nations and of Governments, Parliamentary Debates and the Trend of Public Opinion and Action relating to the World Disarmament Conference, 1932. Geneva, 1931-1932. A fortnightly publication by Geneva journalists giving the various national

positions and views. A good overview of
issues.

593. Engely, Giovanni. The Politics of Naval
Disarmament. London, 1932.

594. Henderson, Arthur. Conference for the
Reduction and Limitation of Armaments:
Preliminary Report on the Work of the Confer-
ence. Geneva, 1936. A full account by the
Conference President.

595. Hoetzsch, Otto. Abrüstung und Sicherheit.
Leipzig, 1932.

596. Lippay, Z. Behind the Scenes of the "Disarmament" Conference. New York, 1932. Leftist
criticism.

597. Litvinov, Maxim. The Soviet's Fight for
Disarmament. New York, 1932.

598. Loosli-Usteri, Carl. Geschichte der Konferenz
für die Herabsetzung und die Begrenzung der
Rüstungen, 1932-1934: ein politischer Welt-
spiegel. Zurich, 1940.

599. Markovitch, Lazare. Le désarmement et la
politique de Belgrade. Paris, 1932. Yugoslav delegate to the Preparatory Commission,
sharing the French position: no disarmament
without security guarantees. Peace based on
the status quo.

600. Noel-Baker, P. J. "Disarmament." International Affairs 13(1934):3-25. Review as of
late 1933. Note Admiral Sydney Fremantle's
view from the discussion: "He believed that
the peace of the British Empire was more
important than the peace of the world."

601. Noel-Baker, P. J. The First World Disarmament Conference 1932-1933 and Why it Failed.
Oxford, 1979. Revealing statement by personal assistant to Henderson, president of
the conference, blaming Hankey, Vansittart,
and Simon for the death of the plan.

602. Riddell, Walter A. World Security by Conference. Toronto, 1947.

130

603. Scialoja, Vittorio. "Obstacles to Disarmament." Foreign Affairs 10(1932):212-19.

604. Scott, James Brown. "Disarmament Through International Organization." Annals of the American Academy of Political and Social Science 126(1926):146-50.

605. Shillock, John C., Jr. "The Post-War Movements to Reduce Naval Armaments." International Conciliation 245(1928):9-92.

606. Temperley, Arthur C. The Whispering Gallery of Europe. London, 1938. One of the authors of the British Draft Treaty before the 1933 conference.

607. Thorne, Christopher. "The Quest for Arms Embargoes: Failure in 1933." Journal of Contemporary History 5(1970):129-50. Britain tried to embargo arms sales to China and Japan in 1933, placing hopes in disarmament and collective security.

608. Toléndano, André. Ce qu'il faut savoir sur le désarmement. Paris, 1932.

609. Wheeler-Bennett, J. W. The Disarmament Deadlock. London, 1934. Good account, with discussions of personalities.

610. Wheeler-Bennett, John W. Disarmament and Security Since Locarno, 1925-1931; Being the Political and Technical Background of the General Disarmament Conference, 1932. London, 1932.

611. Wheeler-Bennett, John W. The Pipe Dream of Peace. London, 1935.

612. Wilson, Hugh R. Disarmament and the Cold War in the Thirties. New York, 1963.

D. Related Issues: Airpower, Gas, and International Police

613. Attlee, Clement R. An International Police Force. London, 1934.

614. Bennett, Edward M. German Rearmament and the West. Princeton, 1979.

615. Bialer, Uri. "'Humanization' of Air Warfare in British Foreign Policy on the Eve of the Second World War." Journal of Contemporary History 13(1978): 79-96.

616. Brown, F. J. Chemical Warfare; A Study in Restraints. Princeton, 1968. Discusses reaction of military elites to use of gas in World War I (which was unfavorable), US reaction in the postwar period, and international efforts to make use of gas illegal, such as the Geneva Gas Protocol and the World Disarmament Conference. A valuable historical study of the evolution and nature of international deterrence schemes.

617. Davies, David. "An International Police Force?" International Affairs 11(1932):76-99. Calls for an international authority to make decisions for international policing.

618. Davies, David. The Problem of the Twentieth Century: A Study of International Relationships. London, 1930. The problem is how to enforce international agreements. The answer: an international police force.

619. Davies, David. Suicide or Sanity? An Examination of the Proposals Before the Geneva Disarmament Conference: The Case for an International Police Force. London, 1932. Argues for an international armed force, with the capacity to make war.

620. Dennis, Peter. Decision by Default: Peacetime Conscription and British Defence, 1919-1939. London, 1972.

621. Douhet, Giulio. The Command of the Air. Trans. Dino Ferrari, New York, 1942. The next war will be won by a first-strike from the air; Europe's cities are vulnerable. Douhet was the period's most systematic theorist of airpower.

622. Fradkin, Elvira K. The Air Menace and the Answer. New York, 1934. Only League control of all aircraft, for League use in time of war, can prevent a rain of gas and chemicals on the world's cities. Needed: disarmament.

623. Gibbs, Norman. Grand Strategy. Volume 1: Rearmament Policy. London, 1976. The official history.

624. Groves, P. R. C. "The Influence of Aviation on International Relations." Journal of the Royal Institute of International Affairs 6(1927):133-52.

625. Groves, P. R. C. "The Influence of Aviation on International Affairs." Journal of the Royal Institute of International Affairs 8(1929):289-305.

626. Hall, Hines H., III. "The Foreign Policy-Making Process in Britain, 1934-1935, and the Origins of the Anglo-German Naval Agreement." Historical Journal 19(1972):477-99.

627. Haraszti, E. H. Treaty Breaker or "Real-politiker"? The Anglo-German Naval Agreement of June 1935. Boppard am Rhein, 1974.

628. Hyde, H. Montgomery. British Air Policy between the Wars, 1918-1939. London, 1976.

629. International Committee of the Red Cross. La protection des populations civiles contre les bombardements. Geneva, 1930. Question: are there rules to protect civilians? Answer, by jurists: No. Existing rules do not apply to air war.

630. Inter-Parliamentary Union. What Would be the Character of a New War? London, 1931. The horrors of modern war, imagined from the destructive power of new weapons.

631. Izard, L., and Cilleuls, J. des. La guerre aéro-chimique et les populations civiles. Paris, 1932. How to deal with gas warfare.

632. Le Goyet, P. "Evolution de la doctrine d'emploi de l'aviation française entre 1919 et 1939." Revue d'histoire de la deuxième guerre mondiale 73(1969):3-41.

633. Liddell Hart, B. "An International Force." International Affairs 12(1933):205-23. Against the French position of national contingents placed at the disposal of the League, argues for a permanent service.

634. McCarthy, Richard D. The Ultimate Folly: War by Pestilence, Asphyxiation and Defoliation. London, 1970. A one-sided philippic by a U.S. Congressman.

635. Martin, William. Disarmament and the Inter-Parliamentary Union. Lausanne, 1931. Good chapter on work of IPU in encouraging popular opinion for disarmament.

636. Morris, A. J. A. "The English Radicals' Campaign for Disarmament and the Hague Conference of 1907." Journal of Modern History 43(1971):367-93.

637. Mumford, P. Humanity, Air Power and War. Wants internationalization of civil aviation and creation of an international air police force.

639. New Commonwealth. The Functions of an International Air Police. London, 1936. The New Commonwealth was founded by Lord Davies in 1932 to argue for an international tribunal to adjudicate all international disputes, and an international police force to prevent aggression and enforce judgments.

640. Pelz, Stephen E. Race to Pearl Harbor: The Failure of the Second London Naval Conference and the Onset of World War II. Cambridge, MA., 1974.

641. Roskill, Stephen. Naval Policy Between the Wars. London, 1968.

642. Shay, Robert Paul, Jr. British Rearmament in the Thirties: Politics and Profits. Princeton, 1977. Shows that N. Chamberlain's insistence on economic stability, "the fourth arm of defence," dominated rearmament policy. He consciously chose to risk defense rather than financial stability, in hope appeasement would spare Britain the need to rearm on a vast scale.

643. Spaight, J. M. "Air Bombardment." British Year-Book of International Law 4(1922/3):21-33.

644. Spaight, J. M. Air Power and the Cities.
     London, 1930. Need new codes regulating air
     action, such as the "Proposed Rules for Regu-
     lating Air Warfare" drafted at The Hague in
     1923.

645. Spaight, J. M. An International Air Force.
     London, 1932.

646. Turner, C. C. Britain's Air Peril. London,
     1933. London the most exposed capital, and
     Britain fifth among air powers.

647. Vauthier, Lt. Col. Le danger aérien et
     l'avenir du pays. Paris, 1930. Suggests
     precautions, such as new layouts for cities
     and buildings.

648. Young, Robert J. "The Strategic Dream:
     French Air Doctrine in the Inter-War Period
     1919-1939." Journal of Contemporary History
     9(1974):57-76.

IX. THE CRISES OF THE 1930s

A. General

649. Aloisi, Pompeo. _Journal, 25 juillet 1932 - 14 juin 1936_. Trans. by M. Vaussard. Paris, 1957. Head of Italian delegation to League. Revealing of Mussolini's tactics.

650. Avon, Earl of (Anthony Eden). _The Eden Memoirs: Facing the Dictators_. London, 1962. Covers Eden's tenure as Minister for League of Nations Affairs, and beyond.

651. Blondel, Jules-François. _Au fil de la carrière: Récit d'un diplomate, 1911-1938_. Paris, 1960.

652. Blum, John M. _From the Morgenthau Diaries: Years of Crisis, 1928-1938_. Boston, 1959.

653. Blum, Léon. _L'histoire jugera_. 2nd ed. Montreal, 1943.

654. Bottai, Giuseppe. _Vent'anni e un giorno_. 2nd ed. Rome, 1949.

655. Bova Scoppa, Renato. _La pace impossibile_. Turin, 1961. Secretary of Italian delegation to League.

656. Butler, J. R. M. _Lord Lothian (Philip Kerr), 1882-1940_. New York, 1960.

657. Cameron, Elizabeth R. "Alexis Saint-Léger Léger." In _The Diplomats, 1919-1939_, edited by Gordon Craig and Felix Gilbert. Princeton, 1953.

658. Cameron, Elizabeth R. _Prologue to Appeasement: A Study in French Foreign Policy_. Washington, 1942.

659. Cato (pseudo.). _Guilty Men_. London, 1940.

137

660. Cecil of Chelwood, Viscount (Robert). All the Way. London, 1949.

661. Chamberlain, Austen. "The Permanent Bases of British Foreign Policy." Foreign Affairs 9(1931):533-46.

662. Chambrun, Charles de. Traditions et souvenirs. Paris, 1952. Reveals little, but some sense of his embassy in Rome.

663. Cross, J. A. Sir Samuel Hoare: A Political Biography. London, 1977.

664. Dalton, Hugh. The Fateful Years: Memoirs, 1931-1945. London, 1957.

665. Debicki, Roman. Foreign Policy of Poland, 1919-1939. New York, 1962.

666. Dodd, William E. Ambassador Dodd's Diary, 1933-1938. Edited by W. E. Dodd, Jr. and Martha Dodd. New York, 1941.

667. Eayrs, James. In Defence of Canada: Appeasement and Rearmament. Toronto, 1965. Solid study of policy turns and troubles,

668. Fabry, Jean. De la place de la concorde au course de l'intendance. Paris, 1942. Laval's centrist minister of war.

669. Fischer, Louis. Men and Politics: An Autobiography. New York, 1941.

670. Flandin, Pierre-Etienne. Politique française, 1919-1940. Paris, 1947. Does not explain the Flandin riddle.

671. François-Poncet, André. The Fateful Years: Memoirs of a French Ambassador in Berlin, 1931-1938. Translated by J. LeClerq. New York, 1949.

672. Giraud, Emile. La nullité de la politique internationale des grandes démocraties, 1919-1939. Paris, 1948. A sustained indictment of non-cooperation by a League official. A fine, perceptive analysis.

673. Hagglof, Gunnar. *Memoirs of a Swedish Envoy in London, Paris, Berlin, Moscow, Washington.* London, 1972.

674. Harvey of Tasburgh, Lord. *The Diplomatic Diaries of Oliver Harvey, 1937-1940.* Edited by John Harvey. London, 1970.

675. Herriot, Edouard. *Jadis, II: D'une guerre à l'autre, 1914-1936.* Paris, 1952. A solid memoir, informative (uses private documents that provide best clues to Council of Ministers), by courageous, pro-British, pro-League French delegate.

676. Hull, Cordell. *Memoirs.* 2 vols. New York, 1948. Revealing of difficulties in maintaining strictly limited support for League.

677. Jablon, Howard. "The State Department and Collective Security, 1933-1934." *Historian* 23(1971):248-63.

678. Kelly, David. *The Ruling Few, or, The Human Background to Diplomacy.* London, 1952.

679. Kennan, George F. *Russia and the West under Lenin and Stalin.* Boston, 1961.

680. Kuhn, Axel. *Hitler's Aussenpolitisches Programm: Entstehung und Entwicklung, 1919-1939.* Stuttgart, 1970.

681. Macartney, C. A., and Palmer, A. W. *Independent Eastern Europe.* London, 1962.

682. Madariaga, Salvador de. *Morning without Noon: Memoirs.* London, 1974. Thin, but with some sense of place and time, by a long-time Spanish diplomat at Geneva and London.

683. Mansergh, Nicholas. *Survey of British Commonwealth Affairs: Problems of External Policy, 1931-1939.* London, 1952.

684. Marquand, David. *Ramsay MacDonald.* London, 1977.

685. Michel, Bernard. "La petite entente et la crise des années 30." *Revue d'histoire de la deuxième guerre mondiale* 77(1970):15-24.

686. Middlemas, Keith, and Barnes, John. Baldwin:
     A Biography. London, 1969. Exhaustive, but
     more still is to be said about Baldwin.

687. Miller, J. K. Belgian Foreign Policy between
     Two Wars, 1919-1940. New York, 1951.

688. Motta, Giuseppe. Testimonia temporum: Series
     secunda, 1932-1936. Bellinzona, 1936. Swiss
     spokesman for foreign affairs, ambivalent
     towards League, especially during Italian
     crisis.

689. Néré, Jacques. The Foreign Policy of France
     from 1914 to 1945. Trans. by C. J. Lowe.
     London, 1975.

690. Nixon, Edgar B., ed. Franklin D. Roosevelt
     and Foreign Affairs. 3 vols. Cambridge, MA,
     1969. Contains speeches, revealing letters,
     but much is left out.

691. Northedge, F. S. The Troubled Giant: Britain
     among the Great Powers, 1916-1939. London,
     1966. An important study, with provocative
     conclusions of how Britain used the Dominions
     to pursue an anticontinental policy in dis-
     agreement with the French.

692. Ormos, Sz. "A propos de la sécurité est-
     européenne dans les années 1930." Acta His-
     torica 16:307-21.

693. Ostrower, Gary B. "American Ambassador to
     the League of Nations--1933: A Proposal Post-
     poned." International Organization 25(1971):
     46-58. A tantalizing proposal, that came to
     nothing.

694. Osusky, Stefan. "The Little Entente and the
     League of Nations." International Affairs
     3(1934):378-93. Czech minister to France
     since 1920.

695. Paul-Boncour, Joseph. Entre deux guerres. 3
     vols. Paris, 1945.

696. Petrie, Charles A. The Life and Letters of
     the Right Hon. Sir Austen Chamberlain. 2
     vols. London, 1939, 1940.

697. Reynaud, Paul. Au coeur de la mêlée 1930-1945. Paris, 1951. One of the few who consistently supported cooperation with Britain as France's necessary connection.

698. Reynaud, Paul. Mémoires, I: Venu de ma montagne. Paris, 1960.

699. Roberts, Henry L. "Maxim Litvinov." In The Diplomats, 1919-1939, edited by G. Craig and F. Gilbert. Princeton, 1953.

700. Rose, Norman. Vansittart: Study of a Diplomat. London, 1978.

701. Roskill, Stephen. Hankey: Man of Secrets. 3 vols. London, 1969-74.

702. Rubinstein, Alvin Z., ed. The Foreign Policy of the Soviet Union. New York, 1960.

703. Salter, Lord Arthur. Personality in Politics. London, 1947.

704. Selby, Walford. Diplomatic Twilight, 1930-1940. London, 1953.

705. Seton-Watson, Hugh. Eastern Europe between the Wars, 1914-1941. London, 1945. 2nd ed. 1946.

706. Somervell, D. C. Stanley Baldwin: An Examination of Some Features of Mr. G. M. Young's Biography. London, 1953.

707. Soulié, Michel. La vie politique d'Edouard Herriot. Paris, 1962.

708. Stimson, Henry L., and Bundy, McGeorge. On Active Service in Peace and War. New York, 1948.

709. Suarez, Georges, and Laborde, G. Agonie de la paix, 1935-1939. Paris, 1942.

710. Szembek, Comte Jean. Journal, 1933-1939. Translated by J. Rzewuska and T. Zaleski. Paris, 1952.

711. Templewood, Viscount (Samuel Hoare). Nine Troubled Years. London, 1954.

712. U.S.S.R. "The Struggle of the U.S.S.R. for Collective Security in Europe during 1933-1935." International Affairs nos. 6, 7, 8, 10. Moscow, 1963.

713. Warner, Geoffrey. Pierre Laval and the Eclipse of France. London, 1968. A full scale criticism of Laval's policies.

714. Wilson, Hugh R. Diplomat between Wars. New York, 1941.

715. Wood, Edward (Earl of Halifax). Fullness of Days. London, 1957.

716. Young, G. M. Stanley Baldwin. London, 1952.

717. Zuylen, Pierre van. Les mains libres: Politique extérieure de la belgique, 1914-40. Brussels, 1950.

B. Manchuria

Japan's expansion in Manchuria in 1931 was brought before the League by China, asserting that a threat of war existed and that its territorial integrity was violated. This was the most significant challenge to the League's authority to date. Its failure in the course of 1931-33 to compel Japanese withdrawal exposed the inability of the League to coerce states to comply with the terms of the Covenant. This shook confidence in the League, as it revealed the difficulty in determining swiftly if aggression had taken place (the investigation of the Lytton Commission took almost a year), the absence of powerful interested parties (the U.S. and the U.S.S.R.) which made comprehensive collective action impossible, the weakness of Britain and its caution in acting more or less alone in the Far East in light of its imperial commitments there, and, as France and other European states stood aloof from Asia's problems, the difficulties of extending the League's writ when internal concerns in Europe and America (depression, diffident leadership) took predominance over any interest in universalizing liberal principles far from home.

718. Borg, Dorothy. The United States and the Far Eastern Crisis of 1933-1938. Cambridge, MA, 1964.

719. Casella, Allessandro. Le conflit sino-japonais et la Société des Nations. Paris, 1968.

720. Chin, Wunsz. China and the League of Nations: The Sino-Japanese Controversy. New York, 1965.

721. Endicott, Stephen Lyon. Diplomacy and Enterprise: British China Policy, 1933-1937. Vancouver, 1975.

722. Kawakami, K. K. Manchoukuo, Child of Conflict. New York, 1969.

723. Koo, V. K. Wellington. Memoranda Presented to the Lytton Commission. 3 vols. New York, 1932-33.

724. Lensen, G. A. The Damned Inheritance: The Soviet Union and the Manchurian Crises, 1924-1935. Tallahassee, 1974.

725. Lytton, Earl of. "The Problem of Manchuria." International Affairs 11(1932):737-56. An exposition of the Report by its author, discussing the procedure of the commission and the situation of the League.

726. Lytton, Earl of. "The Twelfth Assembly of the League of Nations." International Affairs 10(1931):740-56.

727. Ogata, Sadako. Defiance in Manchuria: The Making of Japanese Foreign Policy, 1931-1932. Berkeley, 1964.

728. Rubinow, E. S. Sino-Japanese Warfare and the League of Nations. Geneva, 1938.

729. Smith, Sara R. The Manchurian Crisis, 1931-1932: A Tragedy in International Relations. New York, 1948.

730. Stimson, Henry L. The Far Eastern Crisis. New York, 1936.

731. Thorne, Christopher. Limits of Foreign Policy: The West, the League and the Far Eastern Crisis of 1931-1933. London, 1972.

This is the best single study, superb sources and bibliography.

732. Thorne, Christopher. "Viscount Cecil, the Government and the Far Eastern Crisis of 1931." Historical Journal 14(1971):805-26.

733. Trotter, Ann. Britain and East Asia, 1933-1937. New York, 1975.

734. Willoughby, W. W. The Sino-Japanese Controversy and the League of Nations. Baltimore, 1935.

735. Yoshihashi, Takehiko. Conspiracy at Mukden: The Rise of the Japanese Military. New Haven, 1963.

C. Chaco and Leticia

The failure of the general disarmament conference further discouraged League supporters, but some comfort was derived by the role the League played in two disputes in South America, the war between Bolivia and Paraguay over the Chaco territory and the dispute between Colombia and Peru over the Amazonian area around Leticia. The League's commission of inquiry over Chaco could not end the war, but it recommended an arms embargo (not executed), defined the issues, and helped set the terms for peace eventually agreed to by the exhausted parties. In Leticia, where Colombia's legal position was strong in the face of a clear incursion, the Council exerted pressure on Peru despite some notable non-cooperation by the British and Dutch governments. A change of regime in Lima led to a League commission taking control of Leticia for one year in 1933-34 and with Brazilian assistance the eventual negotiated reestablishment of Colombian authority.

736. Barros, Jayme de. Ocho años de política exterior des Brasil. Rio de Janeiro, 1938.

737. Braden, Spruille. "A Resume of the Role Played by Arbitration in the Chaco Dispute." Arbitration Journal 2(1938):387-95.

738. The Chaco Peace Conference: Report of the Delegation of the United States of America to

the Peace Conference Held at Buenos Aires,
July 1, 1935 - January 23, 1939. Washington,
1940.

739. Cooper, R. M. The Chaco Dispute. Geneva,
1934.

740. Corrêa da Costa, Sergio. A Diplomacia
brasileira na questão de Letícia. Rio de
Janeiro, 1942.

741. Garner, William R. The Chaco Dispute: A
Study of Prestige Diplomacy. Washington,
1966.

742. Hilton, Stanley E. Brazil and the Great
Powers, 1930-1939: The Politics of Trade
Rivalry. Austin, 1975.

743. Hudson, M. O., comp. The Verdict of the
League. Boston, 1933. Reviews and presents
League conclusion.

744. Kirkpatrick, Helen P. The Chaco Dispute, the
League, and Pan-Americanism. Geneva, 1936.

745. Kirkpatrick, Helen P. The Chaco Dispute.
Geneva, 1936.

746. La Foy, Margaret. The Chaco Dispute and the
League of Nations. Ann Arbor, 1946.

747. Lindsay, J. W. "The War over the Chaco."
International Affairs 14(1935):231-40.

748. Mattison, M. The Chaco Arms Embargo.
Geneva, 1934.

749. Meacham, J. Lloyd. The United States and
Inter-American Security, 1889-1960. Austin,
1962.

750. Pérez Serrano, Jorge. El tercero en la dis-
cordia. Quito, 1936. A study of Ecuador's
interest and behavior in dispute.

751. Reyes, Alfonso. La conferencia Colombo-
Peruana para Rio di Janeiro, 25 de octubre de
1933 a 24 de mayo de 1934, el arreglo del
incidente de Leticia. Mexico City, 1947.

752. Rout, Leslie B., Jr. Politics of the Chaco Peace Conference, 1935-1939. Austin, 1970.

753. St. John, R. B. "The End of Innocence: Peruvian Foreign Policy and the United States, 1919-1942." Journal of Latin American Studies 8(1976):325-34.

754. Wood, Bryce. The United States and Latin American Wars, 1932-1942. New York, 1966.

755. Villegas, Silvio. De Ginebra a Río de Janeiro. Bogatá, 1934.

756. Zook, David H., Jr. The Conduct of the Chaco War. New York, 1960.

D. Ethiopia

The test of the system of collective security posed by Italy's invasion of Fthiopia in 1935 was, in Walter's words, "the most important and decisive chapter in the history of the League." (History of the League, 623). Italy's premeditated aggression was in clear violation of the Covenant, and its modern army using airplanes and poison gas horrified a world increasingly fearful of general war. Attention throughout the world focused on the League's response. For the first and only time article 16 was applied. Fifty states participated in limited economic sanctions against Italy, potentially extendable to blockade or restraints on shipments of oil. Collective action worked for over seven months. Yet the reluctance of Britain and France to push opposition to the point of threatening Italy with a war in Europe, the equivocation of Secretary-General Avenol, the swiftness of the Italian military victory, and European preoccupations and uncertainty concerning America qualified all support given at Geneva, and led to appeasement by the League's leaders that undermined the effectiveness of the collective response. The result was a humiliating failure for the League, exposing more clearly than did the Manchurian dispute its institutional weaknesses.

757. Asante, S. K. B. Pan-African Protest: West Africa and the Italo-Ethiopian Crisis, 1934-1941. London, 1977. The powerful effects of League failure felt in West Africa.

758. Asante, S. K. B. "The Catholic Missions, British West African Nationalists, and the Italian Invasion of Ethiopia, 1935-36." African Affairs 73(1974):204-16.

759. Atwater, Elton. Administration of Exports and Import Embargoes by Member States of the League of Nations, 1935-36. Geneva, 1938.

760. Baer, George W. The Coming of the Italian-Ethiopian War. Cambridge, MA, 1967.

761. Baer, George W. "Sanctions and Security: The League of Nations and the Italian-Ethiopian War, 1935-1936." International Organization 27(1973):165-80.

762. Baer, George W. Test Case: Italy, Ethiopia, and the League of Nations. Stanford, 1976.

763. Bartholin, Pierre. Aspects économiques des sanctions prises contre l'Italie. Paris, 1938.

764. Bastin, Jean. L'affaire d'Ethiopie et les diplomates, 1934-1937. Brussels, 1937.

765. Berio, Alberto. "L' 'affare' etiopico." Rivista di studi politici internazionali 25(1958):181-219. In the Secretariat, Berio was liaison between it and Italian delegation.

766. Bianchi, Gianfranco. Rivelazioni sul conflitto italo-etiopico. Milan, 1967.

767. Buccianti, Giovanni. "Hitler, Mussolini, e il conflitto italo-etiopico." Il Politico 37(1972):415-28.

768. Buell, Raymond L. American Neutrality and Collective Security. Geneva, 1935.

769. Buell, Raymond L. The Suez Canal and League Sanctions. Geneva, 1935.

770. Braddick, H. "A New Look at American Policy during the Italo-Ethiopian Crisis, 1935-36." Journal of Modern History 34(1962):64-73.

771. Cohen, Armand. La Société des Nations devant le conflit italo-éthiopien (décembre 1934 - octobre 1935), politique et procédure. Paris, 1960.

772. Colvin, Ian. None So Blind. New York, 1965.

773. De Felice, Renzo. Mussolini il duce. Part 1, Gli anni del consenso, 1929-1936. Turin, 1974.

774. De Wilde, J. The International Distribution of Raw Materials. Geneva, 1936.

775. Divine, Robert A. The Illusion of Neutrality: Franklin D. Roosevelt and the Struggle over the Arms Embargo. Chicago, 1962.

776. Dorigo, P. P. Ginevra o Roma? Pisa, 1934.

777. Doxey, Margaret P. Economic Sanctions and International Enforcement. London, 1971.

778. Feis, Herbert. Seen from E. A., Three International Episodes. New York, 1947. Advisor for International Economic Affairs in Department of State. Part II entitled: "Oil for Italy: A Study in the Decay of International Trust."

779. Forster, W. Arnold. "Sanctions." Journal of the Royal Institute of International Affairs 5(1926):1-15.

780. Funke, Manfred. "Le relazioni italo-tedesche al momento del conflitto etiopico e delle sanzioni della Società delle Nazioni." Storia contemporanea 2(1971):475-93.

781. Funke, Manfred. Sanktionen und Kanonen: Hitler, Mussolini, und der internationale Abessinien Konflikt, 1934-1936. Düsseldorf, 1970.

782. Guariglia, Raffaele. Ricordi, 1922-1946. Naples, 1950. Headed Ethiopian desk in Italian Foreign Ministry during crisis.

783. Géraud, André. "British Vacillations." Foreign Affairs 14(1936):584-97.

784. Gilbert, Felix. "Two British Ambassadors: Perth and Henderson." In The Diplomats, 1919-1939, edited by G. Craig and F. Gilbert. Princeton, 1953. Perth, of course, was Eric Drummond, at this time ambassador in Rome, and his opinions may to some extent be read backward in time to his secretary-general-ship.

785. Harris, Brice, Jr. The United States and the Italo-Ethiopian Crisis. Stanford, 1964.

786. Highley, Albert E. The Actions of the States Members of the League of Nations in Applica-tion of Sanctions against Italy, 1935-1936. Geneva, 1938.

787. Highley, Albert E. The First Sanctions Experiment: A Study of League Procedures. Geneva, 1938.

788. Hoskins, H. "The Suez Canal in Time of War." Foreign Affairs 14(1935):93-101.

789. Istituto per gli Studi di Politica Interna-zionale. Il Conflitto italo-etiopico: Documenti. 2 vols. Milan, 1936.

790. Koren, William. The Italian-Ethiopian Dispute. Geneva, 1935.

791. Kuyper, Pieter Jan. The Implementation of International Sanctions: The Netherlands and Rhodesia. The Hague, 1978. Good chapter on "the Netherlands and the League of Nations," and on the general problem of organizing a sanctions front.

792. La Pradelle, Albert de. Le conflit italo-éthiopien. Paris, 1936.

793. Laurens, Franklin D. France and the Italo-Ethiopian Crisis, 1935-1936. The Hague, 1967. Collection of journal opinions about collective security, etc.

794. Laval, Pierre. Le procès Laval: Compte rendu sténographique. Paris, 1946.

795. Leroux, Eugene-Louis. Le conflit italo-éthiopien devant la S.D.N. Paris, 1937.

796. Lessona, Alessandro. _Memorie_. Florence, 1958.

797. Lothian, Lord. "The Place of Britain in the Collective System." _International Affairs_ 12(1935):622-50.

798. Magistrati, Massimo. "La Germania e l'impresa italiana di Etiopia, Ricordi di Berlino." _Rivista di studi politici internazionali_ 17(1950):563-606.

799. Mallet, Alfred. _Pierre Laval_. 2 vols. Paris, 1955.

800. Margueritte, V. _The League Fiasco_. Trans. by Mrs. N. MacFarlane. London, 1936.

801. Mengesha, Eshetou. _Die Aussenpolitik der äthiopischen Regierung Wahrend der Italo-äthiopischen Krise und das Versagen des Völkerbundes, 1933-1936_. Bonn, 1975.

802. Mitrany, David. _The Problem of International Sanctions_. London, 1925. An earlier study of the sanction problem, concluding only a case of international conflict justifies the risk and burden. In the Ethiopian case, the risk and burden were thought to provoke conflict--the threat without sanctions was minimal, except to the authority of the League.

803. Mori, Renato. "L'impresa etiopica e le sue ripercussioni internazionali." In Augusto Torre et al., _La politica estera italiana dal 1914 al 1943_. Rome, 1963.

804. Mori, Renato. _Mussolini e la conquista dell'Etiopia_. Florence, 1978.

805. Nemours, General Alfred. _Craignons d'être un jour l'Ethiopie de quelqu'un_. Port-au-Prince, 1945.

806. Olson, Richard Stuart. "Economic Coercion in World Politics: With a Focus on North-South Relations." _World Politics_ 31(1979):471-94.

807. Ormesson, Wladimir de, et al. Anglo-French Conference, Bouffémont, December 1935: _La_

sécurite collective à la lumière du conflit italo-éthiopien. Geneva, 1936.

808. Pankhurst, Richard. "The Italo-Ethiopian War and League of Nations Sanctions, 1935-36." Genève-Afrique 13(1974):5-29.

809. Parker, R. A. C. "Great Britain, France, and the Ethiopian Crisis, 1935-1936." English Historical Review 89(1974):293-332.

810. Post, Gaines, Jr. "The Machinery of British Policy in the Ethiopian Crisis." International History Review 1(1979):522-41.

811. Potter, Pitman B. The Wal Wal Arbitration. Washington, 1938.

812. Robertson, Esmonde M. Mussolini as Empire-Builder: Europe and Africa, 1932-36. London, 1977.

813. Robertson, James C. "The British General Election of 1935." Journal of Contemporary History 9(1974):149-64. How far was the British public willing to support rearmament or a strong League policy against Italy?

814. Rousseau, Charles. Le conflit italo-éthiopien devant le droit international. Paris, 1938.

815. Santarelli, Enzo. "Guerra d'Etiopia, imperialism e terzo mondo." Il movimento di liberazione in Italia 21(1969):35-51.

816. Schonfield, Hugh J. The Suez Canal in World Affairs. New York, 1953.

817. Terlinden, Vicomte Charles. Le conflit italo-éthiopien et la Société des Nations. Liege, 1936.

818. Tillett, Lowell R. "The Soviet Role in League Sanctions against Italy, 1935-1936." American Slavic and East European Review 15(1956):11-16.

819. Vaucher, Paul, and Siriex, Paul-Henri. L'opinion britannique, la Société des Nations, et la guerre italo-éthiopienne. Paris, 1936.

820. Wilson, Hugh R., Jr. For Want of a Nail: The Failure of the League of Nations in Ethiopia. New York, 1959.

821. Wright, Quincy. "The Test of Aggression in the Italo-Ethiopian War." American Journal of International Law 30(1936):45-56.

822. Zimmern, Alfred. "The League's Handling of the Italo-Abyssinian Dispute." International Affairs 14(1935):751-68.

823. Zimmern, Alfred. "The Testing of the League." Foreign Affairs 14(1936):373-386.

E. Rearmament, Reform, and Last Acts

The League did nothing about Hitler's denunciation of Locarno, German remilitarization of the Rhineland, the Anschluss, Nazi activity in Danzig, and Hitler's moves against Czechoslovakia. Britain and France rearmed, appeased, and eventually went to war. For the League, these were years of defeat. Proposals for the reform of the Covenant, instructive for the League's successor organization, came to nothing. Efforts in 1937 to establish the integrity of the Sanjak of Alexandretta were thwarted by France and Turkey. In December 1939 the Soviet Union was 'excluded' from the League as a result of its invasion of Finland. But by then anything the League could do was overtaken by events beyond its control. In the second world war the League, as an institution, played no part.

824. Aita, Adman A. Le conflit d'Alexandrette et la Société des Nations. Damascus, 1949.

825. Avenol, Joseph. "The Future of the League of Nations." International Affairs 5(1934):143-58. Important revisionist statement, prudent, cautious. Argues still that disarmament is central issue for League.

826. Balossini, Cajo Enrico. La perte de la qualité de membre de Société des Nations: Cas récents. Geneva, 1945.

827. Barcia Trelles, C. Puntos Cardinales de la politica internacional española. Barcelona, 1939.

828. Benes, Eduard. Memoirs: From Munich to New War and New Victory. Trans. by Godfrey Lias. London, 1954.

829. Blum, Léon. L'oeuvre de Léon Blum, 1934-1937. Paris, 1964.

830. Bourquin, M., ed. Collective Security. London, 1936. Reports submitted to the seventh and eighth International Studies Conference in Paris on collective security, with some suggestive ideas.

831. Cerruti, Vittorio. "Collaborazione internazionale e ragioni dell'insuccesso della Societa delle Nazioni." Rivista di studi politici internazionali 13(1946):50-73.

832. Coghlan, F. "Armaments, Economic Policy, and Appeasement: Background to British Foreign Policy, 1931-1937." History 57(1972):205-16.

833. Collier, Basil. The Defence of the United Kingdom. London, 1957.

834. Dreifort, John E. Yvon Delbos at the Quai d'Orsay: French Foreign Foreign Policy During the Popular Front, 1936-38. Lawrence, KS, 1973.

835. Emmerson, James T. The Rhineland Crisis, 7 March 1936: A Study in Multilateral Diplomacy. London, 1977.

836. Gathorne-Hardy, G. M. "The League at the Cross-Roads." International Affairs 15(1936): 485-505.

837. Gathorne-Hardy, G. M., and Mitrany, D. "Territorial Revision and Article 19 of the League Covenant." International Affairs 14(1935): 818-36. Debate on possibility and value of reform.

838. Ghebali, Victor-Yves. La Société des Nations et la réforme Bruce, 1939-1940. Geneva, 1970. The best study of the Bruce Reform; a Carnegie 50th anniversary monograph.

839. Goodrich, Leland M. "Peace Enforcement Perspective." International Journal 24(1969):
657-72.

840. Gross, Leo. "Was the Soviet Union Expelled
from the League of Nations?" American
Journal of International Law (1945):35-44.

841. Hambro, Carl J. "The Role of the Smaller
Powers in International Affairs Today."
International Affairs 15(1936):167-82.

842. Jakobson, Max. The Diplomacy of the Winter
War: An Account of the Russo-Finnish War,
1939-1940. Cambridge, MA, 1966.

843. Kieft, David Owen. Belgium's Return to Neutrality: An Essay in the Frustrations of
Small Power Diplomacy. Oxford, 1972.

844. La Pradelle, Albert de. "L'appel de la Fin-
lande." Revue des deux mondes (1940):459-73.

845. Laurent, Pierre Henri. "The Reversal of Belgian Foreign Policy, 1936-1937." Review of
Politics 31(1961):370-84.

846. Macleod, Iain. Neville Chamberlain. London,
1961.

847. Mantoux, Paul, et al. The World Crisis.
London, 1938.

848. Mysyrowicz, Ladislas. Autopsie d'une défaite:
Origines de l'effondrement militaire français
de 1940. Lausanne, 1973.

849. Nicolson, Harold. "Has Britain a Policy?"
Foreign Affairs 14(1936):549-62.

850. Peden, G. C. British Rearmament and the
Treasury, 1932-1939. Edinburgh, 1979.

851. Potter, Pitman B. "League Publicity: Cause
or Effect of League Failure?" Public Opinion
Quarterly (1938):399-412.

852. Raschhofer, Hermann. Völkerbund und Münchner
Abkommen. Munich, 1976.

853. Robertson, Esmonde M. "Zur Wiederbesetzung des Rheinlandes 1936." Vierteljahrshefte für Zeitgeschichte 10(1962):178-205.

854. Schmidt, Hugo C. Das Ende des Völkerbundes. Stuttgart, 1956.

855. Stolper, G. "European Kaleidoscope." Foreign Affairs 14(1936):216-26.

856. Upton, Anthony F. Finland in Crisis, 1940-41. A Study in Small Power Politics. London, 1964.

857. Wourinen, John, ed. Finland and World War II, 1939-1944. New York, 1948.

X. ECONOMIC AND FINANCIAL ORGANIZATION

"Looking back, the decision to concentrate the activity of the League in its early years upon the development of international cooperation appears as perhaps the most important single act of policy during the first decade of its existence" (League of Nations, Ten Years of World Co-operation [Geneva, 1930], 179).

Inspired by wartime interallied economic cooperation, with models before it such as the Universal Postal Union (1874), the International Union for the Protection of Industrial Property (1883), and the international agreements on sugar (1902) and bills of exchange (1910), in response to the urgent needs of postwar reconstruction, and in light of the liberal principle of "equitable treatment of the commerce of all Members of the League" in article 23(e) of the Covenant, the Economic and Financial Organization became the largest of the League's technical bodies. In its first decade it concentrated on refugee aid and the supervision of loans and technical assistance to Austria, Bulgaria, Danzig, Estonia, Greece, and Hungary. Other work included efforts to liberalize trade and investment through the removal of tax and tariff barriers and the preparation of statistics, reports, and suggestions to assist trade policy and economic planning. The secretariat of the organization, the Economic and Financial Section, gave dedicated leadership, under the directorships of Arthur Salter (1922-31) and Alexander Loveday (1931-46). The organization was only advisory, offering services and ideas, at the mercy always of the diverse ambitions and capacities of states on whom the world economy depended. It worked closely with the ILO, the International Institute of Agriculture, and other institutions such as the International Chamber of Commerce, and regularly consulted ministries in member countries. The League was never given any responsibilities concerning the major postwar political-economic issues of reparations and war debts.

In the 1930s, with the disintegration of world trading and monetary systems and the decisive return to economic nationalism, the organization turned to more limited work, helping governments with particular problems such as wheat trade agreements, double taxation, and bilateral conventions, and to collecting information on depression-related problems of clearing arrangements, exchange controls, loan contracts, raw material procurements. In the hope of advancing a humanistic understanding of the economic and financial conditions of the time and to make up for its relative neglect of public education, it began explicitly to stress the ultimate interconnections of global prosperity, and turned its attention to migration and population movements, nutrition, housing, and questions of the standard of living.

With the outbreak of war, and following recommendations for reorganization and autonomy of the 1939 "Bruce Committee" (which included S. M. Bruce of Australia, Maurice Bourquin of Belgium, Harold Butler of Britain--late head of the ILO, Charles Rist of France, and C. J. Hambro of Norway) the organization, now entitled the Economic, Financial, and Transit Department, moved to Princeton to keep alive the League's non-political activities in preparation for dealing with the post-war chaos. The value of the League's social and economic services was recognized in the foundation of UNRRA and UNESCO, and in their partial autonomy from the UN's political structure.

A. List of Economic Conferences Convened by the League

1919.   Conference on International Cooperation in Statistics, London.

1920.   International Financial Conference, Brussels.

1922.   Genoa Conference, one aim of which was to simplify customs formalities.

1923.   International Conference on Customs and Other Similar Formalities, Geneva, to whose convention 35 countries adhered.

1927.   International Economic Conference, Geneva. Wide-ranging, with 194 delegates, aimed at collective tariff reduction, the preparation of a Standard Customs Nomenclature, and the codification of most-favored nation treatment.

1927-29.   International Conferences for the Abolition of Import and Export Prohibitions and Restrictions, Geneva.

1928-29. International Conferences on Hides, Skins, and Bones, Geneva.
1928. International Conference on Economic Statistics, Geneva.
1929. International Conference on the Treatment of Foreigners, Paris.
1929. International Conference on Counterfeiting Currency.
1930-31. Conferences with a View to Concerted Economic Action, Geneva.
1930-31. International Conference for the Unification of Laws on Bills of Exchange, Promissory Notes, and Cheques, Geneva.
1932. Stresa Conference, on reconstruction in Central and Eastern Europe.
1933. Wheat Conference, London.
1933. International Monetary and Economic Conference, London. This was to deal with the problems of the depression. Its work, in the confusions of the time and with no cooperation from the United States, came to little, although there were some agreements on commodity exchange and recommendations on monetary policy and credit were sometimes adopted.
1937. Conference on Sugar, Geneva.
1930. European Conference on Rural Life (not convened).

For each conference the organization presented documentation and memoranda on specific issues, and compiled a "report and proceedings" record. These extensive reports and recommendations have a lasting historical value, beyond interest in what agreements were concluded. A list of the most important of these organizational papers is found in Hans Aufricht, Guide to League of Nations Publications (New York, 1951), 217-31.

B. League Publications.

Regular publications of the Economic Intelligence Service included:

Monthly Bulletin of Statistics
Statistical Year-Book
International Trade Statistics
World Production and Prices
Review of World Trade
Money and Banking

World Economic Survey
Survey of National Nutrition Policies

Hans Aufricht, Guide to League of Nations
Publications (New York, 1951), 212-258, gives a list
of documents, and there is a well categorized bibliography in Martin Hill, The Economic and Financial
Organization of the League of Nations: A Survey of
Twenty-Five Years' Experience (Washington, 1946). An
annotated list is contained in League of Nations,
Catalogue of Selected Publications on Economic and
Financial Subjects: A Guide to the Documents of Value
in Connection with the Formulation of Post-War Economic Policies (Geneva, 1943). The following is a
selection of publications of general nature and some
concerned with reconstruction.

> The Development of International Co-Operation
>   in Economic and Social Affairs (1939)
> The Transition from War to Peace Economy:
>   Report of the Delegation on Economic
>   Depressions (1943)
> Economic Stability in the Post-War World
>   (1945)
> Relief Deliveries and Relief Loans, 1919-1923
>   (1943)
> Urban and Rural Housing (1939)
> Principles and Methods of Financial Recon-
>   struction Undertaken Under the Auspices of
>   the League of Nations (1930)
>   Excellent and detailed introduction.
> The League of Nations Reconstruction Schemes
>   in the Inter-War Period (1945)
>   This is the essential book on reconstruction
>   work, written by Royall Tyler who was League
>   representative in Budapest for 14 years.
> The Financial Reconstruction of Austria:
>   General Survey and Principal Documents
>   (1926)
> Reports of the Commissioner of the League of
>   Nations for Bulgaria (1926-39)
> The Financial Reconstruction of Hungary.
>   General Survey and Principal Documents
>   (1926)

C. General Works

858.   Adams, Frederick C. Economic Diplomacy:
        The Export-Import Bank and American Foreign
        Policy, 1934-1939. Columbia, MO., 1976.
        The EIB was founded in 1934. This book
        provides the historical and conceptual

setting for EIB's early years, showing policies and actions towards Soviet Union, China, Latin America, a matter of growing statism, not increased Wilsonianism.

859. Aldcroft, Derek H. "The Development of the Managed Economy before 1939." Journal of Contemporary History 4(1969):117-37. The public sector as an economic force and instrument of economic control.

860. Bain, H. Foster. "Mineral Resources and their Effect on International Relations." Journal of the Royal Institute of International Affairs 9(1930):664-79. A message of current import: there is only one crop.

861. Boadle, Donald G. "The Formation of the Foreign Office Economic Relations Section, 1930-1937." Historical Journal 20(1977): 919-36.

862. Carroll, M. B. "International Double Taxation." In Pioneers in World Order, edited by H. E. Davis. New York, 1944.

863. Cassel, Gustav. The Downfall of the Gold Standard. Oxford, 1936.

864. Clarke, Stephen V. O. Central Bank Cooperation, 1924-1931. New York, 1967.

865. Damalas, Basile. La réorganisation de l'économie mondiale: Les tentatives infructueuses de la SDN et les efforts actuels de l'ONU. Paris, 1947.

866. Davis, Joseph. The World between the Wars, 1919-1939: An Economist's View. Baltimore, 1975.

867. Doxey, Margaret. Economic Sanctions and International Enforcement. London, 1971.

868. Durand, E. "Standardizing World Statistics." In Pioneers in World Order, edited by H. E. Davis. New York, 1944.

869. Ghebali, Victor-Y. La Société des Nations et la réforme Bruce, 1939-1940. Geneva, 1970. The best account.

870. Grady, H. F. "World Economy." In Pioneers in World Order, edited by H. E. Davis. New York, 1944.

871. Guillain, Robert. Les problèmes douaniers internationaux et la Société des Nations. Paris, 1930. Discussion of the economic work of the League, the economic conference of 1927, cartels, and commercial conventions.

872. Helperin, Michael A. "La coopération économique internationale et la sécurité collective." Recueil des cours 68(1939):327-414.

873. Henderson, Arthur. "Chatham House: First Annual Dinner." Journal of the Royal Institute of International Affairs 9(1930):557-98. Speech by the foreign secretary on the importance of economic relations between countries.

874. Hill, Martin. The Economic and Financial Organization of the League of Nations: A Survey of Twenty-Five Years' Experience. Washington, 1946. This is the fundamental introduction.

875. Humphries, A. E. "The International Aspects of the Wheat Market." International Affairs 10(1931):84-102.

876. Jacobsson, Erin E. A Life for Sound Money: Per Jacobsson--His Biography. Oxford, 1979. A public finance expert on the financial committee and later a founder of Bank for International Settlement, with League until 1928. This book, his diaries, contains much inside information about financial committee and the secretariat.

877. Jensen, W. G. "The Importance of Energy in the First and Second World Wars." Historical Journal 11(1968):538-54.

878. Kapp, Karl. The League of Nations and Raw Materials, 1919-1939. Geneva, 1941.

879. Kirk, Dudley. Europe's Population in the Interwar Years. Princeton, 1946. A study sponsored by the League.

880. Leith, C. K. World Minerals and World
Politics: A Factual Study of Minerals in
their Political and International Relations.
New York, 1931. By a well-known geologist,
and includes Thomas Holland's proposed rider
to the Kellogg Pact prohibiting export of
mineral products in case of violation.

881. Loveday, Alexander. "The Economic and Financial Activities of the League." International Affairs 17(1938):788-808. The Director
of the section--a clear exposition.

882. McClure, Wallace M. World Prosperity as
Sought through the Economic Work of the
League of Nations. New York, 1933. A solid
survey of the economic activities of the
League and its auxiliaries.

883. McDougall, F. L. Food and Welfare. League
of Nations Studies on Nutrition and National
Economic Policy. Geneva, 1938.

884. Mond, Alfred. "International Cartels."
Journal of Royal Institute of International
Affairs 7(1927):265-83.

885. Patterson, E. M. "An Economic Approach to
Peace." International Affairs 10(1931):760-
77. A transnational rather than international world-wide approach through economic
connections.

886. Pollard, Sidney. European Economic Integration, 1815-1970. Harmondsworth, 1973.

887. Rappard, William. Post-war Efforts for Freer
Trade. Geneva, 1938.

888. Salter, Arthur, ed. The Economic Conse-
quences of the League. London, 1927.
Articles on the World Economic Conference.

889. Salter, Arthur. Memoirs of a Public Servant.
London, 1961.

890. Sosoin, Carina. Le rôle de la Société des
Nations en matière d'emprunts d'état. Paris,
1934.

891. Sweetser, Arthur. "The Non-Political Achieve-
ments of the League of Nations." Foreign
Affairs 19(1940):179-192.

892. Vagts, A. Mexico, Europa und Amerika unter
besondere Berücksichtigung der Petroleum-
politik. Berlin, 1928. The international
connections. A volume in the series "Politische Wissenschaft" published by the Institut und Deutsche Hochschule für Politik.

893. Zimmern, Alfred. "Fiscal Policy and International Relations." Journal of the British
Institute of International Affairs 3(1924):
20-34. Optimistic about the possibilities
for coordination through the League.

D. Financial and Technical Assistance

894. Antonucci, A. La liquidation financière
la guerre et la reconstruction en Europe
centrale. Paris, 1933. Long association
with Reparations Commission. Says Financial
Committee of February 1919 lost its opportunity, and recommends a great central bank to
take over the external public debts of Succes-
sion States and to arrange reasonable terms
for conversion and amortisation.

895. Aubert, Louis. The Reconstruction of Europe.
New Haven, 1925.

896. Berened, Ivan, and Ránki, Gyorgy. "Economic
Problems of the Danube Region after the
Break-up of the Austro-Hungarian Monarchy."
Journal of Contemporary History 4(1969):169-
86. Good article with excellent bibliography.

897. Bonnet, Georges. "The Economic Reconstruction
of Central and South-Eastern Europe." International Affairs 12(1933):19-36. Chairman of
the committee to study these problems, he
discusses the recommendations laid down at
the Stresa conference in light of world
crisis and agricultural dumping.

898. Campbell, W. K. Technical Collaboration with
China: Co-operation for Economically Undevel-
oped Countries. Geneva, 1938. A League
publication, reviewing one of the technical

assistance missions and reflecting on the
problem as a more general issue.

899. Conze, Werner. "Die Strukturkrise des ost-
lichen Mitteleuropas vor und nach 1919."
Vierteljahrshefte für Zeitgeschichte 6(1953):
319038.

900. Dertilis, Pauagiotis. La reconstruction
financière de la Grèce et la Société des
Nations. Paris, 1929.

901. Eckhardt, Tibor. "The Economic Position in
Central Europe." Journal of the Royal Institute for International Affairs 9(1930):521-8.
Shows problems developing from the terms of
the peace treaties.

902. Edelstein, Robert. Vienne: la situation
économique de l'Autriche de 1918-23. Neuchâ-
tel, 1930. Sees Anschluss the worst way out
of Austria's difficulties. Argues for a
customs union of the secession states.

903. Goode, William. "Austria." Journal of the
British Institute of International Affairs
6(1922):35-54. A moving study of what the
situation was like in this defeated country.

904. Keynes, John Maynard. The Economic Conse-
quences of the Peace. London, 1920. The
classic indictment of the peace settlement,
on the dangers of economic incoherence.

905. Koszul, J. P. La reconstruction financière
de la Bulgarie (1922-1931). Paris, 1932.

906. Meienberger, Norbert. Entwicklungshilfe unter
dem Völkerbund: Ein Beitrag zur Geschichte
der internationalen Zusammenarbeit in der
Zwischenkriegszeit unter besonderer Berücksichtigung der technischen Hilfe an China.
Winterthur, 1965. A fine, thorough study.

907. Mitzakis, Michel. Le relèvement financier de
la Hongrie et la Société des Nations. Paris,
1926.

908. Pasvolsky, Leo. Bulgaria's Economic Position,
with Special Reference to the Reparation

Problem and the Work of the League of Nations.
Washington, 1930.

909. Pietri, Nicole. La Société des Nations et la
reconstruction financière de l'Autriche,
1921-1926. Geneva, 1970. A careful recent
study, based on League archives.

910. Pillet, Maurice. Le relèvement financier de
l'Autriche. Paris, 1928.

911. Poortenaar, A. A. L'oeuvre de la restauration
financière sous les auspices de la Société
des Nations. Amsterdam, 1933. Brings
together League actions in Austria, Hungary,
Greece, Bulgaria, Danzig, and Estonia.
Praises Economic and Financial Committee's
handling of the difficult problems such as
marketing, employment for immigrants and
various matters of national economic reconstruction.

912. Recker, M. L. England und der Donauraum,
1919-1929: Probleme einer europäischen Nach-
kriegsordnung. Stuttgart, 1976.

913. Salter, Arthur. "The Reconstruction of
Hungary." Journal of the British Institute
of International Affairs 3(1924):190-202.

914. Schrecker, Charles. "The Growth of Economic
Nationalism and its International Conse-
quences." International Affairs 13(1934):
208-25.

915. Strakosch, Henry. "The Convention on Financial Assistance." International Affairs
10(1931):208-22.

E. Conferences

916. Feis, Herbert. 1933: Characters in Crisis.
Boston, 1960. About the London Economic
Conference.

917. Foss, William, and Austin, A. B. The World
Conference in Caricature. London, 1933.
Drawings by Nagy.

918. Heineman, John L. "Constantin von Neurath
and German Policy at the London Economic

Conference of 1933: Backgrounds to the Resignation of Alfred Hugenberg." Journal of Modern History 41(1969):160-88. Important for the question of German participation in the early years of Hitler.

919. Layton, W. T. "The Forthcoming Economic Conference of the League of Nations and its Possibilities." Journal of the Royal Institute of International Affairs 6(1927):69-87.

920. Lazar, Oscar. Conférence économique internationale, Genève 1927. Geneva, 1927. Fifty-seven portraits and caricatures of members of the conference by Lazar.

921. McDougall, F. L. "The International Wheat Situation." International Affairs 10(1931): 524-38. A fine discussion of the European situation in relation to the Conference of Wheat Exporting Countries in London, 1931, and the preparatory work of the International Wheat Conference in Rome held under IIA auspices.

922. Nichois, J. P. "Roosevelt's Monetary Diplomacy in 1933" American Historical Review 56(1951): 295-317.

923. Salter, Arthur. "The Economic Conference: Prospects of Practical Results." Journal of the Royal Institute of International Affairs 6(1927):350-67.

924. Salter, Arthur. Recovery: The Second Effort. Rev. ed. London, 1933. Good on the Economic Conference of 1927 and its aftermath.

925. Samuel, Herbert. "The World Economic Conference." International Affairs 12(1933):439-59.

926. Slade, E. J. W. "The Influence of Oil on International Politics." Journal of the British Institute of International Affairs 2(1923):251-58. Asserts the complications introduced into the Genoa Conference by the conflict of oil interests were responsible for its breakdown.

927. Traynor, Dean. International Monetary and
      Financial Conferences in the Inter-War
      Period. Washington, 1949. Best general
      discussion of the London World Economic
      Conference of 1933.

928. Zimmern, A. "Fiscal Policy and International
      Relations." Journal of the British Institute
      of International Affairs 3(1924):20-34.

XI. MANDATES

Article 22 of the Covenant put in trust to the League the supervision of the former colonial territories of the defeated states, as well as some territories previously integral parts of the Ottoman Empire. The League was given no direct control, and it was left to the Supreme Council to declare, according to traditional considerations of great power interests, which states were to assume supervisory authority. The League's jurisdiction remained indirect.

The Council established a Permanent Mandates Commission, to meet twice a year to examine the annual reports each mandatory power was requested to submit to the Council, and to advise the Council. Support was furnished by the Mandates Section of the Secretariat. The PMC was the League's main agent, and the 37 volumes of its sessional minutes, its annual reports to the Council, and its questionnaires are the essential League documents on the subject, and publicity was the only lever of League influence. Hans Aufricht, A Guide to League of Nations Documents (New York, 1951), 152-60, reviews the official literature.

Many questions pertaining to the mandate system deserve study. Why did not the Assembly play a greater role? What can be said about the internal workings of the PMC, the sections, the experts, the political complexion and intent of its members? What were the limitations placed on or accepted in their work? How is one to evaluate Lugard's judgment that one of the reasons for the success of the PMC was its observance of this principle: "Abstention from direct advice or criticism of administration and policy, either in audience to the accredited representative of the mandatory, or by any attempt at local inspection" (cited in H. Duncan Hall, Mandates, Dependencies, and Trusteeships, Washington, 1948, 209). There was a remoteness to its work. No commissioner ever went in an official capacity to a mandated territory for an on-the-spot investigation, and the annual reports of the powers dealt with events already past. The system reveals a lot about the aspirations and the limitations of the League. Quincy Wright called the mandate system "perhaps the most important innovation wrought by the peace treaties and the Covenant in the system of international law" (Mandates under the League of Nations, Chicago, 1930, p. vii). To what extent may the mandate system, a highly visible connection between developed and underdeveloped areas, be viewed as part of a process leading from direct rule to independence? Even in its own terms, how well did the PMC serve to control arms, liquor, and slavery, encourage economic development, and work to improve labor conditions, in part in connection with the ILO?

Members of the PMC were appointed by the Council, membership was permanent, and there was notable continuity of tenure. The more influential commissioners were:

Alberto Theoldi, Italy, served 1921-37, chairman for 16 years.

D. F. W. van Rees, Netherlands, served 13 years.

Pierre Orts, Belgium, sat the entire 18 years of the PMC.

Frederick Lugard, U.K., sat for 13 years.

William Rappard, Switzerland, director of the Mandates Section of the Secret Secretariat, 1921-25, and in 1924 made an extraordinary member of the PMC with voting rights.

The annual reports of the mandatory powers were state documents, not League documents. They are found in appropriate state archives, and are held also in the League library. Only those of 1924 were published. The files of the Mandates Section are in the League Secretariat Archive Group. Each territory has its own colonial history. This was not a matter of international diplomacy, and the bibliography on any given area is beyond our scope. Below are some studies useful in indicating the situation of the PMC.

929. Abendroth, W. Die völkerrechtliche Stellung der B und C Mandate. Breslau, 1936.

930. Albertini, Rudolf von. Dekolonisation: Die Diskussion über Verwaltung und Zukunft der Kolonien, 1919-1960. Cologne, 1966.

931. Albertini, Rudolf von. "The Impact of Two World Wars on the Decline of Colonialism." Journal of Contemporary History 4(1969):17-36. Argues the arrogance of the mandate idea.

932. Albertini, Rudolf von. "Die USA und die Kolonialfrage, 1917-1945." Vierteljahrshefte für Zeitgeschichte 13(1965):1-31.

933. Ambrosini, Gaspare. Paesi sotto mandato: condizioue giuridica degli abitani. Milan, 1932.

934. Amery, L. S. "The Problem of the Cessation of the Mandated Territory." International Affairs 16(1937):3-16.

935. Antonius, George. "Syria and the French Mandate." International Affairs 13(1934):523-39.

936. Asbeck, F. M. van. "Le régime des étrangers dans les colonies." Recueil des cours 61(1937): 5-93.

937. Austen, Ralph A. Northwest Tanzania under German and British Rule: Colonial Policy and Tribal Politics, 1889-1939. New Haven, 1968.

938. Austen, Ralph A. "Varieties of Trusteeship: African Territories under British and French Mandates, 1919-1939." In France and Britain in Africa: Imperial Rivalry and Colonial Rule, edited by P. Gifford and W. R. Louis. New Haven, 1971.

939. Baroudi, M. Les problèmes juridiques concernant l'administration des communautés sous mandat. Geneva, 1949.

940. Beer, G. L. African Questions at the Paris Peace Conference: with Papers on Egypt, Mesopotamia, and the Colonial Settlement. New York, 1923.

941. Bentwich, Norman. England in Palestine. London, 1932. Attorney-general in Palestine, notes the military-administrative aspects of mandate, that soldier governors, however good their intentions, could not effectively tackle troublesome problems of reform in taxation, law, administration, or civil tension.

942. Bentwich, Norman. The Mandates System. London, 1930.

943. Bentwich, Norman. "Ten Years of International Mandates." Political Quarterly 2(1931):564-76.

944. Bentwich, Norman. England in Palestine. London, 1932.

945. Bentwich, Norman. "Colonial Mandates and Trusteeships." Transactions (Grotius Society) 32(1946): 121-34.

946. Bentwich, Norman, and Bentwich, Helen. Mandate Memories, 1918-1945. London, 1965. Largely letters, covering the first 10 years of mandates, especially relating to Palestine.

947. Berthoud, Paul. "Des mandats aux accords de tutelle: La publicité des travaux de la Commission permanente des mandats." Die Friedenswarte 47(1947):233-54.

948. Bethell, Nicholas. The Palestine Triangle: The Struggle Between the British, the Jews and the Arabs, 1935-1948. London, 1979.

949. Buell, Raymond L. The Native Problem in Africa. 2 vols. New York, 1928.

950. Busch, Briton C. Mudros to Lausanne: Britain's Frontier in West Asia, 1918-1923. Albany, 1976.

951. Chowdhuri, R. N. International Mandates and Trusteeship Systems: A Comparative Study. The Hague, 1955. A useful study with an extensive bibliography.

952. Clyde, Paul H. Japan's Pacific Mandate. New York, 1935.

953. Cohen, Michael J. "British Strategy and the Palestine Question, 1936-39." Journal of Contemporary History 7(1972):157-83. Examines British efforts to recover prestige after Italian invasion of Ethiopia, with emphasis on attempts to maintain peace in Palestine.

954. Conover, Helen F. Non-Self-Governing Areas with Special Emphasis on Mandates and Trustee-

ships: A Selected List of References. Washington, 1947.

955. Crozier, Andrew J. "The Establishment of the
Mandates System 1919-1925: Some Problems
Created by the Paris Peace Conference."
Journal of Contemporary History 14(1979):483-
513. Discusses ambiguities of control and
great power freedoms which vitiated rights and
duties the mandate system was supposed to
establish.

956. Davidson, Nigel. "The Termination of the Iraq
Mandate." International Affairs 12(1933):60-
78.

957. Eggleston, Frederic. The Australian Mandate
for New Guinea. Melbourne, 1928.

958. Ekoko, Edho. "The British Attitude Towards
Germany's Colonial Irredentism in Africa in
the Inter-War Years." Journal of Contemporary
History 14(1979): 287-308.

959. Evans, L. H. "The General Principles governing
the Termination of a Mandate." American
Journal of International Law 26(1932):735-58.

960. Feinberg, Nathan. La juridiction de la cour
permanente de justice internationale dans le
système des mandats. Paris, 1930.

961. Fox, Annette. The Disposition of Enemy Dependent Areas. New Haven, 1945.

962. Gardinier, David E. "The British in the
Cameroons, 1919-1939." In Britain and Germany
in Africa: Imperial Rivalry and Colonial Rule,
edited by P. Gifford and W. R. Louis. New
Haven, 1967.

963. Gerig, Benjamin. The Open Door and the
Mandates System: A Study of Economic Equality
Before and Since the Establishment of the
Mandates System. London, 1930.

964. Gilchrist, Huntington. "Dependent Peoples and
Mandates." In Pioneers in World Order, edited
by H. E. Davis. New York, 1944.

965. Grunwald, Kurt. "The Government Finances of the Mandated Territories in the Near East." Bulletin of the Palestine Economic Society 6(1932).

966. Haas, Ernst B. "The Reconciliation of Conflicting Colonial Policy Aims: Acceptance of the League of Nations' Mandate System." International Organization 6(1952):521-36.

967. Hailey, Lord. An African Survey: A Study of Problems Arising in Africa South of the Sahara. London, 1938. The great compendium of information.

968. Hales, J. C. "The Creation and Application of the Mandate System." Transaction (Grotius Society) 25(1939):185-284. Perceptive and thorough.

969. Hales, James C. "The Reform and Extension of the Mandate System." Transactions (Grotius Society) 26(1940):153-210.

970. Hales, James C. "Some Legal Aspects of the Mandate System: Sovereignty--Nationality-Termination, and Transfer." Transactions (Grotius Society) 22(1937):85-126.

971. Hall, H. Duncan. Mandates, Dependencies and Trusteeship. Washington, D.C., 1948. The fundamental introduction.

972. Hancock, W. Keith. Smuts. 2 vols. Cambridge, 1962, 1968. Volume two, The Fields of Force, 1919-1950, sees Smuts' ideas put to the test. This is the major biography, based on the Smuts papers.

973. Hooper, Charles A. L'Iraq et la Société des Nations: Application à l'Iraq du pacte de la Société des Nations. Paris, 1928. An impartial, detailed work on an individual mandate in the early stages.

974. Hyamson, Albert M. Palestine Under the Mandate, 1920-1948. London, 1950.

975. International Colonial Institute. Record of the Meeting of the International Colonial Institute at Brussels, 24, 25, 26 June 1929.

Brussels, 1930. Instructive as to attitudes of colonial powers, such as apprehension of some delegates that impractical requirements might be demanded by activities of non-colonial states represented in the ILO.

976. Kedourie, Elie. The Chatham House Version and Other Middle-East Studies. New York, 1970. Exposes what he takes to be the line taken by the Royal Institute of International Affairs. A controversial criticism.

977. Kent, M. Oil and Empire. London, 1976. The two interests of Britain in the Near East.

978. League of Nations. The Mandates System: Origin - Principles - Application. Geneva, 1945. The official summing up by P. M. Anker.

979. Le Vine, Victor T. The Cameroons from Mandate to Independence. Berkeley, 1964.

980. Logan, Rayford W. The Senate and the Versailles Mandate System. Washington, 1945.

981. Longrigg, Stephen H. Iraq, 1900-1950. London, 1953.

982. Longrigg, Stephen H. Syria and Lebanon under the French Mandate. London, 1958.

983. Louis, Wm. Roger. "African Origins of the Mandates Idea." International Organization 19(1965):20-36.

984. Louis, Wm. Roger. "Australia and the German Colonies in the Pacific, 1914-1919." Journal of Modern History 38(1966):407-21.

985. Louis, Wm. Roger. Great Britain and Germany's Lost Colonies. London, 1967.

986. Louis, Wm. Roger. "Great Britain and the International Trusteeship: The Historiography of the Mandates System." In The Historiography of the British Empire, edited by R. W. Winks. Durham, 1966.

987. Louis, Wm. Roger. "The United Kingdom and the Beginning of the Mandates System, 1919-1922." International Organization 23(1969):73-97.

988. Lugard, F. D. The Dual Mandate in British Tropical Africa. London, 1922.

989. Mejcher, Helmut. Imperial Quest for Oil: Iraq, 1910-1928. London, 1976.

990. Miller, David Hunter. "The Origin of the Mandate System." Foreign Affairs 6(1928):277-89.

991. Moresco, Emanuel, ed. Colonial Questions and Peace. Paris, 1939.

992. O'Connell, D. P. "Nationality in 'C' Class Mandates." British Yearbook of International Law 31(1954):458-61.

993. Olivier, Sidney. The League of Nations and Primitive Peoples. London, 1918.

994. Pechoux, Laurent. Le mandat français sur le Togo. Paris, 1939.

995. Perham, Margery. Lugard: The Years of Authority, 1898-1945. London, 1960. Volume two of her excellent biography. Includes information about Lugard's 13 years of service on the PMC.

996. Potter, Pitman. "Origin of the System of Mandates under the League of Nations." American Political Science Review 16(1922):564-69.

997. Rappard, William E. "Human Rights in Mandated Territories." Annals of the American Academy of Political and Social Sciences 243(1946): 118-123.

998. Rappard, William E. "The Mandates and the International Trusteeship System." Political Science Quarterly 61(1946):408-19.

999. Rappard, William E. "The Practical Workings of the Mandates System." Journal of the British Institute of International Affairs 4(1925): 205-226.

1000. Robinson, Kenneth. The Dilemmas of Trusteeship: Aspects of British Colonial Policy between the Wars. New York, 1965. Suggestive study, repudiating ideological explanations in favor of studies of the bureaucracy.

1001. Roth, Heinz. Das Kontrollsystem der Völker-
bundsmandate. Berlin, 1930.

1002. Royal Historical Society. The British in
Palestine: The Mandatory Government and the
Arab-Jewish Conflict, 1917-1919. London, 1978.

1003. Schact, H. "Germany's Colonial Demands." Foreign Affairs 15(1937):223-34.

1004. Schmokel, Wolfe W. Dream of Empire: German
Colonialism, 1919-1945. New Haven, 1964.

1005. Schmokel, Wolfe W. "The Hard Death of Imperialism: German and British Colonial Attitudes, 1919-1939." In Britain and Germany in
Africa: Imperial Rivalry and Colonial Rule,
edited by P. Gifford and W. R. Louis. New
Haven, 1967.

1006. Schnee, Heinrich. "Entstehung und Entwicklung
des Mandatsystems." Zeitschrift für Politik
13(1924):381-407.

1007. Schoen, Ludwig. Das Koloniale Deutschland:
deutsche Schutzgebiete unter Mandatsherrschaft.
Berlin, 1939.

1008. Shorrock, William. "The Origins of the French
Mandate in Syria and Lebanon: The Railroad
Question, 1901-1914." International Journal of
Middle East Studies 1(1970):133-153.

1009. Silagi, Michael. Von Deutsch-Südwest zu
Zambia: Wesen und Wandlungen des völkerrecht-
lichen Mandats. Ebelsbach, 1977.

1010. Smith, Gaddis. "The British Government and the
Disposition of the German Colonies in Africa,
1914-1918." In Britain and Germany in Africa:
Imperial Rivalry and Colonial Rule, edited by
P. Gifford and W. R. Louis. New Haven, 1967.

1011. Stoyanovski, J. La théorie générale des mandats internationaux. Paris, 1925.

1012. Swanson, Maynard W. "South West Africa in
Trust, 1915-1939." In Britain and Germany in
Africa: Imperial Rivalry and Colonial Rule,
edited by P. Gifford and W. R. Louis. New
Haven, 1967.

1013. Tritonj, Romolo. L'unità dell siria e l'indi-visibilità del suo mandato. Rome, 1934. Attack on French administration, saying the French economic rivalry violates the mandate statutes of economic equality for League members.

1014. Tshisungu, Edouard. Le contrôle de la Société des Nations et l'évolution des mandats fran-çais en Afrique, 1918-1939. Strasbourg, 1970.

1015. Upthegrove, Campbell L. Empire by Mandate: A History of the Relations of Great Britain with the Permanent Mandates Commission of the League of Nations. New York, 1954.

1016. Van Rees, D. F. W. Les mandats internationaux. Le contrôle international de l'administration mandataire. Paris, 1927.

1017. Van Rees, D. F. W. Les mandats internationaux. Les principes généraux du régime des mandats. Paris, 1928.

1018. Wehberg, Hans. "Die Pflichten der Mandat-armächte betreffend die Deutschen Schutzge-bietsanleihen." Weltwirtschaftliches Archiv 25 (1927):136-83.

1019. White, Freda. Mandates. London, 1926. Especially interesting on South West Africa, where rebellion and questionable constitutional practices existed.

1020. Wright, Quincy. Mandates Under the League of Nations. Chicago, 1930. Very complete, and detailed. Appendices have full charter docu-ments, and the enabling statutes of the PMC.

1021. Wyndham, H. A. "The Problem of the West African Liquor Traffic." Journal of the Royal Institute of International Affairs 14(1930): 801-18. Work of Mandates Commission in this regard.

XII. MINORITIES AND REFUGEES

A. Protection of Minorities

"The protection of minorities is one of the
most difficult and delicate tasks which the
Peace Treaties laid on the League and one which
places the greatest responsibility upon the
Members of the Council." (League of Nations,
Ten Years of World Co-operation, [Geneva,
1930], p. 357).

Sixteen states, comprising virtually all those of
central and eastern Europe, from Finland to Iraq,
were bound by treaty to respect the rights--the
social and religious freedoms and civil equality--of
linguistic, racial, and religious minorities in
their territories. By specific agreement the
League was made guarantor of these rights, which
were defined as a matter of international concern.
Here was an early, broad, statement of human
rights--striking in an era of self-determination.
The problems were: who was to interpret these guarantees, how to determine violations, and how, if at
all, enforcement was possible. No state permitted
interference in its internal affairs, and the
League's competence, and its interest, was contin-
ually challenged. The result was minimalist action
by League agencies and even the discouragement of
publicity on minority issues. In the 1930s, its
unwillingness to recognize or consider the plight of
central European Jews revealed the profound and
tragic dimensions of this incapacity or lack of
will. So little was done to give flesh to the
spirit of the minority treaties, so frustrating
seemed the cause of the protection of minority
rights, that when the UN was founded no agency was
included in its structure to continue the notion of
international obligation.
     The minimum the League could do was stated by
treaty, and, procedurally, conceding to the increasingly serious political implications of action, it
limited its own competence even more. No permanent
commission on the order of the Mandates Commission

was ever established. The Council received petitions from minorities seeking redress. A petition
was first submitted for review to the Minorities
Section of the Secretariat, headed notably by the
Norwegian Erik Colban. Then, it might be passed to
an ad hoc three person Minorities Committee of
Council members. These committee meetings, and any
subsequent mediation or semi-official negotiations
with governments, were secret. If satisfaction was
not obtained, an issue could be brought to the
Council, or to the Permanent Court, and even to the
Assembly. Even then all action was only advisory.
Conciliation was always the aim, and minorities and
governments supporting their positions in various
cases complained loudly of the lack of publicity and
of the absence of open confrontation. Some partial
successes were obtained in the settlement period of
the 1920s. In the 1930s the fact that problems were
'delicate' or 'difficult' was an excuse for inaction,
and the eventual abandonment of concern at Geneva.

* * *

The main League archives are in the papers of
the Minorities Section and the "Commission Files."

1022. Azcárate y Florés, Pablo de. The League of
Nations and National Minorities: An Experiment.
Trans. by E. E. Brooke. Washington, 1945. An
evaluation by a League official (Under-Secre-
tary General 1936-1939).

1023. Azcárate y Florés, Pablo de. La Société des
Nations et la protection des minorités.
Geneva, 1969. Three case studies of minority
protection in Czechoslovakia, Rumania, and
Upper Silesia.

1024. Boehm, M. H. Europa Irredenta. Berlin, 1923.

1025. Calderwood, H. B. "Should the Council of the
League of Nations Establish a Permanent Minor-
ities Commission?" American Political Science
Review 26(1933):250-59.

1026. Claude, Inis L., Jr. National Minorities: An
International Problem. Cambridge, MA., 1955.

1027. Devedji, A. L'échange obligatoire des minorités grecques et turques en vertu de la convention de Lausanne du 30 janvier 1923. Paris, 1929.

1028. Dugdale, Blanche. "The Working of the Minority Treaties." Journal of the British Institute of International Affairs 7(1926):79-95.

1029. Feinberg, Nathan. "La jurisdiction et la jurisprudence en matière de mandats et de minorités." Recueil des cours 59(1937):591-705.

1030. Fischer, P. Das Recht und der Schutz der polnischen Minderheit in Oberschlesien. Berlin, 1931.

1031. Haas, Ernst. Human Rights and International Action. Stanford, 1970.

1032. Junckerstorff, Kurt. Die Völkerbundsgarantie des Minderheitenrechts. The Hague, 1930.

1033. Junghann, Otto. Das Minderheitenschutzverfahren vor dem Völkerbund. Tubingen, 1934. A useful survey with documents.

1034. Junghann, Otto. The Origin and Solution of the Problems of National Minorities. Vienna, 1929. Some useful theoretical perspectives.

1035. Korowicz, M. S. Une expérience de droit international: La protection des minorités de Haute-Silésie. Paris, 1946.

1036. Ladas, Stephen P. The Exchange of Minorities: Bulgaria, Greece and Turkey. New York, 1932.

1037. Lamy, Bernhard. Die Minderheiten in Lettland. Riga, 1931. A solid, well-informed account of the complex mix of minorities in Latvia.

1038. Laponce, J. A. The Protection of Minorities. Berkeley, 1960. A general consideration of the problem with a good bibliography.

1039. Lauterpacht, Hersch. International Law and Human Rights. New York, 1950.

1040. Macartney, C. A. National States and National
Minorities. London, 1934. An exhaustive,
scholarly, contemporary study.

1041. Macartney, C. A. "A Select List of References
on Minorities." Journal of the Royal Institute
of International Affairs 9(1930):819-25.

1042. Mair, Lucy. "The Machinery of Minority Protection." Journal of the Royal Institute of
International Affairs 7(1929):256-65. Clear
synopsis of League action.

1043. Mair, Lucy. The Protection of Minorities: The
Working and Scope of the Minorities Treaties
under the League of Nations. London, 1928.
Critical of the League's discouragement of
publicity on minority issues. Considers
minorities issues potentially very disruptive.

1044. Mandelstam, André. La protection internationale
des minorités. Première partie: La protection
des minorités en droit international positif.
Paris, 1931.

1045. Molony, W. O'S. Nationality and the Peace
Treaties. London, 1934. Member of Minorities
Section of the League. This is a very complete
survey. The work of the League and various
voluntary societies.

1046. Monfosca, E. A. Le minoranze nazionali contem-
plate dagli atti internationali. 2 vols.
Florence, 1929. Includes texts of the most
important treaties and national laws respecting
treatment of minorities.

1047. Plieg, Ernst-Albrecht. Das Memelland 1920-
1939. Würzburg, 1962. When Lithuanian troops
moved into Memel in 1923 the German minority
suffered from an effort to 'denationalize' it.
Numerous infringements of the Memel statute
stopped just short of provoking an effective
reaction by the League. This is a thorough
study of the problems faced by the German
minority.

1048. Ramlow, Rudolf. Das Minderheitenschutzverfahren das Völkerbundes. Berlin, 1931.
Discusses reasons behind the minority clause in
the Covenant, and procedure for the protection

of minorities. Concludes a need for revision, with more certain protection.

1049. Ritter, Ernst. Das Deutsche Ausland-Institut in Stuttgart, 1917-1945: Ein Beispiel deutscher Volkstumsarbeit zwischen den Weltkriegen. Wiesbaden, 1976. Institute's purpose was to develop bonds between German minorities under foreign control.

1050. Robinson, Jacob. Das Minoritätenproblem und seine Literatur: Kritische Einführung in die Quellen und die Literature der europäischen Nationalitätenfrage der Nachkriegszeit, unter besonderer Berücksichtigung des völkerrecht-lichen Minderheitenschutzes. Berlin, 1928. A thorough, annotated bibliography.

1051. Robinson, Jacob, et al. Were the Minorities Treaties a Failure? New York, 1943.

1052. Stephens, J. S. Danger Zones of Europe--A Study of National Minorities. London, 1929.

1053. Stone, Julius. International Guarantees of Minority Rights: Procedure of the League of Nations in Theory and Practice. London, 1932.

1054. Stone, Julius. Regional Guarantees of Minority Rights. London, 1933. A study of procedure under the Upper Silesian Convention.

1055. United Nations. The Main Types and Causes of Discrimination. Lake Success, 1949. A biblio-graphy of 1,000 titles.

1056. Winkler, Wilhelm. Statistisches Handbuch der europäischen Nationalitäten. Vienna, 1931. Director of the Institut für Statistik der Minderheitsvolker at the University of Vienna. A survey of the full magnitude of Europe's minority problem--50 million people consciously in minority status. For instance, Germans live in 15 countries outside Germany, Poles in seven outside Poland, Ukrainians in three. This reveals the dense complexity of minorities.

1057. Wurfbain, A. L'échange gréco-bulgare des minorités ethniques. Paris, 1930.

B. Refugees

When a million and a half refugees from Russia settled in Europe governments and volunteer agencies called on the League for help. In 1921 Fridtjof Nansen, the explorer who had recently done work in repatriating prisoners of war and in relief work with the Russian famine, was appointed as High Commissioner for Refugees, to see what could be done to define their legal position, consider their repatriation, or find them employment. Nansen sought to coordinate work already being undertaken by governmental and volunteer agencies such as the ICRC, the International 'Save the Children' Fund, the Russian Relief Association, and the Jewish Colonization Association. The League took a narrow view of its role. Individual states had the responsibility for those who settled in their territory, and the League decided early on to provide not for relief, maintenance, or settlement but to work for international agreements on legal protection, recognition of status, and the capacity of refugees to travel across borders seeking work. The 'Nansen passport' became the standard identity certificate.

Nansen resigned in 1924. The work of his office which concentrated on employment and resettlement questions was transferred to the ILO while the High Commission remained directly responsible to the Council in its concern for the legal status of displaced peoples, which now included refugees of Turkish, Greek, and Armenian origins. In 1930 the High Commissariat was transformed into an autonomous organization called the Nansen International Office for Refugees, which lasted until 1938. In 1933, a new position of High Commissioner for Refugees Coming from Germany (Jewish and Other) was established in London. The first incumbent, James G. McDonald, was nominated by the Council but considered a servant of 'the commission,' not of the League. McDonald resigned at the end of 1935 with a strong attack on the German government's racial policies, and in January 1936 Neill Malcolm was appointed by the Council as High Commissioner for Assistance to Refugees (Jewish and Other) from Germany. From 1939 to 1946 the High Commissioner of the League of Nations for Refugees was Herbert Emerson, who established a closer connection with the League.

The most comprehensive assistance was given refugees who settled in Greece in the early 1920s, the League assisting the Greek government in assimi-

lating a million and a half exiles mainly from
Turkey. This work was undertaken by a special
agency, the Greek Refugee Settlement Board, not by
the High Commissioner, with assistance from the
Health and the Economic and Financial Organizations.
Throughout, all League activities were con-
sidered temporary and ad hoc, and kept on strictly
limited budgets and responsibilities. With the UN,
a better funded institution was established in the
International Refugee Organization.
The fundamental archival collections are: the
Administrative Commissions and Minorities Section of
the Secretariat Archive Group and the "Nansen Mixed
Group" in the League archives in Geneva.
The following periodicals dealt entirely with
minority questions. Nation und Staat: Deutsche
Zeitschrift für das europäische Minoritätenproblem
(Vienna); Bulletin international du droit des
minorités; Les minorités nationales (issued by the
Minorities Commission of the Federation of League of
Nations Associations, Brussels).

1058. Bentwich, Norman. The International Problem of
Refugees. Geneva, 1935. Clear, detailed
statement.

1059. Bentwich, Norman. The Refugees from Germany:
April 1933 to December 1935. London, 1936.
From standpoint of the High Commission for
Refugees from Germany. Shows how international
the problem is, how High Commission was
divorced from League in deference to German
susceptibilities, and the problems of immigra-
tion barriers.

1060. Eddy, Charles. Greece and the Greek Refugees.
London, 1931.

1061. Frings, Paul. Das internationale Flüchtlings-
problem, 1919-1950. Frankfurt a. Main, 1951.
A very good overview.

1062. Hansson, Michael. Flyktningsproblemet og
Folkeforbundet. Oslo, 1938. Account of the
work of the Nansen International Office for
Refugees by the president of its Governing Body.

1063. Häsler, Alfred A. Das Boot ist Voll...Die
Schweiz und die Flüchtlinge, 1933-1945.
Zurich, 1967. Does not go beyond Carl Ludwig's

damning "Rapport ... à l'Assemblée fédérale sur la politique practiquée par la Suisse à l'égard des réfugiés de 1933 à nos jours" (Berne, 1957). A sobering story.

1064. Heuven, Goedhart, G. J. van. "The Problem of Refugees." Recueil des cours 82(1953):261-371.

1065. Holborn, L. W. The International Refugee Organization. London, 1956.

1066. Holborn, L. W. "The Legal Status of Political Refugees, 1920-1938." American Journal of International Law 32(1938):680-703.

1067. Hoyer, Liv Nansen. Nansen og Verden. Oslo, 1955. The standard bibliography.

1068. Institut für Besatzungsfragen. Das DP-Problem. Tübingen, 1950. The second wave--persons displaced in the 1939-45 war.

1069. League of Nations. The Refugees. Geneva, 1938. A concise overview of the situation and the League's role.

1070. Macartney, C. A. Refugees: The Work of the League. London, 1938.

1071. McDonald, James G. The German Refugees and the League of Nations. London, 1936. McDonald was League High Commissioner for Refugees Coming from Germany during 1933-35. His papers are with the Columbia University School of International Affairs. This book speaks to his work.

1072. McDonald, James G. "Refugees." In Pioneers in World Order, edited by H. E. Davis. New York, 1944.

1073. Malin, Patrick M. "The Refugee: A Problem for International Organization." International Organization 1(1947):443-59.

1074. Mandelstam, A. N. La Société des Nations et les puissances devant le problème arménien. Paris, 1925.

1075. Morgenthau, Henry. An International Drama. London, 1930. Was first chairman of League's

Greek Refugee Settlement Commission, charged
with relocating and settling the four million
refugees from Turkey who moved to Greece.
This informative book tells of the difficulties in persuading the League, the Bank of
England, and other agencies, to forward loans
or support for settlement needs.

1076. Nansen, Fridtjof. Armenia and the Near East.
London, 1928.

1077. Nansen International Office for Refugees.
Annual Report of the Governing Body. 9 vols.
Geneva, 1931-39. Includes a special report
for 1936 by Michael Hansson, president of the
Governing Body.

1078. Nourissier, François. L'homme humilié: Sort
des réfugiés et 'personnes déplacées,' 1912-
1950. Paris, 1950. Excellent, thorough
study.

1079. Reale, Egidio. Le problème des passeports.
Paris, 1935. A good study of the work of the
League concerning passports, the Nansen
certificates for stateless persons and refugees, and various other means of identifica-
tions. A complete bibliography.

1080. Reale, Egidio. Le régime des passeports et
la Société des Nations. Paris, 1930. Passports as a problem in international relations,
with special reference to rights of foreign
nationals and political refugees. Advocates
total abolition of passports.

1081. Ristelhuber, R. La double aventure de
Fridtjhof Nansen, explorateur et philanthrope.
Montreal, 1945.

1082. Simpson, John Hope. The Refugee Problem:
Report of a Survey. London, 1939.

1083. Simpson, John Hope. Refugees: A Review of
the Situation since September 1938. London,
1939. Continues the study listed above, in
light of further expulsions and flights from
Nazi Germany.

1084. Simpson, John Hope. "The Work of the Greek
Refugee Settlement Commission." Journal of the

Royal Institute of International Affairs
8(1929):583-604. By vice-president of the
Commission, a study of the main lines of its
work.

1085. Tait, D. Christie. "International Aspects of
Migration." Journal of the Royal Institute
for International Affairs 6(1927):25-46. The
British member of the Migration Service of the
ILO.

1086. Thomashefsky, J. M. The Development of International Protection of Refugees. New York,
1949.

1087. Wyman, D. S. Paper Walls: America and the
Refugee Crisis, 1938-1941. Amherst, 1968.

XIII. SOCIAL AND HUMANITARIAN ACTIVITIES

The records of the League's auxiliary organizations reveal the limits given to or set by the agencies themselves, and the external limitations imposed by the extent of cooperation offered by members, or non-member, states.

The Health Organization existed, not always happily, alongside a pre-existing non-League agency, the Office International d'Hygiène Publique, both, the Health Organization the more actively, to promote campaigns against epidemics, and to standardize terms for the definition and control of disease. The Health Organization was regarded as one of the League's more successful undertakings. The World Health Organization of the UN is its direct successor.

Other agencies established by the Council likewise existed on limited budgets and limited authority, seeking international conventions to limit or abolish inhumane practices, often in the face of dislike and suspicion of officials in states who accused them of meddling in internal affairs. Such agencies included: the Advisory Committee on Traffic in Opium and Other Dangerous Drugs (1921), the Advisory Committee on the Traffic in Women and Children (1922), and the Temporary Slavery Commission (1924) which evolved ten years later into the Advisory Committee of Experts on Slavery.

The International Committee on Intellectual Co-operation, and the International Institute of Intellectual Co-operation established in Paris in 1926 in cooperation with the French government, and the various National Committees of Intellectual Co-operation sought a further understanding of such matters as the teaching of history and to define the role of the press, radio, and cinema in the modern world.

Responding to needs for standardization and common practices imposed by the demands of modern technology, the Organiztaion of Communications and Transit was established at the Barcelona Conference of 1921, with a permanent secretariat, several specialized committees, and the promise of regular

189

general conferences. Early, it concluded two
general conventions standardizing operations of
maritime ports and railways, needs long recognized
of which the settlement had been deferred because of
the war. It also worked on establishing agreements
on inland navigation, road traffic, calendar reform,
passports, and other technical issues. Its hope to
make comprehensive agreements for air traffic and
broadcasting was disappointed, and work on radio and
telecommunications regulations was taken up by
functional agencies outside the League, the International Broadcasting Union (1925) and the International Telegraph Union (1865, renamed the International Telecommunication Union in 1932), the
latter, since 1947, a specialized agency of the UN.

***

The archives of the Health and Social Questions
Section, the Communications and Transit Section, and
the International Cooperation and International
Bureaux Section are in the Secretariat Archive
Group. The archives concerning slavery are in the
Mandates Group. The files of the International
Institute of Intellectual Cooperation, and related
agencies, are in an external archive group in the
Archives Section of UNESCO.

1088. André, Charles. L'organisation de la coopération intellectuelle. Rennes, 1938.

1089. Bailey, S. H. The Anti-Drug Campaign. London,
1936. Documents the elaborate international
machinery, showing the importance of cooperation in this cause. Suggests possible application of similar procedure to disarmament.

1090. Bennett, A. L. The Development of Intellectual
Cooperation under the League of Nations and
United Nations. Urbana, 1950. Thesis for the
University of Illinois.

1091. Besson, Maurice. "La problème de l'esclavage
devant l'opinion et la Société des Nations."
Revue des sciences politiques (1932):439-49.

1092. Borgeaud, Marc-Auguste. L'union internationale
de secours. Paris, 1932. This international
bureau was not under the direction of the
League, but related to it by the convention of

1927 which created the Union. Its connection with the League was dissolved in 1946.

1093. Boudreau, F. G. "International Health Work." In Pioneers of World Order, edited by H. E. Davis. New York, 1944.

1094. Burchall, H. "The Politics of International Air Routes." International Affairs 14(1935): 89-107.

1095. Calan, Charles de. "L'affaire du Libérie devant la Société des Nations." Revue des sciences politiques (1933):590-99.

1096. Castendyck, E. "Social Problems." In Pioneers of World Order, edited by H. E. Davis. New York, 1944.

1097. Crowdy, Rachel. "The Humanitarian Activities of the League of Nations." Journal of the Royal Institute of International Affairs 6(1927):153-69. Author was chief of the Opium and Social Questions Section, and this reviews the many activities of the League such as resettlement, drugs, inquiry into minimum age for marriage, disease, repatriation.

1098. Gorgé, Camille. L'union internationale de secours: Ses origins, son buts, ses moyens, son avenir. Geneva, 1938. The Union's authorized history.

1099. Grumbach, Jacques. La répression de la traite des femmes. Lyon, 1940.

1100. Harris, Henry W. Human Merchandise: A Study of the International Traffic in Women. London, 1928. Resumes the League studies.

1101. International Institute of International Cooperation. Holiday Courses in Europe, 1932. Paris, 1932. An example of the sorts of things the Institute did. Here is a list of 135 holiday courses to be held in 17 countries and in 82 cities.

1102. International Institute of Intellectual Co-operation. La coopération intellectuelle. Its journal.

1103. International Telecommunication Union. From Semaphore to Satellite, 1793-1965. Geneva, 1965.

1104. International Telecommunication Union. 1865-1965--A Hundred Years of International Co-operation. Geneva, 1968.

1105. Llewellyn-Jones, F. The League of Nations and the International Control of Dangerous Drugs. Cambridge, 1931.

1106. May, H. L. "Dangerous Drugs." In Pioneers of World Order, edited by H. E. Davis. New York, 1944.

1107. Moorhead, H. H. International Administration of Narcotic Drugs, 1928-1934. Geneva, 1935.

1108. Mourey, Charles. "La question de l'esclavage devant la Société des Nations. L'Afrique française (1926):213-23.

1109. Northedge, F. International Intellectual Cooperation within the League of Nations: Its Conceptual Basis and Lessons for the Present. London, 1953. Thesis for the University of London.

1110. Pham-Ti-Tu. La coopération intellectuelle sous la Société des Nations. Geneva, 1962.

1111. Pignochet, Anne. L'organisme le plus évolué du droit international, la commission interna-tionale de navigation aérienne. Paris, 1936.

1112. Revest, Marcel. La protection de l'enfance devant la Société des Nations. Paris, 1936.

1113. Rothbarth, Margarete. Geistige Zusammenarbeit im Rahmen des Völkerbundes. Munich, 1931. The founding of the International Institute of Intellectual Cooperation, written by a staff member.

1114. Scialoja, Vittorio. Discorsi alla Società delle Nazioni. Rome, 1932. Was chief Italian delegate to League for a decade. This includes his remarks on the opening of the IICI in Paris in 1926.

1115. Slotemaker, L. H. Freedom of Passage for
International Air Services. Leiden, 1932.
Argues for liberalization in rules of air
communication.

1116. Tombs, L. C. International Organisation in
Europe and Air Transport. New York, 1936.
Full of information, by a long-time official of
the Communications and Transit section, arguing
that national regulations in this field are
foolish.

1117. Wilcox, Francis O. The Ratification of International Conventions. London, 1935. Good
studies of the European Commission of the
Danube, the Permanent Sugar Commission, UPU,
and the International Commission for Air
Legislation.

1118. Wissler, Albert. Die Opiumfrage: eine Studie
zur weltwitschaftlichen und weltpolitischen
Lage der Gegenwirt. Jena, 1931. Extent of
trade and attempts to control. Is inclined to
regard the anti-drug campaign as a means by
which colonial powers divert attention from
their Far Eastern difficulties.

1119. Woods, Arthur. Dangerous Drugs: The World
Fight against Illicit Traffic in Narcotics.
New Haven, 1931.

XIV. PERMANENT COURT OF INTERNATIONAL JUSTICE

Following the instruction of article 14 of the Covenant, to establish a Permanent Court of International Justice "competent to hear and determine any dispute of an international character which the parties thereto shall submit to it," and to "give an advisory opinion upon any dispute or question referred to it by the Council or by the Assembly," the Council in 1920 had drawn up a draft statute. This was unanimously approved by the Assembly, and, in September 1921, upon ratification by a majority of League members, the Court came into force.

Located at the Peace Palace in The Hague (as was the Permanent Court of Arbitration), its 15 judges were elected for terms of nine years by the Assembly and the Council. The League budget paid for the work of the Court, and the Council made over two dozen requests for advisory opinion on issues before the League, such as questions of legal status in minority, frontier, and jurisdictional questions. Any study of Memel, Mosul, Danzig, the Austro-German customs union, or the borders and population transfers concerning Greece must include reference to the evidence presented to the Court. For suspicious critics, the Court was merely a political agency of the League. Some states, notably America and Britain, were reluctant to make certain binding commitments as shown by the diplomatic and political problems associated with adherence to the 'optional clause' (added by the Assembly for compulsory arbitration). Two conferences were held in Geneva (1923 and 1926) to consider revisions of the Court's statute, but no significant changes were made. The acceptance of the statute by a very large number of states, the advice rendered to the League, and the continuous function of a responsible and respected central international tribunal for 18 years, led to a renewed appreciation and active discussion of international law, and some fundamental support to the League. Its value was recognized by the creation, as an integral part of the UN, of the Court's successor organization, the International Court of Justice.

A list of documents concerned with the founding of the Court, conferences of signatories, and a list of judgments, orders, and advisory opinions, is found in Hans Aufricht, Guide to League of Nations Publications (New York, 1951), pp. 386-97. Two journals that contain many important discussions of the Court are the British Year Book of International Law, and the Recueil des cours of the Académie de Droit International de la Haye, a collection of lectures held at the Academy between 1923-1939 and published in 69 volumes.

1120. Bentwich, Norman. "The Jurisdiction of the International Court of Justice over Concessions in a Mandated Territory." The Law Quarterly Review 44(1928):450-63.

1121. Bustamente y Sirvén, Antonio de. The World Court. Trans. by Elizabeth F. Read. New York, 1925. A Court judge from Cuba. Contains an interesting exposition of the Central American Court of Justice (est. 1907 by five Central American republics) and an account of the work of the Advisory Committee of Jurists who prepared the Court's Statute.

1122. Douma, J. Bibliography on the International Court, including the Permanent Court, 1918-1964. Leyden, 1966. Volume IV-C of the series The Case Law of the International Court by Eduard Hambro. The major compendium of titles by the former librarian of the Court.

1123. Fachiri, Alexander. The Permanent Court of International Justice: Its Constitution, Procedure and Work. 2nd ed. London, 1932. A clear evaluation.

1124. Fachiri, Alexander P. "Repudiation of the Optional Clause." British Year Book of International Law 20(1939):52-57. Paraguay withdrew from the League after legal hassle over "optional clause."

1125. Fawcett, J. E. S. "The Development of International Law." International Affairs Special Issue (1970):127-37.

1126. Feinberg, Nathan. La juridiction de la cour permanente de justice internationale dans le système des mandats. Paris, 1930. Conscientious analysis of each aspect of this matter.

1127. Feinberg, Nathan. La juridiction de la cour permanente de justice internationale dans la protection internationale des minorités. Paris, 1931. Too theoretical--little touch with reality.

1128. Feinberg, Nathan. "La juridiction et la jurisprudence de la Cour permanente de Justice internationale en matière de mandats et de minorités." Recueil des cours 59(1937):587-708.

1129. Fleming, D. F. The United States and the World Court, 1920-1966. Rev. ed. New York, 1968.

1130. Fischer, Georges. Les rapports entre l'organisation internationale du travail et la cour permanente de justice internationale: Contribution à l'étude du problème de la séparation des pouvoirs dans le domaine international. Paris, 1946.

1131. Fockema Andreae, J. P. An Important Chapter from the History of Legal Interpretation: The Jurisdiction of the First Permanent Court of International Justice, 1922-1940. Leyden, 1948. A fine overview.

1132. Fontes Iuris Gentium (Berlin). Digest of the Decisions of the Permanent Court of International Justice, 1922-1930. Berlin, 1930.

1133. Fontes Iuris Gentium (Berlin). Digest of the Decisions of the Permanent Court of International Justice, 1931-1934. Berlin, 1935.

1134. Francqueville, Bernard de. L'oeuvre de la cour permanente de justice internationale. 2 vols. Paris, 1928.

1135. Goodrich, Leland M. "The Nature of the Advisory Opinions of the Permanent Court of International Justice." American Journal of International Law 32(1939), 738-58.

1136. Hambro, Eduard, ed. The Case Law of the International Court: A Repertoire of the Judgements Advisory Opinions and Orders of the Permanent Court of International Justice and of

the International Court of Justice. 2 vols.
Leyden, 1952 (vol. 1) and 1960 (vol. 2).

1137. Hambro, Eduard. L'exécution des sentences
internationales. Paris, 1936.

1138. Hammarskjöld, Aake. Juridiction internationale. Leiden, 1938. By the Court's Registrar.

1139. Hammarskjöld, Aake. "The Permanent Court of
International Justice and the Development of
International Law." International Affairs
14(1935):797-817. Argues the Court needs time
for it to become effective.

1140. Hammarskjöld, Aake. "The Permanent Court of
International Justice and its Place in International Relations." Journal of the Royal
Institute of International Affairs 14(1930):
467-97.

1141. Hudson, Manley O. International Tribunals,
Past and Future. Washington, 1944. A basic,
authoritative overview covering a wide range
such as the Court, the Permanent Court of
Arbitration, commissions, and other tribunals.

1142. Hudson, Manley O. The Permanent Court of
International Justice, 1920-1942. New York,
1943. Hudson, an American, sat on the Court
from 1936. This is the best study of the
institution.

1143. Hudson, Manley O. The Permanent Court of
International Justice and the Question of
American Participation, with a Collection of
Documents. Cambridge, MA., 1925.

1144. Hudson, Manley O. "The Revision of the Statute
of the World Court." Foreign Affairs 9(1931):
341-345.

1145. Hudson, Manley O. "Ten Years of the World
Court." Foreign Affairs 11(1932):81-92.

1146. Hudson, Manley O., ed. World Court Reports: A
Collection of Judgements, Orders, and Opinions
of the Permanent Court of International
Justice. 4 vols. Washington, D. C., 1934-43.

1147. Jenks, C. W. The Prospect of International Adjudication. London, 1964. Has a sound discussion of the Court.

1148. Jessup, Philip C. "The Acceptance of the Senate Reservations." International Conciliation 273(1931):9-28.

1149. Jessup, Philip C. Elihu Root. 2 vols. New York, 1938.

1150. Lauterpacht, Hersch. The Development of International Law by the Permanent Court of Justice. London, 1934.

1151. Lauterpacht, Hersch. International Law: Being the Collected Papers of Hersch Lauterpacht. Volume 2: The Law of Peace. Part 1: International Law in General. Edited by F. Lauterpacht. London, 1975. Among the papers, an attack on E. H. Carr's The Twenty Years Crisis, and articles from the British Year Book of International Law, which Lauterpacht edited.

1152. McNair, Arnold D. "The Council's Request for an Advisory Opinion from the Permanent Court of International Justice." British Year Book of International Law 7(1926):1-13.

1153. Marek, K., Furrer, H.P., and Martin, A. Les sources du droit international. Geneva, 1967. An exhaustive, 1286-page review of the decisions and presentations before the Court, 1922-1945.

1154. Maza, Herbert. "William Randal Cremer: Les origines de la Cour permanente internationale d'arbitrage et de justice." In Neuf meneurs internationaux, edited by H. Maza. Paris, 1965.

1155. Permanent Court of International Justice. Ten Years of International Jurisdiction, 1922-1932. Leyden, 1932. Introduction by the President of the Court, M. Adatci; note by the Registrar Aake Hammarskjöld.

1156. Permanent Court of International Justice. Publications of the Permanent Court of International Justice. Leyden, 1922-46. Series A. Collection of Judgements. Series B. Collection of Advisory Opinions. Series A/B. Collection of Judgements, Orders, and Advisory Opinions. Series C. Pleadings, Oral Statements, and Documents. Series D. Acts and Documents Concerning the Organization of the Court. Series E. Annual Reports. Series F. General Indexes.

1157. Phillimore, Walter G. F. "The Permanent Court of International Justice." International Affairs 1(1922):113-23.

1158. Politis, Nicolas. La justice internationale. Paris, 1924.

1159. Pomerance, Michla. The Advisory Function of the International Court in the League and UN Eras. Baltimore, 1973. A fine recent comparative study.

1160. Root, Elihu. "The Permanent Court of International Justice." American Society of International Law Proceedings 17(1923):1-14.

1161. Schindler, D. "Les progrès de l'arbitrage obligatoire depuis la création de la Société des Nations." Recueil des cours 25(1928):237-361.

1162. Schwarzenberger, George. International Law. 3 vols. 3rd ed. London, 1957. The first edition, 1945, is also worth consulting.

1163. Schiffer, Walter. Repertoire of Questions of General International Law Before the League of Nations, 1920-1940. Geneva, 1942.

1164. Scott, James Brown, ed. The Hague Court Reports. 2 vols. New York, 1916 (vol. 1) and 1932 (vol. 2).

1165. Scott, James Brown. The Project of a Permanent Court of International Justice and Resolutions of the Advisory Committee of Jurists. Washington, 1920.

1166. Silva, Pereira da. La réforme de la cour permanente de justice internationale: Le protocole de 1929 et le veto de Cuba. Paris, 1931.

1167. Syatauw, J. J. G. Decisions of the International Court of Justice: A Digest. Leyden, 1969.

1168. Verzijl, J. H. W. International Law in Historical Perspective. 5 vols. Leyden, 1968-72. Vol. I., General Subjects, is a case by case analysis of the work of the Court, 1922-1940. The other volumes deal with: International Persons, State Territory, Stateless Domain, Nationality and Other Matters Relating to Individuals.

1169. Visscher, Charles de. "Les avis consultatifs de la Cour Permanente de Justice Internationale." Recueil des cours 26(1929):5-75.

1170. Visscher, Charles de. La justice internationale et les limites présentes de son action. Rome, 1935.

1171. Visscher, Charles de. Theory and Reality in Public International Law. Rev. ed. P. E. Corbett, trans. Princeton, 1968. A translation of the 3rd French edition of 1960.

1172. Wheeler-Bennett, John, and Fanshawe, Maurice. Information on the World Court, 1918-1925. London, 1929. Asserts the organic connection between the Court and the League. A good discussion of the optional clause.

XV. INTERNATIONAL LABOR ORGANIZATION

The ILO's charge was to promote social justice through the creation of humane working conditions in industrial societies. Autonomous as to its external activities, and a legally independent entity, it was branched to the League through generally overlapping membership, common internationalist purposes, its site in Geneva, its right to call on the assistance of the Secretary-General, and a supporting budget from the League's general fund. The autonomy of the ILO increased as it defined its role in ways concerned mainly with the internal policies of its members, while the League was wrenched with international political tensions. Still, close collaboration took place between the Secretariat and the administrative Office of the ILO, whose representative sat with the League when labor issues were discussed, whose initiative was behind the Economic Conference of 1933, and which took over functions dealing with the settlement and employment of refugees. Some issues the ILO never resolved, such as how to deal with a situation as in the Soviet Union where the state was the fundamental employer, or the terms of legislation where the labor force in a state was based in a non-industrial economy.

The ILO comprised an annual General Conference of Representatives of the Members based on a famous system of tripartite representation (four delegates from each member state, two representing governments, one representing workers, one representing employers); a Governing Body of 24 persons (again tripartite - twelve representing governments, six workers, six employers); and the central administrative International Labor Office. The Director of the Office set the tone of the organization, and the competence, energy, and vision of these men gave continuity, recognition, and prestige throughout the Organization's history. The Directors in our period were:

Albert Thomas, France, 1920-32
Harold Butler, U.K., 1932-38
John G. Winant, U.S.A., 1938-41
Edward J. Phelan, Ireland, 1941-48.

The tripartite arrangements were a new form of international cooperation. The ILO's fact-finding studies, statistical reports, 80 draft conventions, and 80 recommendations gave guidance for standards of labor conditions, and with the publicity of the annual meetings, and the example of a permanent organization that was part of the League system, set the terms for just treatment of industrial labor in this age.

The U.S. became a member in 1934. In 1940, following the need to relocate and the refusal of the U.S. to receive the headquarters, the Office moved to Montreal. After the difficult and frustrating war years the ILO was, in 1946, reconstituted, along essentially its original lines, as a specialized agency of the UN.

1173. Alcock, Antony. History of the International Labour Organisation. London, 1971. The best single work, the authorized history based on ILO archives.

1174. Argentier, Claude. Les résultats acquis par l'organisation permanente du travail de 1919 à 1929. Paris, 1930. A solid survey.

1175. Arnou, André. L'organisation internationale du travail et les catholiques. Paris, 1933.

1176. Ballaloud, Jacques. Le tribunal administratif de l'organisation internationale du travail et sa jurisprudence. Paris, 1967. Need in League and ILO of officials for some sort of legal tribunal concerning disputes over contracts, disciplinary issues, pensions. Could not appeal courts of own countries. In 1920 got right to appeal to Council or Governing Body of ILO. But these could not give dispassionate rulings, as both judges and interested parties. So, after 1927, Administrative Tribunal to hear and decide appeals was created by League Assembly. Now has been recognized widely.

1177. Beddington-Behrens, Edward. The International Labour Office: A Survey of Certain Problems of International Administration. London, 1924. A detailed study of inner workings and its problems of adaptation and guidance.

1178. Beguin, Bernard. "ILO and the Tripartite System." <u>International</u> <u>Conciliation</u>, 523 (1959):405-446.

1179. Berenstein, Alexandre. <u>Les</u> <u>organisations</u> <u>ouvrières:</u> <u>leurs</u> <u>compétences</u> <u>et</u> <u>leur</u> <u>role</u> dans <u>la</u> <u>Société</u> <u>des</u> <u>Nations</u> <u>et</u> <u>notamment</u> <u>dans</u> <u>l'organisation</u> <u>internationale</u> <u>du</u> <u>travail</u>. Paris, 1936. An informative survey.

1180. Brand, G. "International Labor Organization in Transition." <u>World</u> <u>Affairs</u>, 12(1946):81-89.

1181. Brandeisz, Maximilian. <u>Sozialpolitisches</u> <u>im</u> <u>Friedensvertrag</u>. Vienna, 1923.

1182. Butler, H. B. <u>Confident</u> <u>Morning</u>. London, 1941. Former deputy Director and then Director succeeding Albert Thomas.

1183. Butler, H. B. <u>The</u> <u>Lost</u> <u>Peace</u>. London, 1941.

1184. Dietz, Theodor. <u>Aufbau,</u> <u>Aufgaben</u> <u>und</u> <u>Ergeb-</u> <u>nisse</u> <u>der</u> <u>Internationalen</u> <u>Arbeitsorganisation</u>. Munich, 1934.

1185. Dillon, Conley Hall. <u>International</u> <u>Labor</u> <u>Conventions</u>. Chapel Hill, 1942.

1186. Drechsel, Max. <u>Le</u> <u>traité</u> de <u>Versailles</u> <u>et</u> <u>le</u> <u>mécanisme</u> <u>des</u> <u>conventions</u> <u>internationales</u> <u>du</u> <u>travail</u>. Brussels, 1926.

1187. Fernbach, Alfred. <u>Soviet</u> <u>Coexistence</u> <u>Stra-</u> <u>tegy:</u> <u>A</u> <u>Case</u> <u>Study</u> <u>of</u> <u>Experience</u> <u>in</u> <u>the</u> <u>Inter-</u> <u>national</u> <u>Labor</u> <u>Organization</u>. Washington, 1960.

1188. Fine, Martin. "Albert Thomas: A Reformer's Vision of Modernization, 1914-1932." <u>Journal</u> <u>of</u> <u>Contemporary</u> <u>History</u> 12(1971):545-64.

1189. Fischer, Georges. <u>Les</u> <u>rapports</u> <u>entre</u> <u>l'organi-</u> <u>sation</u> <u>internationale</u> <u>du</u> <u>travail</u> <u>et</u> <u>la</u> <u>cour</u> <u>permanente</u> <u>de</u> <u>justice</u> <u>internationale:</u> <u>Contri-</u> <u>bution</u> <u>à</u> <u>l'étude</u> <u>du</u> <u>problème</u> <u>de</u> <u>la</u> <u>séparation</u> <u>des</u> <u>pouvoirs</u> <u>dans</u> <u>le</u> <u>domaine</u> <u>international</u>. Paris, 1946.

1190. Follows, J. W. Antecedents of the International Labor Organisation. Oxford, 1951.

1191. Fried, John H. E. "Relations between the United Nations and the International Labor Organiztaion." American Political Science Review, 41(1947):963-77.

1192. Gompers, Samuel. Seventy Years of Life and Labor. New York, 1925.

1193. Goodrich, Carter. "The International Labor Organization." In Pioneers in World Order. Edited by H. E. Davis. New York, 1944.

1194. Haas, Ernst B. Beyond the Nation-State: Functionalism and International Organization. Stanford, 1964. A classic investigation.

1195. Haas, Ernst B. Human Rights and International Action: The Case of Freedom of Association. Stanford, 1970.

1196. Hillery, Brian. Ireland in the International Labor Organization. Dublin, 1969.

1197. International Labor Office. The Admission of Germany and Austria to the International Labour Organisation. Geneva, 1920.

1198. International Labor Office. Albert Thomas, 1878-1932. Annemasse(Haute-Savoie), 1932.

1199. International Labor Office. Bibliography on the International Labour Organization. Geneva, 1959.

1200. International Labor Office. Catalogue of Publications in English of the International Labour Office, 1919-1950. Geneva, 1951.

1201. International Labor Office. The I.L.O. and Asia. New York: International Secretariat, Institute of Pacific Relations, 1954.

1202. International Labor Office. The International Labour Organisation: The First Decade. London, 1931. Objective, authoritative, by senior staff officers. An important work of reference.

1203. International Labor Office. "The International Labour Organization Since the War." International Labour Review 67(1953):109-155.

1204. International Labour Review. Geneva, 1921-. Monthly.

1205. International Labour Office. Subject Guide to Publications of the International Labour Office, 1919-1964. Geneva, 1967.

1206. International Labor Organization Yearbook. Geneva, 1930.

1207. International Labor Office. A New Era: The Philadelphia Conference and the Future of the ILO. Montreal, 1944.

1208. International Labor Office. L'organisation internationale du travail: Trente ans de combat pour la justice sociale, 1919-1949. 2nd ed. Geneva, 1950.

1209. Jacobson, Harold Karan. "The USSR and the ILO." International Organization 14(1960): 402-428.

1210. Jenks, C. Wilfred. "Constitutional Changes in the ILO." British Yearbook of International Law 23(1946):303-317.

1211. Jenks, C. Wilfred. Britain and the I.L.O. The David Davies Memorial Institute of International Studies. Annual Memorial Lecture, 1969. London, 1969. Jenks served the ILO for nearly 40 years as legal adviser and Director-General.

1212. Jenks, C. Wilfred. "The International Labour Organisation and Peaceful Change." World Affairs 4(1939):361-379.

1213. Jenks, C. Wilfred. Social Justice in the Law of Nations: The I.L.O. Impact After Fifty Years. London, 1970. The Hersch Lauterpacht Lectures.

1214. Johnston, George A. International Social Progress: The Work of the International Labour Organisation of the League of Nations. New York, 1924.

1215. Johnston, George A. The International Labour Organization: Its Work for Social and Economic Progress. London, 1970.

1216. Kakkar, N. K. India and the I.L.O.: The Story of Fifty Years. Delhi, 1970.

1217. Landelius, Torsten. Workers, Employers and Governments: A Comparative Study of Delegations and Groups at the International Labour Conference, 1919-1964. Stockholm, 1965. Assumed equality of states at conferences of international organizations is illusory.

1218. Landy, E. A. The Effectiveness of International Supervision: Thirty Years of I.L.O. Experience. London, 1966. Respect for treaty obligations tested by the way parties live up to commitments. Studies whether systematic supervision can produce compliance.

1219. Lorwin, Lewis I. Labor and Internationalism. New York, 1929.

1220. Lusignan, Guy de. L'organisation internationale du travail (1919-1959). Paris, 1959.

1221. Michelis, G. de, ed. L'Italia nell' orgàni-zazione internazionale del lavoro della società delle nazioni. Rome, 1930.

1222. Milhaud, Edgard. La journée de huit heures et ses résultats d'après l'enquête sur la production. Geneva, 1927.

1223. Mondaini, G., and Cabrini, A. L'evoluzione del lavoro nelle colonie e la società delle nazioni. Padua, 1931.

1224. Montreau, Marc. L'organisation internationale du travail (B.I.T. et O.I.T.). 2nd ed. Paris, 1964.

1225. Morse, David A. The Origin and Evolution of the I.L.O. and its Role in the World Community. Ithaca, 1969.

1226. Phelan, Edward J. "Some Reminiscences of the ILO." Studies (Dublin), (1954):241-270. "The ILO sets up its Wartime Centre in Canada." Studies (Dublin), (1955):151-70. "The ILO

Turns the Corner." Studies (Dublin), (1956): 160-86. "After Pearl Harbour: ILO Problems." Studies (Dublin), (1957):193-206.

1227. Phelan, Edward Joseph. Yes and Albert Thomas. London, 1936. Thomas as Director, by his collaborator and successor.

1228. Phelan, V. C. "Human Welfare and the ILO." International Journal 9(1954):24-33.

1229. Pillai, P. P. India and the International Labour Organisation. Patna, 1951.

1230. Price, John. The International Labour Movement. New York, 1945.

1231. Raeburn, Walter. "Features and Development of the International Labour Organization." Transactions (Grotius Society) 35(1949):57-71.

1232. Scelle, Georges. L'organisation internationale du travail et le B.I.T. Paris, 1930.

1233. Shaper, B. W. Albert Thomas--Trente ans de réformisme social. Assen, 1959.

1234. Shkunaev, V. G. The International Labor Organization: Past and Present. Moscow, 1969.

1235. Shotwell, James T. Diary of a Research Expedition to Europe. New York, 1931.

1236. Shotwell, James T. The Origins of the International Labour Organisation. 2 v. New York, 1934. Volume one is the history, volume two the documents.

1237. Société des Amis d'Albert Thomas. Albert Thomas vivant. Geneva, 1957.

1238. Stewart, M. Britain and the ILO--The Story of Fifty Years. London, 1969. A fine official history.

1239. Thomas, Albert. Histoire anecdotique du travail. Paris, 1925.

1240. Thomas, Albert. International Social Policy. Geneva, 1948.

1241. Thomas, Elbert D. "Report on the Paris Conference of the International Labor Organization."
Institute of World Affairs Proceedings
21(1945): 118-22.

1242. Tidmarsh, Kyril. The Soviet Union and the
I.L.O. Oxford, 1957.

1243. Vogel-Polsky, Elaine. Du tripartisme à
l'organisation internationale du travail.
Brussels, 1966. The principle of universality
sometimes prevailed over freedom of association, but tripartism stood the test.

1244. Wilson, F. G. Labor in the League System: A
Study of the ILO in relation to International
Administration. London, 1952.

1245. Windmuller, John P. American Labor and the
International Labor Movement, 1940-1953.
Ithaca, 1954.

XVI. INTERNATIONAL ORGANIZATIONS
OUTSIDE THE LEAGUE

Of the hundreds of IGOs and NIGOs of the period, humanitarian, functional, regulatory or political, regional, universal, or multilateral, ideological or popular, official or unofficial, a few are selected to represent the range of interests and types of associations.

The Universal Postal Union, founded 1874, facilitates cooperation between various national postal systems, seeking standardization and efficient regulation of the international mails. A central office, the International Bureau in Berne, keeps member governments informed of changes needed. Representatives meet periodically in a Congress to review agreements.

The International Institute of Agriculture was founded in 1905 to collect information on agricultural production and facilitate cooperation among farmers and farm groups. By 1939 the Institute served the representatives of 68 governments. It became part of the FAO in 1946. Today its collection forms the nucleus of the David Lubin Archives and Memorial Library in the FAO headquarters in Rome.

The British Commonwealth of Nations was not universal in membership. Its members owed allegiance to the British crown. It is instructive for the study of the redefinition, during these years, of empire, as some colonies took on new statutes of association. The Commonwealth was always an important consideration in British policy in this period. The Commonwealth states were the largest organized bloc in the League, but their interests, and votes, sometimes differed.

The Inter-Parliamentary Union, established 1888, called on members of national legislatures to "study all questions of an international character suitable for settlement by parliamentary action." After the war the Union gave its main attention to support of the League. In 1938 it had some 5,000 members from 31 states.

Article 25 of the Covenant admonished members to "promote the establishment and co-operation of

duly authorized voluntary national Red Cross
organizations having as purposes the improvement of
health, the prevention of disease and the mitiga-
tion of suffering throughout the world." During
our period the international aspects of the Red
Cross comprised three main parts: the League of
Red Cross Societies founded in 1919 and headquartered at Geneva, the federation of national societies; an International Conference, a meeting of
representatives of participating states to discuss for
instance the management and revision of the Geneva
Conventions; and the International Committee of the
Red Cross. The ICRC was the founder organization,
established in 1863, independent, neutral, composed
of Swiss citizens, but international in its work.
The presidents of the ICRC in our period were:
Gustave Ador (1910-1928), Max Huber (1928-1945),
and Carl J. Burckhardt (1945-1948).

The ICRC acted on its own initiative as
neutral intermediary in questions of humanitarian
nature, in favor of war victims, including prisoners of war and displaced persons, and to further
the purposes of the Geneva Conventions for aid to
war wounded. Administratively it gave recognition
to new national societies, promoted humanitarian
law, and sought ways to protect civilian populations from the anticipated horrors of another war.
In the 1930s, for example, there were many informative articles in the monthly Revue internationale
de la Croix-Rouge on the dangers of air bombardment
and poison chemicals. The ICRC sent missions of
investigation to Ethiopia during the Italian invasion and determined the use of poison gas there.
Ostensibly non-political, the shadow of the ICRC
(located just yards away from the Palace of
Nations) can be discerned in several international
affairs during this time.

Peace associations were of many kinds. The
International Federation of League of Nation Societies, meant to influence public opinion, was a
loose federation of national societies. It had a
small office in Brussels, established by the pacifist and philosopher Theodore Ruyssen. The most
important of the national societies was the League
of Nations Union in Britain, led by Robert Cecil.
It had 841,208 members in 1930, sponsored the
'Peace Ballot' in 1935, and published Headway.
There were also religiously inspired organizations,
information centers, and pressure groups to encourage the idea of peaceful settlements. The Carnegie
Endowment for International Peace, in New York with

a European branch, was exemplary with its many
authoritative studies of current problems and its
stress on the value of international organization,
as was the Geneva Research Center (founded 1920)
with its competent monograph series, 'Special
Studies.' Projects to break down language barriers, such as the Esperanto movement, had world
peace as their objective. Ruyssen concluded: "The
sentiments aroused in men's souls by the pacifists'
appeal never had the same depth or strength of the
clarion calls of 'patriotism'" but the influence of
these associations in shaping opinion must not be
underestimated.[1]

Of other popular, ideological, and coopera-
tivist bodies note may be taken of the Communist
Third International (from 1919, dominated by Soviet
Russian policy), the spiritual and political
activities of the Vatican under Popes Pius XI and
Pius XII, the Pan-Europe movement, and the role of
the press. Groups devoted to supposedly non-
political internationalism included the International Olympic Committee (1894), the International
Confederation of Students (1919), the International
Federation of Trade Unions (organized 1901, reconstituted 1919), the Workers' Sport International,
the World's Alliance of YMCAs (one of the oldest
international non-governmental organizations--
1855), the International Chamber of Commerce, and
dozens of others. Internationalism was a theme,
and often a necessity, of the age.

A. General Bibliography

1246. Burton, John W. World Society. Cambridge,
1972.

1247. Adam, H. T. Les organismes internationaux
spécialisés: Contribution à la théorie générale des établissements publics internationaux.
2 vols. Paris, 1965. Discusses organizations
of limited but practical value, with many
interesting examples analyzed.

1248. Berman, M. R., and Johnson, J. E. Unofficial
Diplomats. New York, 1977. Recent work by
the Carnegie Foundation, the ICRC, the World
Council of Churches, and others. Indicative
of the range of interest of such bodies.

1. Ruyssen is quoted in P. Renouvin and J. P.
Duroselle, Introduction to International Relations,
p. 233.

1249. Feld, Werner J. Nongovernmental Forces and World Politics: A Study of Business, Labor, and Political Groups. New York, 1972.

1250. Harley, J. E. International Understanding: Agencies Educating for a New World. Stanford, 1931.

1251. Huntington, Samuel P. "Transnational Organizations in World Politics." World Politics 25(1973):333-68.

1252. Jacobson, Harold K. Networks of Interdependence: International Organizations and the Global Political System. New York, 1979.

1253. Kaiser, Karl. "Transnational Politics: Toward a Theory of Multinational Politics." International Organization 25(1971):803-17.

1254. Kaufmann, Wilhelm. "Les unions internationales de nature économique." Recueil des cours II(1924).

1255. Keohane, Robert O., and Nye, Joseph S., Jr. "Transgovernmental Relations and International Relations." World Politics 27(1974): 39-62.

1256. Keohane, Robert O., and Nye, Joseph S., Jr. Transnational Relations and World Politics. Cambridge, MA, 1972.

1257. League of Nations. Handbook of International Organizations. Geneva, 1921-1938. Seven editions published during this time, noting the various groups and organizations.

1258. League of Nations. The (Quarterly) Bulletin of Information on the Work of International Organizations. Geneva, 1922-1939. A quarterly 1922-1931, published irregularly 1931-1939.

1259. Luard, Evan. International Agencies: The Emerging Framework of Interdependence. London, 1976.

1260. Lyons, F. S. L. Internationalism in Europe, 1815-1914. Leyden, 1963. An important book, published under the auspices of the Council of Europe, exploring all aspects of the historical background of our subject.

1261. Maza, Herbert, ed. Neuf meneurs internationaux: De l'initiative individuelle dans l'institution des organisations internationales. Paris, 1965. Includes studies of the work of David Lubin, Frédéric Passy, W. R. Cremer, S. O. Levinson, and J. T. Shotwell.

1262. Potter, Pitman B. The League of Nations and other International Organisations. Geneva, 1934.

1263. Skjelsbaek, K. "The Growth of International Non-governmental Organization in the Twentieth Century." International Organization 25(1971): 420-442.

1264. Union of International Associations. La Société des Nations et l'union des associations internationales. Brussels, 1926.

1265. Union of International Associations. La vie internationale. Brussels, 1912-1921. Twenty-six issues of the Association's journal.

1266. White, Lyman C. International Non-Governmental Organizations. Their Purposes, Methods, and Accomplishments. New York, 1968. A fine introduction to various major INGOs.

1267. White, Lyman C. The Structure of Private International Organizations. Philadelphia, 1933.

1268. Whitton, John B. The Re-organization of the Geneva Research Centre. Geneva, 1937.

B. International Governmental Organizations and International Non-Governmental Organizations

1. Universal Postal Union

1269. Boisson, Henri. La Société des Nations et les bureaux internationaux des unions universelles postale et télégraphique. Paris, 1932.

1270. Bühler, Hans. Der Weltpostverein: eine Völkerrechtsgeschichtliche und wirtschaftspolitische Untersuchung. Berlin, 1930.

1271. Codding, George A., Jr. The Universal Postal Union: Co-ordinator of the International Mails. New York, 1964. Examines the economic, political, and technical situation in which the UPU was created, and gives its history, structure, and function.

1272. Mench, M. A. K. Universal Postal Union. New York, 1965.

1273. Sly, J. F. "The Genesis of the Universal Postal Union: A Study in the Beginnings of International Organization." International Conciliation 233(1927):9-57.

1274. Union postale universelle. L'union postale universelle, sa fondation et son développement, 1874-1949: Mémoire. Berne, 1949.

1275. Williamson, F. H. "The International Postal Service of the Universal Postal Union." Journal of the Royal Institute of International Affairs 9(1930):68-78.

2. International Institute of Agriculture

1276. Agresti, Olivia R. David Lubin. Berkeley, 1941.

1277. Food and Agriculture Organization. Bibliography of the History and Activity of the International Institute of Agriculture. Rome, 1945.

1278. Hobson, Asher. The International Institute of Agriculture: An Historical and Critical Analysis of its Organisation, Activities and Policies of Administration. Berkeley, 1931.

1279. Maza, Herbert. "David Lubin: La fondation de l'Institut International Agriculteur." In Neuf meneurs internationaux, by H. Maza. Paris, 1965.

3. Commonwealth

1280. Amery, L. S. "The Imperial Economic Confer-
      ence: Before the Meeting at Ottawa."
      International Affairs 9(1932):678-99.

1281. Angell, Norman. "The British Commonwealth in
      the World Order." Annals of the American
      Academy of Political and Social Science
      228(1943):65-70.

1282. Ball, Margaret. The "Open" Commonwealth.
      Durham, 1971.

1283. Berriedale, Arthur. Dominion Autonomy in
      Practice. London, 1929.

1284. Bulwer, Peter McGennis. Commonwealth
      History. London, 1967.

1285. Carter, Gwendolen M. The British Common-
      wealth and International Security: The Role
      of the Dominions, 1919-1939. Toronto, 1947.

1286. Charteris, A. H. "The British Commonwealth
      Relations Conference at Toronto, 1933."
      Transactions (Grotius Society) 19(1933):137-
      53.

1287. Cheng, Seymour. Schemes for the Federation
      of the British Empire. New York, 1931.

1288. Chevallier, Jean Jacques. "La société des
      nations britanniques." Recueil des cours
      64(1938):237-344.

1289. Colonial Office. Catalogue of the Colonial
      Office Library, London. 15 vols. Boston,
      1964.

1290. Cross, Colin. The Fall of the British
      Empire, 1918-1968. New York, 1969.

1291. Cross, J. A. Whitehall and the Commonwealth:
      British Departmental Organisation for Common-
      wealth Relations, 1900-1966. London, 1967.

1292. Dafoe, J. W. "Canada, the Empire, and the
      League." Foreign Affairs 14(1936):297-306.

1293. Dawson, Robert. The Development of Dominion
      Status, 1900-1936. London, 1937.

1294. Drummond, Ian M. Imperial Economic Policy,
1917-1939: Studies in Expansion and Protection. London, 1974.

1295. Eastman, S. M. Canada at Geneva. Toronto,
1946.

1296. Eayrs, James. "Confrontation of the Prophets:
Competing Conceptions of the Commonwealth,
1944-45." The Round Table, 241(1971):101-
115.

1297. Edwards, Cecil. Bruce of Melbourne: Man of
Two Worlds. London, 1965.

1298. Elliott, William Y., and Hall, Duncan, eds.
The British Commonwealth at War. New York,
1943.

1299. Ellis, A. D. Australia and the League of
Nations. New York, 1922.

1300. Fisher, Allen G. B. "The Commonwealth's
Place in the World Economic Structure."
International Affairs 20(1944):32-41.

1301. Fitzhardinge, Lawrence F. "Hughes, Borden,
and Dominion Representation at the Paris
Peace Conference." Canadian Historical
Review 49(1968):160-69.

1302. Fitzhardinge, Lawrence F. "W. M. Hughes and
the Treaty of Versailles, 1919." Journal of
Commonwealth Political Studies 5(1967):130-
42.

1303. Flint, J. E. Books on the British Empire and
Commonwealth. London, 1968.

1304. Frost, R. A., ed. The British Commonwealth
and World Society. New York, 1947.

1305. Garner, Joe. The Commonwealth Office, 1925-
68. Exeter, NH, 1978. An inside account.
Author joined in 1930 five years after Amery
created it as the Dominions Office as a
branch of the Colonial Office. It became the
Commonwealth Relations office in 1947, autonomous and separate from the Colonial Office,
and took the name Commonwealth Office in
1966, incorporating the old Colonial Office--

the wheel having moved full circle, leaving one department again responsible for commonwealth affairs.

1306. Gathorne-Hardy, G. M. "The British Commonwealth Relations Conference, 1933." International Affairs 12(1933):763-74.

1307. Griffiths, P. J. Empire into Commonwealth. London, 1969.

1308. Hall, H. Duncan. "The British Commonwealth as a Great Power." Foreign Affairs 23(1945): 594-608.

1309. Hall, H. Duncan. "The British Commonwealth and Trusteeship." International Affairs 22(1946):199-213.

1310. Hall, H. Duncan. Commonwealth: A History of the British Commonwealth of Nations. London, 1971. A comprehensive, 1015 page, study by a former senior League official (1927-39) who served on the British raw materials commission during the Second World War, and attended most of the Commonwealth Parliamentary Conferences after as special adviser.

1311. Hancock, W. Keith. Survey of British Commonwealth Affairs, 1918-1939. 2 vols. London, 1937, 1941. Volume one entitled: "Problems of Nationality, 1918-1936." Volume two entitled: "Problems of Economic Policy, 1918-1939."

1312. Hauser, Oswald. "Das britische Commonwealth zwischen nationaler Souveränität und imperialer Integration 1917-1931." Vierteljahrshefte für Zeitgeschichte 16(1968):230-46.

1313. Hewitt, Arthur R. Guide to Resources for Commonwealth Studies in London, Oxford, and Cambridge. London, 1957.

1314. Joyner, Conrad. "W. M. Hughes and the 'Powers' Referendum of 1919: A Master Politician at Work." Australian Journal of Politics and History 5(1959):15-23.

1315. Kendle, John E. The Round Table Movement and Imperial Union. Toronto, 1975.

1316. Kerr, Philip H. "The British Empire, the League of Nations and the United States." The Round Table 10(1920):221-53. This journal was subtitled: Commonwealth Journal of International Affairs.

1317. Key, L. C. "Australia and the Commonwealth." International Affairs 21(1945):60-73.

1318. Livingston, William S. Federalism in the Commonwealth: A Bibliographical Commentary. London, 1963.

1319. Macadam, I. S. "Canada and the Commonwealth." International Affairs 20(1944):519-26.

1320. McCarthy, John M. "Australia and Imperial Defence: Co-operation and Conflict, 1918-1939." Australian Journal of Politics and History 17(1971):19-32.

1321. McCarthy, John M. "Singapore and Australian Defence, 1921-1942." Australian Outlook 25(1971):165-80.

1322. McIntyre, David. The Commonwealth of Nations: Origins and Impacts, 1869-1971. Minneapolis, 1977.

1323. Mansergh, Nicholas. The Commonwealth Experience. London, 1969. Close to a full synthesis.

1324. Mansergh, Nicholas. Documents and Speeches on British Commonwealth Affairs 2 vols. London, 1953.

1325. Mehrotra, S. "On the Use of the Term 'Commonwealth.'" Journal of Commonwealth Political Studies 2(1963):1-16.

1326. Moore, William H. "The Dominions of the British Commonwealth in the League of Nations." International Affairs 10(1931):372-91.

1327. Parkinson, Cosmo. The Colonial Office from Within, 1909-1945. London, 1947.

1328. Ram, V. S., and Sharma, B. India and the League of Nations. Lucknow, 1932.

1329. Robinson, Kenneth. The Dilemmas of Trusteeship: Aspects of British Colonial Policy between the Wars. London, 1965. A perceptive and serious consideration of problems of economic development, institutional change, and social impact.

1330. Royal Commonwealth Society, Library. Subject Catalogue of the Royal Commonwealth Society, London. 7 vols. Boston, 1971.

1331. Sales, Peter M. "W. M. Hughes and the Chanak Crisis of 1922." Australian Journal of Politics and History 17(1971):392-405.

1332. Smuts, Jan Christian. Selections from the Smuts Papers. Edited by Jean van der Poel. London, 1973. This refers to volumes V, covering 1919-1934, and VI, 1934-1945, showing Smuts trapped between his faith in international cooperation (the League, the Commonwealth) and domestic opinion which alone could give him authority.

1333. Stroud, John. Annals of British and Commonwealth Air Transport, 1919-1960. London, 1962.

1334. Toynbee, A. J., ed. British Commonwealth Relations: Proceedings of the First Unofficial Conference on British Commonwealth Relations held at Toronto from September 11th to 21st, 1933. London, 1934.

1335. Underhill, F. H. The British Commonwealth: An Experiment in Co-operation among the Nations. Durham, 1956.

1336. Watt, D. C. "Imperial Defence Policy and Imperial Foreign Policy, 1911-1939: The Substance and the Shadow." In Personalities and Policies: Studies in the Formation of British Foreign Policy in the Twentieth Century, by D. C. Watt. Notre Dame, 1965.

1337. Watts, R. L. New Federations: Experiments in the Commonwealth. Oxford, 1966.

1338. Wheare, K. C. The Statute of Westminster, 1931. London, 1933.

1339. Zimmern, Alfred. "Is there an Empire Foreign Policy?" International Affairs 13(1934):303-24. An instructive article on such an association, concluding, with respect to the League, that "where there is a choice to be made between rival principles of universality and morality, between symmetry and virtue, then the claims of formal order must yield to the higher claims of inward order."

4. Inter-Parliamentary Union

1340. Anderson, Stanley V. The Nordic Council: A Study of Scandinavian Regionalism. Seattle, 1967. Nordic Inter-Parliamentary Union formed 1907, amid early suspicions, gradually, and especially after World War II, evolved into a group encouraging common laws, ties, agreements.

1341. Douglas, James. Parliaments across Frontiers. A Short History of the Inter-Parliamentary Union. London, 1975.

1342. France, Assemblée nationale, Bibliothèque. Exposition Frédéric Passy à l'occasion de la 59e conférence interparlementaire. Paris, 1971.

1343 Inter-Parliamentary Union. The Inter-Parliamentary Union, 1889-1939. Geneva, 1939.

1344. Maza, Herbert. "Frédéric Passy: La fondation de l'union interparlementaire." In Neuf meneurs internationaux, by H. Maza. Paris, 1965.

1345. Passy, Paul. Un apôtre de la paix: La vie de Frédéric Passy. Paris, 1927.

5. International Committee of the Red Cross

1346. Brown, Sidney H. Für das Rote Kreuz in Aethiopien. Zurich, 1939.

1347. Chapuisat, Edouard. Le comité international de la Croix-Rouge et la guerre. Geneva, 1944.

1348. Coursier, Henri. _La Croix-Rouge et la paix._ Paris, 1968.

1349. Coursier, Henri. _The International Red Cross._ Trans. by M. C. S. Phipps. Geneva, 1961.

1350. Davis, Gerald H. "Prisoners of War in Twentieth-Century War Economies." _Journal of Contemporary History_ 12(1977):623-34. Helpful for understanding the Geneva Conventions of 1929 and 1949.

1351. Durand, André. _De Sarajevo à Hiroshima._ Geneva, 1978. Volume 2 of the official ICRC history published by the Henri Dunant Institute.

1352. Forsythe, David P. _Humanitarian Politics: The International Committee of the Red Cross._ Baltimore, 1978. Sees the ICRC as "impartial on the side of the victim," too weak to be feared, and that is a source of its strength. A fine modern study.

1353. Forsythe, David P. "The Red Cross as Transnational Movement: Conserving and Changing the Nation-State." _International Organization_ 30(1976):607-30.

1354. Freymond, Jacques. _Guerres, révolutions, Croix-Rouge: réflexions sur le rôle du comité international de la Croix-Rouge._ Geneva, 1976.

1355. Freymond, Jacques. "The International Committee of the Red Cross within the International System." _International Review of the Red Cross_ 134(1972):245-66.

1356. Haan, Hugo von. _Organisation und arbeitsmethoden des Roten Kreuzes in Genf._ Zurich, 1942.

1357. Huber, Max. _Principes, tâches et problèmes de la Croix-Rouge dans le droit des gens._ Geneva, 1944.

1358. Joyce, James A. _Red Cross International._ London, 1959.

1359. Junod, Marcel. Le troisième combattant: De l'ypérite en Abyssinie à la bombe atomique d'Hiroshima. Paris, 1947.

1360. Junod, Marcel. Warrior without Weapons. Translated by Edward Fitzgerald. New York, 1951. Translation of Le troisième combattant.

1361. Moreillon, Jacques. Le comité international de la Croix-Rouge et la protection de détenus politiques. Lausanne, 1973. A high official, explaining how the ICRC operates, and its political premises.

1362. Mueller, Eitelz-Erhard. Das Internationale Rote Kreuz. Göttingen, 1951.

1363. Noailly, Frédérique. La Croix-Rouge au point de vue national et international, son histoire, son organisation. Paris, 1935.

1364. Reimann, Max. Quasi-konsularische und schutzmachtähnliche Funktionen des Internationalen Komitees von Roten Kreuz ausserhalb bewaffneter Konflikte. Geneva, 1971.

1365. Ringgenberg, C. M. Die Beziehungen zwischen dem Roten Kreuz und dem Völkerbund. Bern, 1970.

1366. Vogelsanger, Peter. Max Huber. Recht, Politik, Humanität aus Glauben. Stuttgart, 1967.

1367. International Committee of the Red Cross. Catalogue of Publications, 1864-1975. Geneva, 1975.

1368. International Committee of the Red Cross. La Convention de Genève de 1929: Commentaire par Paul des Gouttes. Geneva, 1930.

1369. International Committee of the Red Cross. Inter arma caritas: The Work of the International Committee of the Red Cross during the Second World War. Geneva, 1947.

1370. International Committee of the Red Cross. Intellectual Relief. Geneva, 1944.

6. Holy See

1371. Alix, Christine. Le Saint-Siège et les nationalismes en Europe 1870-1960. Paris, 1962. Church is in favor of moderation, legality, constitutionalism, and fearful of compromising its concordats with states.

1372. Cardinale, Hyginus Eugene. The Holy See and the International Order. Gerrards Cross, 1976. Apologetics.

1373. Cardinale, Hyginus Eugene. Le Saint-Siège et la Diplomatie: Aperçu historique, juridique et practique de diplomatie pontificale. Paris, 1962.

1374. Charles-Roux, François. Huit ans au Vatican, 1932-1940. Paris: Flammarion, 1947.

1375. Clonmore, Lord. Pope Pius XI and World Peace. New York, 1938.

1376. Delzell, Charles F. "Pius XII, Italy, and the Outbreak of War." Journal of Contemporary History 2(1967):137-161.

1377. Engel-Janosi, Friedrich. Vom Chaos zur Katastrophe: Vatikanische Gespräche 1918 bis 1938, vornehmlich auf Grund der Berichte des österreichischen Gesandten beim heiligen Stuhl. Vienna, 1971.

1378. Fabrègues, J. de. "The Re-establishment of Relations between France and the Vatican in 1921." Journal of Contemporary History 2(1967):163-82. The diplomatic measures taken by Briand to restore relations.

1379. Friedlander, Saul. Pie XII et le IIIe Reich. Paris, 1964.

1380. Giovannetti, Albert. Der Vatikan und der Krieg. Cologne, 1962. By a church official, this expands on the original Italian edition to include additional documents.

1381. Graham, Robert A. Vatican Diplomacy: A Study of the Church and State on the International Plane. Princeton, 1959.

225

1382. Herberichs, Gérard. Théorie de la paix selon
    Pie XII. Paris, 1964.

1383. Holy See. Actes et documents du Saint Siège
    relatifs à la seconde guerre mondiale.
    Vatican City, 1965 ff. The published collec-
    tion of the Vatican's diplomatic documents.

1384. Kent, G. "Pope Pius XII and Nazi Germany:
    Some Aspects of German-Vatican Relations."
    American Historical Review 70(1964):59-78.

1385. Lewy, Guenter. The Catholic Church and Nazi
    Germany. New York, 1964.

1386. McCormick, Anne O'Hare. Vatican Journal,
    1921-1954. Edited by M. T. Sheehan. New
    York, 1957.

1387. Pius XI. Discorsi di Pio XI. Edited by
    Domenico Bertetto. 3 vols. Turin, 1960.

1388. Rhodes, Anthony. The Vatican in the Age of
    the Dictators, 1922-1945. London, 1973.

1389. Salvemini, Gaetano. "The Vatican and the
    Ethiopian War." In Neither Liberty nor
    Bread. Edited by F. Keene. New York, 1940.

1390. Sturzo, Luigi. Chiesa e stato: Studio socio-
    logico-storico. 2 vols. Bologna, 1958,
    reissue.

1391. Teeling, L. William. The Pope in Politics.
    London, 1937.

1392. Vallier, Ivan. "The Roman Catholic Church: A
    Transnational Actor." International Organi-
    zation 25(1971):479-502.

7. Comintern

1393. Borkenau, Franz. The Communist Interna-
    tional. London, 1938.

1394. Braunthal, Julius. Geschichte der Inter-
    nationale. 2 vols. Hanover, 1962-63.

1395. Buber-Neumann, Margarete. Kriegsschauplätze
    der Weltrevolution: Ein Bericht aus der
    Praxis der Komintern, 1919-1943. Stuttgart,

1967. Personal reminiscences, observations, reflections, and some firsthand research in little used sources.

1396. Degras, Jane. The Communist International, 1919-1943. 3 vols. London, 1957, 1960 & 1965.

1397. Drachkovitch, Milorad M., ed. The Revolutionary Internationals, 1864-1943. Stanford, 1966. Nine original essays of interpretive importance.

1398. Kriegel, Annie. Les internationales ouvrières, 1864-1943. Paris, 1964.

1399. McKenzie, Kermit G. Comintern and World Revolution, 1928-1943: The Shaping of Doctrine. New York, 1964.

1400. Sworakowski, Witold S. The Communist International and its Front Organizations: A Research Guide and Checklist of Holdings in American and European Libraries. Stanford, 1965.

8. Peace Associations

1401. Alkinson, Henry A. Theodore Marburg: The Man and his Work. New York, 1951.

1402. Allen, Devere. The Fight for Peace. New York, 1930.

1403. Angell, Norman. After All: The Autobiography of Norman Angell. London, 1951.

1404. Best, Ethelwyn, and Pike, Bernard. International Voluntary Service for Peace, 1920-1946. London, 1948.

1405. Birn, Donald S. "The League of Nations Union and Collective Security." Journal of Contemporary History 9(1974):131-59.

1406. Bramsted, Ernest. "Apostles of Collective Security: The League of Nations Union and Its Functions." Australian Journal of Politics and History 13(1967):347-64.

1407. Brock, Peter. Twentieth-Century Pacifism.
New York, 1970.

1408. Bussey, Gertrude, and Tims, Margaret. Women's
International League for Peace and Freedom,
1915-1965. London, 1965.

1409. Butow, R. J. C. The John Doe Associates:
Backdoor Diplomacy for Peace, 1941. Stanford, 1975. Informal-activities of Catholic
clergy and Japanese in America via Japanese
Ambassador Nomura, to immunize the Pacific
from war.

1410. Carr, E. H. "The League of Peace and Freedom, an Episode in the Quest for Collective
Security." International Affairs 14(1935):
837-44.

1411. Cecil, Lord (Robert). A Great Experiment.
London, 1941.

1412. Chickering, Roger. Imperial Germany and a
World without War. Princeton, 1975.

1413. Cook, B. W. Bibliography on Peace Research
in History. Santa Barbara, 1969.

1414. Holcombe, Arthur N. "Edwin Ginn's Commitment
to World Government." International Organization 20(1966):419-29. Founder of World
Peace Foundation and peace through law.

1415. Holcombe, Arthur H. "Edwin Ginn's Vision of
World Peace." International Organization
19(1965):1-19.

1416. Hudson, Darril. The Ecumenical Movement in
World Affairs. London, 1969. Action in the
1930s was too little and too late.

1417. Hudson, Darril. The World Council of
Churches in International Affairs. Leighton
Buzzard, 1977.

1418. International Peace Bureau. The International Peace Bureau. Geneva, 1977. Founded
in 1892 to serve as permanent secretariat to
the Universal Peace Congresses, it was later
secretariat to the International Union of
Peace Societies, until dissolved in 1959.

1419. Knowles, G. W., ed. Quakers and Peace. London, 1927.

1420. Kuehl, Warren F. "The World Federation League: A Neglected Chapter in the History of a Movement." World Affairs Quarterly 30(1960):349-364.

1421. Lange, Christian L. "Histoire de la doctrine pacifique et de son influence sur le développement du droit international." Recueil des cours 13(1927):171-426.

1422. Latané, John H., ed. Development of the League of Nations Idea: Documents and Correspondence of Theodore Marburg. 2 vols. New York, 1932.

1423. Ligt, Barthelemy de. La paix créatrice: Histoire des principes et des tactiques de l'action directe contre la guerre. Paris, 1934.

1424. Livingstone, Adelaide. The Peace Ballot: The Official History. London, 1935.

1425. Lukowitz, David C. "British Pacifists and Appeasement: The Peace Pledge Union." Journal of Contemporary History 9(1974):115-27.

1426. Madariaga, Salvador de. "Gilbert Murray and the League." In Gilbert Murray: an Unfinished Autobiography, edited by Jean Smith and Arnold Toynbee. London, 1940.

1427. Murray, Gilbert. The League of Nations Movement: Some Recollections of the Early Days. London, 1955.

1428. Nelson, John K. The Peace Prophets: American Pacifist Thought, 1919-1941. Chapel Hill, 1967.

1429. Rappard, William E. The Quest for Peace Since the World War. Cambridge, MA, 1940.

1430. Redlich, Marcellus von. "Résumé of the Movement for World Peace." Transactions (Grotius Society) 22(1936):137-49.

1431. Robbins, Keith. The Abolition of War: the "Peace Movement" in Britain, 1914-1919. Cardiff, 1976. Shows ideological issues closely related to military and political developments.

1432. Romains, Jules. Cela dépend de vous. Paris, 1939.

1433. Ruyssen, Theodore. "La propagande internationale pour la Société des Nations." In Les origines et l'oeuvre de la Société des Nations, edited by P. Munch. Copenhagen, 1924.

1434. Ruyssen, Theodore. Les sources doctrinales de l'internationalisme. Grenoble, 1954.

1435. Stevenson, Lilian. Towards a Christian International. Rev. ed. Paris and London, 1936.

1436. Thompson, J. A. "Lord Cecil and the Pacifists in the League of Nations Union." Historical Journal 20(1977):949-59.

1437. Wank, Solomon, ed. Doves and Diplomats: Foreign Offices and Peace Movements in Europe and America in the Twentieth Century. Westport, CT, 1978.

9. Press and Public Opinion

1438. Allen of Hurtwood, Lord. "Public Opinion and the Idea of International Government." International Affairs 13(1934):186-207.

1439. Azcárate, Pablo de, ed. William Martin: Un grand journaliste à Genève. Geneva, 1970. A journalist for the Journal de Genève, very involved in League affairs. His papers are in the League archives.

1440. Butter, Oscar. La presse et les relations politiques internationales. Paris, 1934.

1441. Cano, S., de Jouvenel, H., et al. Le rôle intellectual de la presse. Paris, 1934. The International Institute of Intellectual Cooperation asked journalists how the press influenced international understanding, and their views are published here.

1442. Carlisle, Rodney. "The Foreign Policy Views of an Isolationist Press Lord: W. R. Hearst and the International Crisis, 1936-1941." Journal of Contemporary History 9(1974):217-27. Suspicion of foreign states did not mean to be anti-war. Militant nationalism and anti-communism propelled Hearst.

1443. Carr, E. H. "Public Opinion as a Safeguard of Peace." International Affairs 15(1936):846-62.

1444. Davison, W. Phillips. Mass Communication and Conflict Resolution: The Role of the Information Media in the Advancement of International Understanding. New York, 1974.

1445. Gallup, George H. The Gallup Poll: Public Opinion, 1935-1971. New York, 1972.

1446. Grandin, T. The Political Use of the Radio. Geneva, 1939.

1447. Hiett, Helen. Public Opinion and the Italo-Ethiopian Dispute: The Activity of Private Organizations in the Crisis. Geneva, 1936.

1448. Huddleston, Sisley. Popular Diplomacy and War. Rindge, NH, 1954.

1449. Knapp, Wilfrid. "Fifty Years of Chatham House Books." International Affairs, Special Issue (1970):138-49.

1450. League of Nations. Revue des commentaires de la presse sur la Société des Nations. Geneva, daily.

1451. Long, B. Esperanto: Its Aims and Claims. London, 1930. Shows how this artificial auxiliary language can be used in all sorts of circumstances to promote harmony.

1452. Marwick, Arthur. "Middle Opinion in the Thirties: Planning, Progress, and Political 'Agreement.'" English Historical Review 79(1964):285-98.

1453. Moe, R. Le Prix Nobel de la Paix et l'Institut Nobel Norvégien: Rapport historique et descriptif, accompagné d'une histoire du mouvement pacifiste de 1896 à 1930. Oslo, 1932. By director of the institute, peace seems defined by humanitarian sentiment, not a matter grounded in diplomacy, finance, sovereignty and the rest.

1454. Nicolson, Harold. "British Public Opinion and Foreign Policy." Public Opinion Quarterly 1(1937):53-63.

1455. Nicolson, Harold. "Modern Diplomacy and British Public Opinion." International Affairs 16(1935):599-618.

1456. Olson, Kenneth E. The History Makers: The Press of Europe from its Beginnings through 1965. Baton Rouge, 1966.

1457. Perkins, Dexter. "The Department of State and American Public Opinion." In The Diplomats, 1919-1939, edited by G. Craig and F. Gilbert. Princeton, 1953.

1458. Pool, Ithiel de Sola. The "Prestige Papers": A Survey of Their Editorials. Stanford, 1951.

1459. Pool, Ithiel de Sola. Symbols of Democracy. Stanford, 1952.

1460. Pool, Ithiel de Sola. Symbols of Internationalism. Stanford, 1951.

1461. Privat, Edmond. The Life of Zamenhof, Inventor of Esperanto. London, 1931. Author leading Esperanto advocate--an interesting story.

1462. Pronay, Nicholas. "British Newsreels in the 1930's: Their Policies and Impact." History 57(1972):63-72.

1463. Seabury, William M. Motion Picture Problems, the Cinema and the League of Nations. New York, 1925.

1464. Saerchinger, César. "Radio as a Political Instrument." Foreign Affairs 16(1938):244-59.

1465. Shenton, H. N., Sapir, Edward, and Jespersen, O. International Communication. London, 1931. Shenton describes activities of International Auxiliary Language Association and its experiments with Esperanto.

1466. Waelder, R. Psychological Aspects of War and Peace. Geneva, 1939.

1467. Waugh, Alec. "History Text Books as a Factor in International Relations." International Affairs 15(1936):877-96. The creation of national images.

1468. Willert, Arthur. "Publicity and Propaganda in International Affairs." International Affairs 17(1938):809-26.

10. Other International Associations

1469. Allen, A. M. Sophy Sanger: A Pioneer in Internationalism. Glasgow, 1958. Origins and aspirations of International Association for Social Progress, founded in 1925 with merging of precursors of the ILO, the International Association for Labor Legislation, the Permanent Committee for Social Insurance, and the International Association for the Struggle against Unemployment.

1470. Altbach, Philip G. "The International Student Movement." Journal of Contemporary History 5(1970):156-74.

1471. Arnou, A. L'organisation internationale du travail et les catholiques. Paris, 1933.

1472. Brown, J. W. "The International Trade Union Movement." Journal of the Royal Institute of International Affairs 7(1928):29-41. Secretary of the International Federation of Trade Unions at Amsterdam.

1473. Comité International Olympique. Les jeux olympiques. Lausanne, 1958.

1474. Fimmen, Edo. The International Federation of Trade Unions. Amsterdam, 1922.

1475. Haas, E. B., Williams, M. P., and Babai, D.
Scientists and World Order: The Uses of
Technical Knowledge in International Organi-
zations. Berkeley, 1978.

1476. International Institute of Intellectual Cooperation. Les associations internationales
d'étudiants. Paris, 1931.

1477. Langley, J. Ayo. "Pan-Africanism in Paris,
1924-1936." Journal of Modern African
Studies 7(1967):69-94.

1478. Luza, Radomir. The History of the International Socialist Youth Movement. Leyden,
1970. From foundation of its precursor,
Socialist Youth International in 1907,
through vacillations of 1920s to new enthu-
siasm for United Europe and 3rd world after
1945. Well meaning, but lost touch.

1479. Ridgeway, George L. Merchants of Peace:
Twenty Years of Business Diplomacy through
the International Chamber of Commerce, 1919-
1938. New York, 1938.

1480. Schroeder-Gudehus, Brigitte. Les scientifiques et la paix: La communauté scientifique
internationale au cours des années 20.
Montreal, 1978. History does not support
contention that science bridged international
conflicts more easily than politics.

1481. Steinberg, David A. "The Workers' Sport
Internationals, 1920-28." Journal of Contemporary History 13(1978):233-52. Sport movement by far largest working class cultural
movement in 1920s, but no unity, remaining
divided because major elements would not
accept communist domination.

1482. Watkins, W. P. The International Co-opera-
tive Alliance, 1895-1970. London, 1970.

XVII. THE SECOND WORLD WAR--PLANNING FOR PEACE

"From the moment when Hitler's invasion of
Poland revealed the bankruptcy of all existing
methods to preserve the peace, it became evident to
us in the State Department that we must begin
almost immediately to plan the creation of a new
system. This, profiting by the failures of the
past, had to erect a viable and practical structure
by which the peace of the world could be successfully maintained....The United States was thus
committed from the very moment when chaos descended
upon Europe to devote her influence toward developing a postwar world in which peace could be assured."
(Cordell Hull, The Memoirs of Cordell Hull, vol. 2
[New York, 1948] p. 1625).

Throughout the war this planning was centered
in the State Department and the nature of a post-
war organization was a feature of increasing importance in conferences and interchanges between the
allied powers, including the Atlantic Charter
discussions of 1941, the Declaration of the United
Nations signed on 1 January 1942, the United Nations
Conference on Food and Agriculture at Hot Springs
in 1943, the United Nations Relief and Rehabilitation Conference in Atlantic City in 1943, the
International Labor Conference in Philadelphia in
1944, the United Nations Monetary and Financial
Conference at Bretton Woods in 1944, the foundation
conference at Dumbarton Oaks in 1944 where proposals
were sketched for the structure of a permanent
organization, and the culminating United Nations
Conference on International Organization in San
Francisco in 1945 which gave final form to the
Charter of the United Nations Organization.

Planning for peace was systematically pursued,
and second in American eyes only to the winning of
the war. It played a part at the wartime meetings
at Quebec, Moscow (in October 1943, agreeing to the
establishment of some 'general international organization'), Cairo, Teheran, Malta, and Yalta (where
agreement was reached on voting procedures in the
Security Council). While the planning took place
largely under American sponsorship, proposals were
always of a world-wide dimension, and were both

part of and transcending the allied cooperation
undertaken for victory in the war.

A. Wartime Conference Diplomacy

1483. Alperovitz, Gar. Atomic Diplomacy: Hiroshima
and Potsdam. New York, 1965.

1484. Beloff, Max. "The Anglo-French Union Project
of June 1940." In Mélanges Pierre Renouvin:
Etudes d'histoire des relations internationales. Paris, 1966.

1485. Byrnes, James F. Speaking Frankly. New
York, 1947.

1486. Cadogan, Alexander. The Diaries of Sir
Alexander Cadogan, O. M., 1938-1945. Edited
by D. Dilks. London, 1971.

1487. Campbell, T. M., and Herring, G. C., eds. The
Diaries of Edward R. Stettinius, Jr., 1943-
1946. New York, 1975.

1488. Churchill, Winston S. The Second World War.
6 vols. Boston, 1948-1953.

1489. Clemens, Diane. Yalta. New York, 1970. The
best single volume, with attention given to
the Soviet side, and a fine bibliography of
Russian sources.

1490. Conte, Arthur. Yalta, ou le portage du
monde. Paris, 1966.

1491. Dallek, Robert. Franklin D. Roosevelt and
American Foreign Policy, 1932-1945. New
York, 1979.

1492. Deuerlein, E., Fischer, A., Mensel, E., and
Wettig, G. Potsdam und die deutsche Frage.
Cologne, 1970.

1493. Divine, Robert A. Roosevelt and World War
II. Baltimore, 1969.

1494. Eden, Anthony. The Eden Memoirs: The Reckon-
ing. London, 1965.

1495. Eubank, Keith. The Summit Conferences, 1919-
1960. Norman, OK, 1966. Summit conferences
directly connected to democratic government.

1496. Faust, Fritz. Das Potsdamer Abkommen und
seine volkerrechtliche Bedeutung. 4th rev.
ed. Frankfurt a. M., 1969.

1497. Feis, Herbert. Between War and Peace: The
Potsdam Conference. Princeton, 1960.

1498. Feis, Herbert. Churchill-Roosevelt-Stalin:
The War They Waged and the Peace They Sought.
Princeton, 1957.

1499. Fischer, Louis. The Road to Yalta: Soviet
Foreign Relations, 1941-1945. New York,
1972.

1500. Gaddis, John Lewis. The United States and
the Origins of the Cold War, 1941-1947. New
York, 1972.

1501. Gimbel, John. The Origins of the Marshall
Plan. Stanford, 1976. Focus is on the
problems of four-power government in Germany,
and the plan as a crash program to dovetail
German economic recovery with general European
recovery programs to make German recovery
politically acceptable.

1502. Gomaa, Ahmed M. The Foundation of the
League of Arab States: Wartime Diplomacy and
Inter-Arab Politics, 1941 to 1945. London,
1977.

1503. Harriman, W. Averell, and Abel, Elie. Special
Envoy to Churchill and Stalin, 1941-1946.
London, 1976.

1504. Holborn, Louise, ed. War and Peace Aims of
the United Nations. 2 vols. Boston, 1943,
1948.

1505. Hull, Cordell. Memoirs. 2 vols. New York,
1948.

1506. Hymans, Paul. Memoires. 2 vols. Brussels,
1958.

1507. Jaksch, Wenzel. Europe's Road to Potsdam. Trans. by K. Glaser. London, 1964.

1508. King, F. P. The New Internationalism: Allied Policy and European Peace, 1939-1945. Hamden, CT, 1973.

1509. Knight, Jonathan. "Russia's Search for Peace: The London Council of Foreign Ministers, 1945." Journal of Contemporary History 13(1978): 137-63.

1510. Kolko, Gabriel. The Politics of War. New York, 1968.

1511. Leiss, Amelia, ed. European Peace Treaties After World War II. Boston, 1954.

1512. Lipgens, Walter. Europa-Föderationspläne der Widerstandsbewegungen 1940-45. Munich, 1968.

1513. Louis, Wm. Roger. Imperialism at Bay, 1941-1945: The United States and the Decolonization of the British Empire. London, 1977.

1514. Mastny, Vojtech. "Soviet War Aims at the Moscow and Teheran Conferences of 1943." Journal of Modern History 47(1975):480-504.

1515. McNeill, William H. America, Britain, and Russia: Their Cooperation and Conflict, 1941-1946. Oxford, 1953.

1516. Mee, Charles L. Jr. Meeting at Potsdam. New York, 1975.

1517. Monnet, Jean. Memoirs. Trans. by Richard Mayne. New York, 1978.

1518. Mosely, Philip E. "Peace-Making, 1946." International Organization 1(1947):21-32.

1519. Nelson, Daniel J. Wartime Origins of the Berlin Dilemma. University, AL, 1978.

1520. Neumann, William. Making the Peace, 1941-1945: The Diplomacy of the Wartime Conferences. Washington, D. C., 1950.

1521. Rempel, Richard A. "The Dilemmas of British Pacifists during World War II." Journal of

Modern History 50(1978):ii. No mass following and divided platforms.

1522. Ressing, Gerd. Versagte der Westen in Jalta
und Potsdam? Frankfurt a. M., 1970.

1523. Sharp, Tony. "The Origins of the 'Teheran
Formula' on Polish Frontiers." Journal of
Contemporary History 12(1977):381-93.

1524. Sherry, Michael S. Preparing for the Next
War: American Plans for Postwar Defense,
1941-45. New Haven, 1977.

1525. Sherwood, Robert E. Roosevelt and Hopkins.
New York, 1948.

1526. Sherwin, Martin. A World Destroyed. New
York, 1975.

1527. Smyth, Henry D. Atomic Energy for Military
Purposes: The Official Report on the Development of the Atomic Bomb. Princeton, 1945.

1528. Spaak, Paul-Henri. Combats inachevés. 2
vols. Paris, 1969.

1529. Stettinius, Edward R. Jr. Roosevelt and the
Russians: The Yalta Conference. Garden City,
NY, 1949.

1530. Stoler, Mark A. The Politics of the Second
Front: American Military Planning and Diplomacy in Coalition Warfare, 1941-1943. Westport, CT, 1977.

1531. Sündermann, Helmut. Potsdam 1945: Ein
kritischer Bericht. Leoni am Starnberger
See, 1963.

1532. Thomson, David. The Proposal for Anglo-
French Union in 1940. Oxford, 1966.

1533. Toynbee, A. J., and Toynbee, V., eds. The
Realignment of Europe, 1939-1946. London,
1955.

1534. United States Department of State. Foreign
Relations of the United States. These include
for our period volumes on:

The Conferences at Washington, 1941-1942, and Casablanca, 1943.
The Conferences at Washington and Quebec, 1943.
The Conferences at Cairo and Tehran, 1943.
The Conference at Quebec, 1944.
The Conferences at Malta and Yalta, 1945.

1535. U.S.S.R. "Documents: The Crimea and Postdam Conferences of the Leadres of the Three Great Powers," International Affairs (Moscow) 6-10(1965).

1536. U.S.S.R. The Tehran, Yalta and Potsdam Conferences: Documents. Moscow, 1969.

1537. Warner, Geoffrey. "From Teheran to Yalta: Reflections on F.D.R.'s Foreign Policy." International Affairs 43(1967):530-6.

1538. Welles, Sumner. Seven Decisions that Shaped History. New York, 1951.

1539. Wettiq, Gerhard. Entmilitarisierung und Wiederbewaffnung in Deutschland, 1943-1955: Internationale Auseinandersetzungen um die Rolle der Deutschen in Europa. Munich, 1967.

1540. Wheeler-Bennett, J. W., and Nicholls, A. The Semblance of Peace: The Political Settlement After the Second World War. London, 1972.

1541. Wilson, Theodore A. The First Summit. Roosevelt and Churchill at Placenta Bay, 1941. Boston, 1969.

1542. Yergin, Daniel. Shattered Peace. The Origins of the Cold War and the National Security State. Boston, 1978.

B. Establishing the United Nations

1543. Acheson, Dean. Present at the Creation: My Years in the State Department. New York, 1969.

1544. Bentwich, Norman. From Geneva to San Francisco. An Account of the International Organization of the New Order. London, 1946.

1545. Bindoff, S. T., and Clark, G. N. Charles Kingsley Webster, 1886-1961. London, 1963.

1546. Bromberger, Merry and Serge. Jean Monnet and the United States of Europe. Trans. by E. P. Halperin. New York, 1969.

1547. Campbell, Thomas M. Masquerade Peace: America's UN Policy, 1944-1945. Tallahassee, 1973.

1548. Chamberlain, W., Hovet, T., Jr., and Hovet, E. A Chronology and Fact Book of the United Nations, 1941-1969. Dobbs Ferry, NY, 1970.

1549. Codding, George A. "The Relationship of the League of Nations and the United Nations with the Independent Agencies: A Comparison." Annals of International Studies (Geneva) (1970):65-87.

1550. Combacau, Jean. Le pouvoir de sanction de L'O.N.U.: Etude théorique de la coercion non militaire. Paris, 1974.

1551. Commission to Study the Organization of Peace. Building Peace: Reports of the Commission to Study the Organization of Peace, 1939-1972. 2 vols. Metuchen, NJ, 1973. All the signed reports of the commission, 22 in total, from 1940 to 1972, plus 20 unnumbered statements.

1552. Commission to Study the Organization of Peace. A Ten Year Record: 1939-1949. New York, 1949.

1553. Cowell, F. R. "Planning the Organization of UNESCO, 1942-1946: A Personal Record." Journal of World History 10(1966):210-56.

1554. Divine, Robert. Second Chance: The Triumph of Internationalism in America during World War II. New York, 1967. A fine study of internationalist pressure groups, their interaction and influence, polls, and elections.

1555. Donelan, M. D., and Grieve, M. J. International Disputes: Case Histories, 1945-1970. London, 1973.

1556. Fhni, Reinhart. Die Schweiz und die Vereinigten Nationen von 1944-1947. Tübingen, 1967.
Memories of the League were alarming and
uncongenial, and conditioned Swiss hesitation
and reluctance to join the U.N.

1557. Eichelberger, Clark M. Organizing for Peace:
A Personal History of the Founding of the
United Nations. New York, 1978.

1558. Finkelstein, Lawrence S. "The United Nations:
Then and Now." International Organization
19(1965):367-93.

1559. Gardner, Richard. Sterling-Dollar Diplomacy:
Anglo-American Collaboration in the Reconstruction of Multilateral Trade. Oxford,
1956.

1560. Geneva Research Center. "The United States
and the League, the Labour Organization, and
the World Court in 1939." Geneva Studies
11(1940):1-67.

1561. Ghebali, Victor-Yves. La France en guerre et
les organisations internationales, 1939-1945.
Paris, 1969.

1562. Ghebali, Victor-Yves. "Aux origines de
l'ECOSOC: l'évolution des commissions et
organisations techniques de la Société des
Nations." Annuaire français de droit international (1972).

1563. Gilchrist, H. "Colonial Questions at the San
Francisco Conference." American Political
Science Review 39(1945):982-92.

1564. Goodrich, Leland M. "From League of Nations
to United Nations." International Organization 1(1947):3-21.

1565. Green, James F. "The Dumbarton Oaks Conversations." U.S. Department of State Bulletin,
11(1944).

1566. Haas, Ernst. "The Attempt to Terminate
Colonialism: Acceptance of the United Nations
Trusteeship System." International Organiza-
tion 71(1973):1-21.

1567. Hackworth, Green. "The International Court of Justice." U.S. Department of State Bulletin, 13(1945).

1568. Hajnal, Peter I. Guide to United Nations Organization, Documentation and Publishing. Dobbs Ferry, NY, 1978.

1569. Hambidge, Gove. The Story of the FAO. New York, 1955.

1570. Hostiou, René. Robert Schuman et l'Europe. Paris, 1969.

1571. Hughes, E. J. "Winston Churchill and the Formation of the United Nations Organization." Journal of Contemporary History 9(1974):177-94.

1572. James, Alan. The Politics of Peace-Keeping. London, 1969.

1573. Kindleberger, Charles. "Bretton Woods Reappraised." International Organization 5(1951): 32-47.

1574. Krill de Capello, H. H. "Die Gründung der UNESCO." Vierteljahrshefte für Zeitgeschichte 16(1968);1-14. Best account, based on archives, shows how CAME conference not called by Butler to establish an international organization. English translation of article appears as "The Creation of the United Nations Education, Scientific and Cultural Organization," International Organization 24(1970):1-30.

1575. Krylov, S. B. Materials for the History of the United Nations. V. 1, Framing the Text of the Charter of the United Nations. Moscow, 1949.

1576. Kuklick, Bruce. "The Genesis of the European Advisory Commission." Journal of Contemporary History 4(1969):189-201. U.S. restricting and undermining British attempts to broaden scope.

1577. League of Nations. The League Hands Over. Geneva, 1946. The story of the transition.

1578. Lee, Dwight E. "The Genesis of the Veto." International Organization 1(1947):33-42.

1579. Myers, Denys P. "Liquidation of the League of Nations' Functions." American Journal of International Law (1948):320-354.

1580. Mylonas, Denis. La genèse de l'Unesco: La conférence des ministres alliés de l'éducation (1942-1945). Brussels, 1976.

1581. Nathan-Chapotot, Roger. Les Nations Unies et les réfugiés. Paris, 1949.

1582. Opie, Redvers, et al. The Search for Peace Settlements. Washington, D. C., 1951.

1583. Reynolds, P. A., and Hughes, E. J. The Historian as Diplomat: Charles Kingsley Webster and the United Nations, 1939-1946. London, 1977. Based on diary Webster kept while serving at heart of British planning, with six appendices of various drafts for the Charter. An important record.

1584. Rhodes James, Robert. Staffing the United Nations Secretariat. Brighton, 1970.

1585. Rosen, S. McKee. The Combined Boards of the Second World War: An Experiment in International Administration. New York, 1951.

1586. Russell, R. B. A History of the United Nations Charter--the Role of the United States, 1940-1945. Washington, D. C., 1958. This is the major account, very thorough study of State Department planning.

1587. Shoup, Laurence H., and Minter, William. Imperial Brain Trust: The Council on Foreign Relations and United States Foreign Policy. London, 1977.

1588. Smouts, Marie-Claude. Le Secrétaire Général des Nations Unies: son rôle dans la solution des conflits internationaux. Paris, 1971.

1589. Solomon, Robert. The International Monetary System, 1945-1976. New York, 1977.

1590. Sweetser, Arthur. "The United States and the League, the Labour Organization, and the World Court During 1940." Geneva Studies 11(1940): 1-19.

1591. Toussaint, C. Edwards. The Trusteeship System of the United Nations. London, 1956.

1592. Twitchett, K. J. "The Colonial Powers and the United Nations." Journal of Contemporary History 4(1969):167-185. The transition from the Mandates System to the System of Trusteeships, with emphasis on the resistance of the colonial powers to the anti-colonial pressures.

1593. United States Department of State. Charter of the United Nations: Report to the President on the Results of the San Francisco Conference. Washington, D. C., 1945.

1594. United States Department of State. The International Court of Justice; Selected Documents Relating to the Drafting of the Statute. Washington, D. C., 1946.

1595. United States Department of State. Postwar Foreign Policy Preparation, 1939-1945. Washington, D. C., 1950.

1596. United Nations. Documents of the United Nations Conference on International Organization, San Francisco, 1945. 20 vols. New York, 1945.

1597. Vandenberg, Arthur H., Jr., ed. The Private Papers of Senator Vandenberg. Boston, 1952.

1598. Walters, F. P. "Dumbarton Oaks and the League." International Affairs 21(1945):141-54.

1599. Webster, Charles K. "The Making of the Charter of the United Nations." History 32(1947):16-38.

1600. Whitton, J. R. "Chairmanship of the San Francisco Conference." American Journal of International Law 39(1945).

1601. Woodbridge, George. UNRRA. New York, 1950.

1602. Woodward, Llewellyn. British Foreign Policy
in the Second World War. Volume V. London,
1976. An official history, this volume,
revised by M. E. Lambert, discusses planning
concerning a world organization.

1603. Young, J. P. "Developing Plans for an International Monetary Fund and a World Bank,"
United States Department of State Bulletin,
23(1950).

INDEX OF AUTHORS

INDEX OF AUTHORS

Date Due

APR 2 1 2009			